Strategisches Lernen

Jahrbuch Strategisches Kompetenz-Management

Herausgeber von Band 6 des Jahrbuchs:
Wolfgang H. Güttel
Stefan Konlechner

Wolfgang H. Güttel
Stefan Konlechner
(Hrsg.)

Strategisches Lernen

Rainer Hampp Verlag München, Mering 2012

Bibliografische Information der Deutschen Nationalbibliothek

Die Deutsche Nationalbibliothek verzeichnet diese Publikation in der Deutschen Nationalbibliografie; detaillierte bibliografische Daten sind im Internet über http://dnb.d-nb.de abrufbar.

ISBN 978-3-86618-833-4 (print)
ISBN 978-3-86618-933-1 (e-book)
Jahrbuch Strategisches Kompetenz-Management: ISSN 1864-5402
DOI 10.1688/978-3866189331
1. Auflage, 2012

Rainer Hampp Verlag München und Mering
Marktplatz 5 D – 86415 Mering

www.Hampp-Verlag.de

∞ *Dieses Buch ist auf säurefreiem und chlorfrei gebleichtem Papier gedruckt.*

Liebe Leserinnen und Leser!
Wir wollen Ihnen ein gutes Buch liefern. Wenn Sie aus irgendwelchen Gründen nicht zufrieden sind, wenden Sie sich bitte an uns.

Vorwort

Das aktuelle Wirtschaftsgeschehen ist in vielen Branchen und Bereichen durch intensive Konkurrenz, volatile Märkte und steigenden Innovationsdruck gekennzeichnet. Dem strategischen Management organisationaler Kompetenzen kommt in dieser Situation besondere Bedeutung zu. Nur Unternehmen, die es bewerkstelligen organisationale Lern- und Veränderungsprozesse strategisch zu steuern, können unter solchen Bedingungen nachhaltig erfolgreich sein. Vor diesem Hintergrund fokussieren die Beiträge des vorliegenden Jahrbuchs unter Rückgriff auf vielfältige konzeptionelle Brillen auf unterschiedliche Aspekte des strategischen Lernens von Organisationen.

Die Beiträge wurden anlässlich der 7. Konferenz zu Strategischem Kompetenz-Management (SKM 2011) an der Johannes Kepler Universität Linz zum Thema „Strategisches Lernen" präsentiert und intensiv diskutiert. Die hier vorgestellten Beiträge wurden im Anschluss über mehrere Runden eines double-blind review-Verfahrens weiter optimiert und schließlich final angenommen. Insgesamt wurden 12 Beiträge für diesen Band eingereicht, womit eine Annahmequote von 50 Prozent erreicht wurde.

Der erste Beitrag dieser Ausgabe beschäftigt sich auf empirischer Basis mit Pfadbruchstrategien in der Musikindustrie. *Kristian Kunow, Martin Gersch und Jochen Koch* zeigen dabei, wie insbesondere das intendierte Herbeiführen einer Situation temporärer Inkompetenz die Erneuerung organisationaler Kompetenzen begünstigen kann. Gerade vor dem Hintergrund einer zunehmenden Marktdynamisierung, die Unternehmen vermehrt vor die Herausforderung stellt, ihre Ressourcen- und Kompetenzbasis, teilweise radikal, zu erneuern, kommt den Erkenntnissen der Autoren zum strategischem (In)Kompetenz-Management besondere Bedeutung zu.

Mit Aspekten der Adaption der organisationalen Kompetenzbasis beschäftigt sich auch *Torsten Klein*. In seinem konzeptionellen Beitrag setzt er sich mit dem Thema der Ressourcenflexibilität als notwendige Voraussetzung für die dynamische Anpassung bestehender Ressourcenkonfigurationen auseinander. Die Konzeption eines dynamischen Ansatzes des Ressourcencontrollings zeigt, wie Unternehmen Ressourcenflexibilität zur Sicherstellung ihrer Wettbewerbsfähigkeit herstellen können. Das vorgelegte Modell weist dabei insbesondere auf die Rolle von Überschussressourcen und inaktiven Ressourcenfunktionen für die dynamische Ressourcenrekonfiguration von Unternehmen hin.

Auf die Förderung der organisationalen Anpassungsfähigkeit fokussiert auch der Beitrag von *Tanja Schulze, Annett Schädlich und Silke Geithner*. Die Autorinnen beleuchten aus einer Dynamic Capabilities-Perspektive den Wert von Mitarbeiterbefragungen zur Förderung reflexiven Lernens. Die Befunde aus zwei mittelständischen Unternehmen beleuchten vor allem die organisationalen

Kontextbedingungen unter denen Mitarbeiterbefragungen als Lerninstrument genutzt werden können.

Auf die Bedeutung unterschiedlicher Kopplungsformen von Exploration und Exploitation zur Gestaltung organisationaler Wandelprozesse fokussieren *Birgit Renzl, Martin Rost und Jürgen Kaschube*. Die Ergebnisse der präsentierten Fallstudie eines Technologieführers in der Automobilzulieferbranche beleuchten die Möglichkeiten der Förderung kontextueller und struktureller Ambidextrie. Durch die Analyse der Ansprüche, die das Herstellen von Ambidextrie an Führungskräfte stellt, tragen die Autoren mit ihrem Beitrag auch zum Verständnis des strategischen Managements der Kopplung von Exploration und Exploitation bei.

Wolfgang Burr und Antje Koch fokussieren in ihrer explorativen Studie auf Strategien beim Ablauf von Patenten in der Pharmabranche. Vor dem Hintergrund, dass Pharmaunternehmen in solchen Situationen mit Exploitation (Verteidigung des bestehenden Wirkstoffs gegen Imitation) und Exploration (Erforschen neuer Wirkstoffe) unterschiedliche Strategieoptionen zur Verfügung stehen, wird mit Fallstudien gezeigt wie führende deutsche Pharmaunternehmen mit unternehmensspezifischen Bündeln von exploitativen und explorativen Maßnahmen auf den Ablauf wichtiger Patente reagieren. Die Ergebnisse der Untersuchung geben damit auch Aufschlüsse über ambidextre Strategien, die Unternehmen zur Abwehr einer Bedrohung ihrer überlegenen Ressourcenposition einsetzen können.

Michael W. Busch und Dietrich von der Oelsnitz befassen sich in ihrem Beitrag mit der Rolle individueller Kompetenzen als Grundlage strategischer organisationaler Kompetenzen und arbeiten dabei die Literatur zum Themengebiet Expertenwissen systematisch auf. Die Autoren fokussieren auf die Fragen, wie Expertenwissen entsteht, welche Maßnahmen zur Bewahrung Organisationen ergreifen können und wie es letztlich auch transferiert werden kann. Gerade diese Transferierbarkeit ist es auch, die im Rahmen des strategischen Kompetenz-Managements von Organisationen eine zentrale Rolle spielt.

Schließlich möchten wir dieses Vorwort auch nutzen, um unseren Dank auszusprechen. Wir bedanken uns bei den Mitarbeiterinnen und Mitarbeitern des Instituts für Human Resource & Change Management der JKU Linz, ohne die die Durchführung der SKM Konferenz 2011 nicht möglich gewesen wäre. Wir möchten auch allen Autorinnen und Autoren danken, die uns mit Ihren Einreichungen die Auswahl der Beiträge für diese Jahrbuchsausgabe sehr schwer gemacht haben. Nicht zuletzt gilt unser besonderer Dank auch den vielen Gutachterinnen und Gutachtern, ohne deren Mühe und Arbeit dieses Jahrbuch nicht zustande gekommen wäre.

Inhaltsverzeichnis

Temporary Incompetence as a Path-breaking Strategy: Two Major Record Companies' Efforts to Escape their Competence Lock-In

Kristian Kunow, Martin Gersch und Jochen Koch

Zusammenfassung

Das Festhalten an ehemals Erfolg bringenden Kompetenzen kann als eines der größten Probleme von Unternehmen in dynamischen Umwelten mit tiefgreifenden Transformationsprozessen angesehen werden. Über das Ausbrechen aus einem solchen Kompetenz-lock-in ist bisher relativ wenig bekannt. Der Beitrag analysiert und vergleicht die Kompetenzentwicklung sowie die strategischen Trajektorien von zwei großen Tonträgerunternehmen vor dem Hintergrund organisationaler und strategischer Pfade. Beide Unternehmen sehen sich aufgrund von tiefgreifenden Veränderungen in der Wettbewerbsumwelt einem hohen Veränderungsdruck ausgesetzt. Unsere Vergleichsstudie zeigt, dass ein erfolgreiches Ausbrechen aus einem Kompetenzpfad dann möglich erscheint, wenn ein Unternehmen sich bewusst und mit Nachdruck in einen Zustand der temporären Inkompetenz begibt. Darüberhinaus zeigen wir, welche Art von strategischen Aktivitäten ergriffen werden müssen, um einen solchen Zustand zu erreichen und über einen bestimmten Zeitraum aufrecht zu erhalten. Damit beschreitet der Beitrag einen neuen Weg in Richtung eines empirisch informierten Verständnisses von temporärer Inkompetenz als Form einer Pfadbruch-Strategie.

Schlüsselwörter: Pfadabhängigkeit, Pfadbruch, Organisationale Kompetenzen, Inkompetenz, Musikindustrie

Abstract

The tendency to stick with once successful competences is one of the major problems of many firms' strategic and organizational development when facing the challenges posed by dynamic fields in the process of fundamental change and transformation. However, as yet little is known about overcoming such competence lock-ins. The paper analyzes and compares the competences and the strategic trajectory of two major record companies from the perspective of path dependence. Due to recent fundamental changes in their market environment, both companies are confronted with high demands on flexibility. By comparing the strategic activities of both firms we explore the deliberate acceptance of a temporal state of incompetence as a conceivable strategy to escape a competence lock-in. We further explain what kind of strategic activities a firm has to adopt in order to build up a temporary incompetence. Thereby the paper contributes to a better understanding of path breaking by introducing the idea of temporary incompetence.

Keywords: Path Dependence, Path Breakage, Organizational Competences, Incompetence, Music Industry

1. Introduction

Firms' competitiveness rests upon their readiness to non-randomly produce a valuable output and to employ capture mechanisms (Freiling et al. 2008; Teece 2010), and their competences are the source of their ability to add value. Being competent and activating competences by accomplishing stable action patterns are fundamental to firms' success. In contrast, proving incompetent to produce a valuable output clearly seems to be disadvantageous for a firm. By drawing on a case study in the music industry we aim to add another interpretation of organizational incompetence for a specific situation a firm may face: a path-induced competence lock-in. The case study was conducted by raising two research questions that are interconnected: How and why do firms find themselves locked in to a certain competence, and what do they do in order to overcome such a lock-in?

To answer these research questions we studied the strategic trajectory of two major record companies. These firms represent one of the most popular examples raised when talking about collapsing business models in the digital age (Teece 2010). Therefore, it seems worthwhile to investigate their competence development and how they have tried to adjust to a radically changing environment. We have engaged in this endeavor by performing a two-step longitudinal case study. The first step is explanatory and focuses on the identification of a competence lock-in. The second step is exploratory and designed to answer the second part of the research question that is central to this paper. By contrasting the strategic development of both firms we will explore and explain why one of the firms is able to overcome its competence lock-in whereas the other is not. We explain this difference by introducing the idea of temporary incompetence. Finally, we discuss this concept against the background of the literature on strategic and organizational change.

2. Competence Development and Rigidities

Despite the breadth and diversity of the field of competence and capability research which emerged in the last two decades, two common ideas can be identified. First, a firm's set of resources and routines can be understood as an organizationally embedded pattern developed over time (Barney 1991; Helfat/Peteraf 2003). Hence these patterns are historical and are inscribed into the organizational body of a firm (Koch 2011). Secondly, what once served as a competence may turn into rigidity and hinder a firm in reconfiguring its set of resources and routines (Leonard-Barton 1992).

Thus it is not surprising that many scholars argue that the development of a firm's resources and capabilities is subject to path-dependent processes (e.g. Daneels 2010; Zollo/Winter 2002; Freiling et al. 2008; Teece et al. 1997). Nevertheless, what is still widely missing in the debate on capability level change, resource recombination and the development of (new) competences is a thorough understanding of path dependence as a type of process with specific consequences in the long run (Sydow et al. 2009). As most scholars still adopt a kind of metaphorical interpretation of path dependence, they rather consider every competence to be developed along an "evolutionary path" (Helfat/Peteraf 2003; Teece 2007). However, by taking into consideration all those aspects of path dependence we know from economics (David 1985; Arthur 1989), some research on competence has already applied a clear-cut definition of path dependence, as explicated in the following section (Schreyögg/Kliesch 2007; Vergne/Durand 2011; Koch 2011). Such research marks path-dependent competence building as specific and highlights the outcome of lock-in as an extreme form of rigidity.

2.1 A Thorough Understanding of Path Dependence

Path dependence is a broadly applied theoretical model in many research areas, including economics (e.g. Shapiro/Varian 1999) and political science (e.g. Pierson 2000). Recently scholars of organization studies and strategy have also adopted the theoretical model to this research area and thereby gone beyond the widespread metaphorical use of the notion (Schreyögg/Sydow 2011. Garud et al. 2010; Vergne/Durand 2010). According to the theoretical model these scholars put forward, path dependence is a non-ergodic process that may lead to a hyperstable organizational solution. This solution might prove to be inferior in the long run, but is almost impossible to overcome. The process itself is defined as having three constitutive elements which can be assigned to three different phases (Sydow et al. 2009, Dobusch/Kapeller 2011).

Phase I: "Small event"

The first phase of a path-dependent process is characterized by a situation of unpredictable courses of organizational action or decisions. Within this phase events are expected to happen (action taken/choices made) that seem to be "small" at the moment of their occurrence, but have big effects because they trigger positive feedback mechanisms.

Phase II: Self-reinforcement

Within the second phase the path is formed by the constitutive element: self-reinforcement. During this phase a firm's action pattern emerges clearly and is continuously refined. Unfolding positive feedback effects push this pattern far ahead of others, and their regime of forming the organizational solution distinguishes the process of path dependence from other related concepts such as imprinting or inertia (Schreyögg/Sydow 2011), and from the simple notion of "history matters" (Dobusch/Kapeller 2011; Teece 2007). Research on organizational and strategic path dependence so far has considered four effects to reinforce an organizational solution: learning effects, complementarity, coordination and adaptive expectations (Sydow et al. 2009). Each of these effects and their interactions are expected to drastically narrow the scope of actions and give rise to the dominance of a certain, ever more attractive pattern (Koch 2008).

Phase III: Lock-in

The transition to phase three is marked by a further constriction in scope, resulting in a (quasi-) deterministic situation. Therefore, the third constitutive element of path-dependent processes — the lock-in — is found in this phase. While with regard to technological standards an almost complete lock-in may be the case, in the social realm of firms such a completely rigid situation cannot be expected. Instead, a lock-in can be regarded as a sort of "action corridor" (Sydow et al. 2009) or "trajectory" (Dosi 1982). Such a corridor/trajectory does restrict a firm's overall choices and actions, but leaves some scope for variation. Nevertheless, locked-in firms are always in danger of finding themselves bound to a solution that turns out to be inferior.

Implications for Competence Research

Besides positive feedback effects, which encompass some sort of accumulation over time and have already been considered in research on competence and capability building (Teece 2007; Helfat/Peteraf 2003), two other constitutive elements of path-dependent processes come to the fore, which could inform competence research. When assuming that firms' competences might emerge and develop further in keeping with a path-dependent process, attention should be paid not only to positive feedback effects. Instead the process model presented above puts equal weight on two other constitutive elements: small events and lock-in. These constitutive elements account for non-ergodicity and extremely rigid outcomes and point to the flip side of path dependent competence building. When this flip side is taken seriously, path breakage becomes a pressing matter for competence research, especially in changing or transforming environments. Unfortunately only little is known so far regarding delocking, and the theoretical model of path dependence still lacks an explanation for the empirical fact that some firms obviously manage to break their (competence) path.

2.2 Breaking a (Competence) Path

As pointed out above, it is difficult to conceive of firms' competence building being completely locked in. Still, a competence lock-in constitutes a drastic reduction in flexibility and restriction to a corridor of variation that might become obvious only when the environment surrounding the company calls for a shift to competences that lie beyond the firm's limited scope (Koch 2008).

Considering this risk, some authors call for capability monitoring in order to avoid path-induced competence lock-ins, conceptualizing such monitoring as an organizational function in its own right (Schreyögg/Kliesch 2007). However, while this concept might help firms to observe path-dependent competence building at earlier stages, it does not provide insight into how to break a path that has already reached the locked-in state.

One of the few theoretical concepts of path breakage is that of "path dissolution." Path dissolution might occur due to an enormous external shock (Sydow et al. 2009; also see Arthur 1994). But such a shock is beyond the control of the organization and could result in economic failure of the firm as such. Burgelman (2002; 2008) shows that path dissolution might also be triggered internally. But even Burgelman's presentation of the strategic development of Intel shows that the firm de-locked more or less by chance. As Koch (2009) demonstrates, the resource allocation routine that forced Intel to change its "strategic vector" was not established deliberately. Rather, path breakage in the case of Intel can be considered as a sort of side effect. For management scholars these conceptualizations of path breakage must be regarded as "fatalistic" and having "at least a passive flavor" (Sydow et al. 2009). Nevertheless, it shows that a competence lock-in is unlikely to be broken merely by efforts to build new competences. Instead, it suggests that breaking competence paths and developing new competences have to be considered in turn, as two different sides of the same coin.

3. Research Design, Case Selection, Data Collection and Analysis

Most empirical research on organizational path dependence to date has been retrospective and based on case study methodology. This fact has recently become the starting point of a debate on empirical evidence concerning its hypothetical statements and its testability in general (Vergne/Durand 2010). Dobusch and Kapeller (2011) recently showed that the conceptual building blocks of the theoretical model call for different methodological approaches. They argue that only the lock-in phase allows clear-cut hypothetical statements to be tested. However, research on both path formation and path breakage needs to apply ideographic methods due to the lack of testable mechanisms (Dobusch/Kapeller 2011; Garud et al. 2010).

Therefore, in studying major record companies' competence building and development from the perspective of path dependence, our empirical research applied a longitudinal case study approach (Yin 2009; Gerring 2007). The selection of cases followed theoretical sampling (Eisenhardt 1989). Two German subsidiaries of global record companies were identified to serve as embedded cases. In the following these firms are referred to as firm A and firm B. The case selection rationale was the following. Regarding the assumption of a competence lock-in, both firms were considered critical cases. The two-case study adopts a literal replication design (Yin 2009) in order to explain the path-dependent development of competences resulting in a specific form of rigidity. Furthermore, one of the two cases, firm B, was considered to represent an extreme case since 2008 (Yin 2009; Siggelkow 2007). To explore how firm B was actually able to break its competence lock-in we contrasted it with the recent development of firm A.

In order to operationalize competence development we build on an understanding of competences that is specified by the Competence-based Theory of the Firm. Following this approach a firm's competence is defined as "a repeatable, non-random ability to render competitive output" (Freiling et al. 2008:1151). This ability of a firm is based on its knowledge as well as on formal and implicit rules that guide the firm's actions. Therefore emergence, changes and stability of competences were traced by observing the strategic action patterns of firms A and B.

Following the case study design and case selection we engaged in data collection and analysis. These steps of conducting the case study were performed by adhering to an interactive approach, with consecutive steps of data gathering, interpretation, further gathering, (re-)interpretation and so forth (Gersch et al. 2009). The data collected were fed into a database set up especially for our case studies.

Documents	**#**	**Time period covered**
Trade magazines	1216	1959-2010
Print and online press	131	1999-2010
books	23	(approx.) 1900-2010
Publications of industrial association	63	1992-2010
Documents	**1433**	
Interviews	**#**	**Length***
Firm A	9	08:44:00
Firm B	9	08:52:48
Industry experts	9	07:28:59
Interviews	**27**	**25:05:47**
Observations (non-participant)	**#**	**Length***
Firm A	5	17:30:00
Firm B	4	13:45:00
Industry conventions**	4	(approx.) 60:00:00
Observations	**13**	**(approx.) 91:15:00**

*HH:MM:SS

**With representatives of firms A and B discussing business trends etc.

Table 1: Synopsis of case study database

First we conducted nine problem-centered interviews with industry experts and visited industry trade fairs and conventions to validate and refine our assumption of competence lock-in (stable action pattern of releasing and exploiting recorded pop music) and to generate propositions of positive feedback effects regarding the two firms in question. On that basis we collected extensive documental data (mainly archival trade magazine reports) and identified relevant interview partners in firms A and B (in this case former staff members) with whom we conducted guided interviews. Applying a pattern coding and matching procedure (Miles/Huberman 1994), we further refined our proposition of a locked-in action pattern in both cases along with positive feedback mechanisms stabilizing this pattern, and then triangulated the data.

The second step in conducting the case study was based on further archival data collection and analysis. In order to trace the process of competence development and the triggering events of unfolding positive feedback effects, we used a narrative strategy of analysis combined with temporal bracketing (Langley 1999).

Finally, once we arrived at an explanation of path-dependent competence development and lock-in, we conducted another round of problem-centered interviews. This time we selected interview partners from firm A (mainly members of the business development unit) and firm B, whom we identified as being central to the efforts of building new competences. The interviews were accompanied by non-participant observations after and between the scheduled interviews; field notes were taken during these meetings and informal conversations. To explore what is done differently in the case of firm B, and to grasp what allows for deviation from the competence development paths, we followed open coding and categorizing procedures (Glaser/Strauss 1967; Langley 1999).

The following table summarizes the case study design and the steps taken in data collection and analysis. The subsequent presentation of findings roughly follows these steps.

Steps of data collection, analysis	Step 2: origins of stabilizing mechanisms and path formation	Step 1: validation of competence path assumption (action pattern & positive feedback mechanisms)	Step 3: terms of path breakage
Research interest	Explanation	Explanation	Exploration
Case selection rationale	Firms A and B as critical cases; literal replication	Firms A and B as critical; literal replication	Firm A as critical case, firm B as extreme case
Main source of data	Documents	Interviews/documents	Interviews/observations
Method of Analysis	(Case) Narrative	Pattern coding and matching	Inductive coding

Table 2: Summary of research steps

4. The Competence Path – Hit Creation and the Exploitation of Hit Records

The need to organize the recording, production and distribution that came along with technologies that capture sound on discs brought record companies into existence. What became obvious when analyzing firm A and B's competences and tracing their historical development is that, at least for these major record companies, competence is poorly described in terms of the recording, production and distribution of music (see also Garofalo 1999). With advances in recording, post-production and distribution technologies (especially with their digitization starting in the 1980s) it has become even more feasible for artists (or their management) to organize production and distribution themselves. This development is also reflected in the type of contracts the record companies have concluded with artists. While up to the 1990s firms A and B bound artists mainly through so-called "artist contracts" in order to control the selection of performed compositions and record production, they have increasingly signed "tape-lease deals" since then. Such deals mean that a completed master record is handed over to the label, which organizes the record release and exploitation.

Consequently, in investigating the development of their competence, the focus should lie on how these firms organize the release and exploitation of recorded music rather than its production and distribution. In tracing back how specific action patterns emerged in the realm of marketing, promotion and sales in firms A and B, we identified two main routines – Chart (Entry) Optimizing and Promoting Songs/Selling Bundles – that represent their competence of creating hit records and capturing the value of this effort.

We will describe these two routines and their origins in greater detail as it seems necessary to answer the first of our research questions ("How and why do firms find themselves locked in to a certain competence?"). Only a "thick description" can illustrate firms' specific organizational competences and how they have deeply informed any actions taken and are stabilized by positive feedback effects. By contrasting these competences it is possible to identify the recent development in firm B as breaking a lock-in.

4.1 Step 1: Stable Action Pattern and Positive Feedback Mechanisms in Releasing Recorded Music

At first glance, a very rough structure of the record companies' routine for releasing music can be described as *recording music, reproducing copies, distributing copies, marketing and promoting the music*. But a closer look at the actions that used to be involved in the cases of firms A and B reveals more specific connections and timing.

Chart (Entry) Optimizing and Coordination Effects

A quote from a former product manager of firm B points to the fact that these specific action pattern and timing of actions are most important in releasing recorded music.

> *You try to release the record so that the highest possible demand is triggered at the release date. This is done by focusing all marketing and promotion activities on a short period. There is this factor of uncertainty: the consumer. Sometimes a song is not popular even though it is pressed into the market with a lot of money. But ultimately it is a question of coordination and timing...*

As for the "Chart (Entry) Optimizing" routine reflected in the quote, it is almost irrelevant whether the firm was responsible for production, recording etc., or whether it released the music on the basis of a tape-lease deal. First, a budget is set and, the calculation of which depends on estimated sales numbers, meaning the number of items sold within a given period of time, usually 6 to 12 months. Such estimates are usually produced in a joint meeting of Artist and Repertoire (A&R) specialists, product and sales managers. In case of an established performing artist, the sales numbers of former releases are considered in estimating sales of the current release. If the artist is new or has not sold many records yet, the budgeting decision is based mainly on "gut feeling." A certain proportion of the budget (the main part) is committed to marketing and promotion. The total amount of this part of the budget may not fall short of what is considered to be necessary to enter the charts (weekly bestseller ranking, see below). Therefore, even for not yet established artists estimated sales must exceed a certain minimum. After defining the budget, the record and the artist are presented to media outlets and retailers. Specialists promote the record and the artist to radio and television programmers and producers, and to the press, by providing samples of the record and selling the "story" of the record and the artist. Samples are sent out in the hope of airplay on the radio or reviews in the press. One main argument for convincing persons in charge of programming is the "company's seriousness in supporting the release" (a phrase often used by interviewees from both companies). In this context, "seriousness" means budget and manpower committed on the part of the record label. The same type of argument is used in convincing retailers to order and prominently display the record, and to cooperate with advertising. The reactions of media outlets and retailers are closely observed, collected by the product manager and diffused across the firms' departments in order to be used in further marketing and promoting activities. Hence, another argument presented to programmers, journalists and retailers are the previous (positive) reactions of other media and trade outlets (programming, stocking etc.). This process of promoting and marketing, evaluating feedback and adjusting is repeated until the official street date. Hence, when these marketing and promotion actions take place the record is not yet available for sale. Most marketing and promotion investments and manpower are concentrated within a few weeks before the record's sales launch. When the record is finally made available in retail outlets, the media presence of the record and the artist is expected to have been maximized in keeping with the allotted budget and manpower. Accomplishing the routine means triggering demand accumulation. This is expected to result in many record sales in the first week after the official record release and therefore a high chart entry.

For firms A and B, high chart entry used to be an event that could be organized, and was expected to set in motion dynamics resulting in the emergence of a hit. Therefore Chart (Entry) Optimizing might be considered a proxy for the hit creation competence of firms A and B. The routine served as an ideal goal for both investigated firms. In most cases, routine performances fell short of matching the ideal action pattern (most releases failed to enter the Top 40). Nevertheless, both organizations strived towards the ideal almost every time the routine was accomplished (every time a music product had been released) and regularly realized high chart entries.

This "continuously striving for the ideal" of an action pattern can be seen as a reason why the routines of both firms, and hence their competence reproduction, remained relatively stable (cf. Pentland/Feldman 2005). The reason for the stability of the action pattern is that Chart (Entry) Optimizing produces a high degree of internal and external coordination, for a positive feedback effect (Sydow et al. 2009). The routine provides rules about what kind of music to release (minimum estimated sales) and how much money and manpower should be invested (as a proportion of estimated sales). Furthermore, it specifies what type of actions can be expected (and when) from other actors inside and outside the company during the release process. For example, sales force agents expect the product manager to provide information on the media presence achieved, which then can be used as an argument when presenting the record to a retailer. Similarly, radio promoters are expected to send out samples before official release dates.

Promoting Songs/Selling Bundles and Complementarity

Striving for the ideal of Chart (Entry) Optimizing when releasing a record and the associated coordination effects can be seen as a trigger of competence stability, as these mechanisms drive out alternative actions and refine the existing pattern. For example, making the record available for sale at the moment radio promotion starts is not considered to be practical timing. But including an upcoming private radio station on a list of the first promotion partners to receive a sample is a common variation of the routine.

However, there is another positive feedback effect that used to cause stability in reproducing the competence of firms A and B. It is the complementarity between Chart (Entry) Optimizing and the exploitation routine, which we refer to as "Promoting Songs/Selling Bundles." The complementarity effect arises because both patterns of action are interconnected so that it becomes ever more attractive to exploit the synergies (Schreyögg/Sydow 2010).

The product configurations of recorded music brought to the market by both firms can be divided roughly into two types: singles and albums. The album configuration contains a compilation of songs performed in a studio or live in concert by one artist or a group of artists. It also could be a compilation of songs performed by different artists (hit compilation, e.g. "Best of the 90s" or "Summer Hits '94"). The name "single" as a product configuration suggests a record that contains only one song. But firms A and B have hardly released any records with just one song since the introduction of the compact disc (CD) in the early 1980s. In fact, what has been sold on physical records over the last three decades was always a bundle. Throughout the 1990s and 2000s both companies sold "Maxi-Singles" or at least "2-Tracks." These records usually contained one hit song along with other slightly different versions (different mainly in post-production).

Still, the subject of the Chart (Entry) Optimizing routine is usually only a single song. This song "is pressed into the market with a lot of money" (see quote by firm B's A&R Manager above). Even in the "golden era" of the 1990s, this money could seldom be recouped by sales of actual singles. Although the smaller "single bundles" generated more income than selling the single song, it rarely recouped the investment in hit creation. The routine to recoup the investments while aiming to generate a hit we observed in both companies was a specific course of action for selling records. This routine can best be described as a cascade of promotion, bundling and selling actions: first the song, second the single, third the album. Promotion of a hit song is followed up by selling a single. Selling a single in turn promotes the album that contains the single. Releasing the album is the final step. This routine of "Promoting Songs/Selling Bundles" is expressed in the response of a manager at firm A when we confronted him with our interpretation of the company's action pattern:

> *That is the practice. Please show me a single that recouped the money invested. The album still represents the returns, this is still an album-centered business. We push the album with the single. The single itself is a promotion tool for the album.*

The complementarity of both routines, "Chart (Entry) Optimizing" and "Promoting Songs/Selling Bundles," becomes obvious when looking at how both action patterns are interconnected. Budget calculations for a record release are based mainly on estimated sales of the album configuration, although promotion and marketing investments are directed mainly toward creating chart entry for a single track from that album. The release of a single is followed by the release of the album, in the hope of the single's promotion effect for the album. It turns out that achieving chart entry is ever more valuable for the firm and, hence, more efficient as the cascade of promotion and sales proceeds.

4.2 Step 2: "Small Events" and Formation of the Competence Path

Two "small events" gave rise to the dynamic of the music industry in which both firms and their action pattern that embodies their competence are embedded. Wikström (2006; 2010) calls this dynamics the "media-audience –engine." The more media presence is achieved for a certain recording, the more consumers are expected to be willing to buy the record.

The initial triggering event for the expectation of this dynamic we found in firms A and B in Germany dates back to the introduction of broadcasting rights. Based on the almost accidental experiences noted in the U.S., that radio airplay has a positive effect on record sales (cf. Dowd 2006), German copyright legislation in 1964 assured broadcasting rights for any prerecorded music. From this time on broadcasting stations have been authorized to play any record that is available in the market place without asking for permission of the copyright holders. In return, radio and TV stations are obliged to compensate copyright holders. Nevertheless, income from compensation had always been insignificant and well outside the strategic focus of firms A and B. The copyright legislation in 1964 represents a critical juncture (Sydow et al. 2009) for the path-dependent formation of firms' competences and hence their routines for releasing and exploiting music. It marks the critical point in the struggle of how to treat radio airplay and all other uses of recorded music apart from purchased records: as a substitute for record sales, and hence as a autonomous income source, or as a record promotion vehicle.

The second event that shaped the competence building of firms A and B was the introduction of official music charts by the music industry association in cooperation with a newly formed market research institute in 1977. The idea and practice of systematically charting music have had a deep influence on the firms' practice of releasing and exploitation (cf. Anand 2006; Anand/Peterson 2000 for U.S. record companies). Since then, in order to enhance audience reach, especially commercial media outlets have been expected to refer to chart positions when making decisions on programming and reporting. Also, retailers are expected to make purchase and stock decisions on the basis of actual chart positions. These expectations were omnipresent in meetings and whenever interviewees from firms A and B talked about how they make decisions on music selection, budgets and how to organize promotions, marketing and sales. A quote from a manager at firm A illustrates these expectations:

> *[...] and then there is this mechanism: you promote the single, it gets ranked in the charts, other radio stations start playing the single, you are higher ranked in the charts, you are visible in the outlets, the people know you and buy, and so forth. That's a kind of snowball effect.*

When referring to the charts as a "self-invented tool," the interviewees gave a literal impression of how they developed a competence that is geared towards setting in motion a dynamic that puts one artist's recording far ahead of others (cf. Rosen 1981; Adler 1984). As Pentland and Feldman (2005) refer to them, the official music charts can be understood as an artifact — a somewhat physical trace of the firms' competences reproduced in the pattern of actions. This artifact should not be confounded with the routines themselves. Rather, it guided the organization of releasing records in firms A and B. On the one hand, the charts reflect the dynamics expected in the music industry and its "winner-take-all" tendency. On the other hand, the charts are the point of reference for the major label's action patterns and used as an instrument for creating hits.

Competence Lock-in and the Rationality Shift

The above described events that took place in the music industry gave rise to the very similar action pattern and competence constellations we observed in both studied firms. The competence of hit creation was reproduced in the 1990s and still holds true for firm A today. As we showed above, it can be assumed to have become stabilized and finally locked-in by coordination effects and complementarity driving out alternative courses of actions. Nevertheless, the efficiency of the "Promoting Songs/Selling Bundles" routine is on shaky ground today, casting doubt on the benefits presented by this competence.

This becomes obvious from data we gathered at both companies. Representatives of both firm A and firm B implicitly pointed to this rationality shift that occurs when starting to engage in efforts of systematically generating income from hit creation by using music products other than records (e.g. branded entertainment); interviewees complained that while they create value ("we make the hits"), other companies were profiting more and more from their resource investments (most frequently named were the prospering concert agencies).

Data on sales of recorded music product configurations provided by the industry further support the assumption of a rationality shift in the action pattern. Physical singles have lost almost all relevance in the German market and have been largely replaced by track downloads, i.e. "real singles." Furthermore, sales of albums (both physical and non-physical) are still declining as single-track download numbers increase (BMVI 2011). In a nutshell, this means less profit contribution from every step in the cascade of "Promoting Songs/Selling Bundles," as consumers obviously prefer to buy songs rather than bundles (see also Elberse 2010).

4.3 Step 3: Efforts to Escape the Competence Lock-in

We now move on to answer our second research question as to what both firms did to escape their competence lock-in. The presentation of our findings so far has shown that firms A and B formed competences that are reflected by action patterns of releasing music and recouping investments in hit creation. Even though the data reveal indications for differences in details regarding routine performances over time, the pattern of competence development and reproduction closely matches across cases until 2008. Both firms' competence formation was equally affected by small events that took place in the industry (treating airplay as records promotion and chart entry as an ideal goal). The assumption of a competence path holds in both cases until very recently.

What makes the comparison of these two cases even more promising for research on competence paths is that starting in 2008 the cases begin to differ dramatically regarding competence reproduction. For four years, firm B had been part of a joint venture with another major record company until firm B's holding sold its interest in the joint venture in 2008 and formed a "new organization." On the one hand, this re-organization could be seen as starting up a new venture for investing in music and music exploitation. On the other hand, it was not started completely from scratch, as a large portion of the copyrights on records were transferred to the new organization; it still invests in releasing recorded music and operates under the name of firm B.

When asking interviewees from firm B about the reason for leaving the joint venture and forming a new organization, they reported that it would be impossible to transform this organization into "something that works nowadays" as it still concentrates on generating income from selling physical records instead of every possible use of their music copyrights. A quote from a senior manager illustrates how they perceive themselves as being different today:

> *The demand for music has never been as great as today. We perceive ourselves as a service provider for the use of music. We are willing to license and provide music everywhere as long as it is paid for. And that is not only selling physical records.*

Interestingly, very similar statements were made by managers and staff working for firm A. For example, a manager stated:

> *From our point of view: Everything is content today. Especially on the internet. Nobody should get our music for free. They can bawl 'then we do not do anything for your artists.' But if there is no good deal for us, no adequate financial compensation, no deal.*

Both statements reflect firms' endeavors to generate alternative income in order to compensate for lower numbers of (bundle) sales and thus build new business opportunities. Both firms engaged in forming alternative action patterns to realize profit compensation beyond the routine presented here as "Promoting Songs/Selling Bundles." However, they differ in their success. While in firm A all efforts to engage in new activities were soon governed by the old "Chart (Entry) Optimizing" routine, firm B had managed to refrain from exercising this activation of its hit creation competence and thereby broaden its scope of potential actions.

Firm A: Path-Induced Negative Effects on the Development of New Business Opportunities

In the case of firm A, the point of reference for how to organize record releases is still high chart entry. This ideal still guides how records are released. The ongoing routine still exhibits the coordination effects described above, but also negative effects with regard to actions now taken to generate income from new sources and uses of music. A quote from a business development manager at firm A gives an impression of how such negative effects unfold:

> *[...] a label manager comes from the CD business, and he makes the most transparent calculation he can. He says, I think I will sell as much as X records and digital downloads with this artist, that is conceivable, that is the basis for marketing and promotion. To come from the opposite site, calculating with licensing and merchandising, in terms of calculation and experience, is much more difficult for him. There are exceptions but they are still rare. In the end we are making chart performers who sell a lot of CDs and digital downloads and thereafter we try to extend our business. That's the situation. Whether it is the right way, that's another question.*

When selecting music for release and defining their budgets, firm A still relies on the rules and procedures provided by the routine of "Chart (Entry) Optimizing." Only after having realized a good chart performance are actions taken to generate alternative income from, e.g. merchandising or licensing. Ultimately, all actions taken are based on the number of records sold.

But besides this indirect negative effect, direct negative effects also unfold between the tasks for "Chart (Entry) Optimizing" and actions taken to expand firm A's exploitation of music. One way to generate income from music would be to systematically license this music to manufacturers of other goods as to support their branding. But this option is contradicted by firm A's product managers, who interact with such manufacturers only to harness their efforts in support of the "Chart (Entry) Optimizing" releasing routine:

> *Today we say we have to generate income out of this (branded music entertainment). But that's impossible for the product manager. He is responsible for dozens of releases and unable to realize such income. He says, dear brand, I need you. But then the willingness to pay on the part of the brand is very low. He is still searching for promotion partners, because he works in a release-oriented way. That makes business for us very difficult. (Business Development staff member, firm A)*

Obviously, it is not only positive feedback in and between routines (e.g. coordinating the release of dozens of records every month) that drives out alternative action patterns in firm A, but negative effects as well. Action patterns specific to "Chart (Entry) Optimizing" (promoting songs by cooperating with brands in terms of record promotion), and hence the locked-in reproduction of the hit creation competence, negatively affects additional actions intended to compensate for declining profits (e.g. income generation through "brand cooperation"). These negative effects can, on the one hand, be assumed to reproduce the competence lock-in of firm A despite the rationality shift reflected by the organization and its members. On the other hand, the still diminished scope of feasible action drives out potential for forming new competences (cf. Page 2006, Vergne/Durand 2011).

Firm B: Establishing Counteractions to Replace the Old Competences

In contrast, firm B nowadays calculates budgets for record releases not only on the basis of licensing potentials and long-term profit contributions. Neither does the organization engage in producing records itself, nor in the promotion, marketing and sale of records. Instead it provides the artists and their management with budgets to invest in these activities. In addition, firm B offers contacts to specialized service agencies and makes plans of expenditure jointly with the artists and their management. These plans now cover an extended period of at least two years. But once it realized that even so most budgets were being invested within much shorter periods, the "new recordings" department of firm B began splitting budgets into payments distributed over the period defined by the plan of expenditure. This new action pattern of financing record releases signifies a process that forgoes the focus on the firm's traditional hit-creation competence. By outsourcing marketing, promotion and sales and even splitting up the budgets for these activities, firm B circumvents organizing record releases as it did in the past and, as shown above, as firm A still does. Letting artists invest a budget at their disposal to release their own records it much less likely that financed music recordings will enter the charts, as the control of the process lies outside the organization. Thus the firm's coordination mechanism ceases to function. The likelihood of a high chart entry is even further diminished by splitting up the provided budget for releasing music on records over periods that were almost irrelevant before. However, now that it is incapable of organizing high chart entries, firm B enjoys the flexibility needed to set up new action patterns and thereby form new competences.

While firm B still takes a share of the artists' income from selling singles and albums of recorded songs, its focus lies on licensing copyrights. As a senior manager of firm B explains:

> *As you know, we have contracts with TV and film producers. They use music and we provide creative advice. Thereby we license our rights. There is not just the CD. It still has importance. But for us it is important that the artist also performs live. It must be music that is good for licensing to film, TV and advertising. Instead of dozens of promoters and marketing experts we now have music supervisors and song pluggers...*

When contracting new music and defining budgets for release, firm B no longer focuses solely on the estimated numbers of record sales, but also on artists' potential for performing live and whether or not the music might fit into films, television series and commercial advertising. In the process of making decisions on what music to contract and how to define budgets for record releases, the staff responsible for licensing the music to firms other than record manufacturers and distributors is integrated early on. These music supervisors offer firm B's music copyrights mainly to television, film and advertising producers. Instead of forcing them to license music that is about to be released on records in hopes of "breaking into" the charts, which requires a major media presence, they recommend music that matches the substance of films, programs and ads, offering a sort of music consulting service. On the one hand, this seems to have made firm B into a distinguished service partner, as it now has exclusive contracts with most of Germany's major film and television producers. Furthermore, the newly formed competence of recommending music for films, TV and ads becomes more and more attractive for artists as it represents a significant and constant income flow. On the other hand, this new competence emerged over a period of almost two years, during which time firm B was incapable of engaging in its traditional competence of hit creation.

This short description gives an account of how a firm B was able to form a new competence while simultaneously establishing a process that counteracted the reproduction of the old one. The counteractions (stretching expenditure plans, outsourcing marketing, promotion and sales tasks, splitting up budgets over longer periods) are designed to preclude the traditional competence of reliable hit creation. Comparable action patterns in firm A were not observed in the study. The main reason for this difference seems to be not that only firm B reflected the rationality shift regarding the locked-in competence and the path-induced restriction of its potential to form a new one. Rather, firm B managed to make its organization "incompetent" by counteracting the elements of the hit creation action pattern. Organizing record releases in firm B is no longer guided by "Chart (Entry) Optimizing." Thereby the negative effects we observed in case of firm A with regard to the formation of reliable action patterns to generate alternative income were ultimately avoided in firm B.

	Firm A	**Firm B**
Reflection of rationality shift	Yes	Yes
New competence building actions	Yes	Yes
Negative effects on competence building	Yes	Yes
Reactions on negative effects	None	Yes
Situation after reflection of rationality shift	Permanently competent due to lock-in	Temporarily incompetent due to counter-actions

Table 3: Comparison of path breaking efforts

5. Discussion

The empirical study of two firms' competence development shows that going back to the origins of their given paths, namely the small, but nevertheless critical events, can explain why each path was taken. It is a competence path that seems at least questionable regarding its efficiency in the digital age (e.g. record sales as the sole income source), but is still difficult to break. It thereby highlights the somewhat dangerous implication of a competence path that is often left unstudied when concentrating on how a path-dependent development of competence and the underlying positive feedback effects lead to firm's unique competitiveness (Teece 2010). Forming a competence for hit creation, by using radio airplay and later every media use of (recorded) music copyrights solely to promote records, was neither the only feasible option for firms A and B, nor was it inefficient early on. It seemed very rational at that point in time. The resulting threat of rigidity was not predictable, as the whole process was non-ergodic (Arthur 1989; Sydow et al. 2009). Although small events directed the process of competence development, rigidity came in later on. Even the consequent lock-in of both firms' competences and action pattern became problematic only when the environment changed fundamentally due to the ongoing digitization of media and the widespread use of such technologies by music consumers. Thus it seems almost impossible for a firm to avoid the formation of a competence path and lock-in. It does not even seem very clever to conduct path avoidance, as this would mean losing out on the positive feedback that unfolds during the process (e.g. coordination and complementarities) and often is at the very heart of a firm's unique competences.

This makes it all the more important for competence research applying the model of path-dependent processes to answer the question of how to break a competence path in the lock-in phase. Such findings would be especially relevant for firms that find themselves in this phase and are confronted with a rationality shift which means that the competence no longer yields satisfactory success in the market process. Some authors point to a kind sort of "organizational reflexivity" as a precondition for path breakage (Sydow et al. 2009). Following this argumentation, it is imperative to reflect on a (superior) alternative and the drivers that keep the competence reproduction on track. Mainly this means being aware of the positive feedback mechanisms that exclude actions beyond the scope of the competence path. But reflecting on the drivers of rigidity is not the same as gaining new flexibility to develop new competences. According to Sydow et al. (2009), the sufficient condition for leaving a path of ongoing competence reproduction can be seen only in stopping those mechanisms from directing competence development.

What makes our empirical findings particularly interesting is that they highlight the importance of studying negative effects in research on (how to break) competence paths. As Page (2006) and Vergne and Durand (2011) theoretically argue, negative effects with regard to alternative courses of action render the path-dependent reproduction of paths inefficient in the long run. Sensitized by this argumentation, we concluded that it is the negative effect that forced firm B to actively dismiss its locked-in competence in order to pave the way to forming a new one.

Both firms' competence paths analyzed in this paper are based on positive feedback mechanisms. Actions taken to release a record were ever better coordinated between A&R, product management, promotion and sales departments, and the ideas for how to create the value (hit song) and how to capture this value (through bundling) are complementary.

As can be seen in the case of firm A, exploring new action potentials and courses of action (e.g. actively licensing released music to brands) sooner or later becomes negatively affected by the ongoing exploitation of deeply inscribed ideas and rules about how to act and how to sequence these actions (brand as a promotion partner to organize a media presence for unreleased music).

In contrast, for firm B it can be shown that stopping these very mechanisms of a competence reproduction for this organization constituted the first steps toward becoming incompetent. Incompetent, that is, compared with what used to be considered a necessary capability to succeed in the music recording market. Nevertheless it seemed necessary, as competence reproduction was not only governed by positive feedback, but at least in our cases yielded negative effects on the endeavor of simultaneously building new business opportunities.

By comparing the recent contrast in how firms A and B adapted to the music market after the rationality shift, we aim to make a first contribution to the question of how to actually break a competence path. We found in both firms a high degree of reflexivity regarding the positive feedback mechanisms driving their competence reproduction. We also found an awareness of the negative effects that hindered the exploration of new action potentials in both cases. But only firm B managed to start a process that was geared towards working against a further reproduction of the hit creation competence and hence broke its path.

This path breakage was a process in itself, as it first gave rise to an action pattern that aimed to counter path-induced action patterns and thereby makes the firm incapable of creating hits — incompetent compared to its past action potentials. Only after setting this process of counteractions into motion could firm B explore the potential for forming new business opportunities (music consulting service and licensing).

5.1 Providing for Temporary Incompetence as Taking an Anti-Stance and Forcing Unlearning

Putting the process of becoming incompetent in motion began with the decision of firm B's parent company to leave the joint venture formed with another major record company only four years earlier. A group of experienced music managers were mandated to form a new organization. Within a couple of weeks they developed a vision of to how to create value (providing music services) and how to capture value (licensing music rights). However, they still faced uncertainty as to which competences had to be developed and how to do so. During interviews it was often emphasized that they do not think they have a ready-made solution at hand, but still need to figure out what works and what does not. But taking the existence of this vision into account, we cannot really speak of "strategy absence" in the case of firm B (Inkpen/Choudgury 1995). And what became obvious was an anti-stance taken against almost everything that fell into the traditional strategic scope of firm B. In our interviews with two managers of this group we were told that during their initial meetings they discussed in equal parts what the new organization "has to do" and what it "should not longer do." As a result, for example, the chart positions of their financed music releases were declared to be parameters almost irrelevant to success.

At the same time, when trying concretize and implement the vision of a new organizational competence by initializing a new action pattern for releasing and exploiting music, in firm B they set up procedures that counteract the firm's traditional way of doing this business. In so doing the anti-stance was put into action. At the same time firm B accepted that it would become incompetent as regards the action potentials it had before, and for which it was known within the industry. This became very clear when we talked to industry experts and artists about firm B. They could hardly make sense of what firm B was doing. Firm B obviously no longer met their expectations of what a record company can do. Correspondingly, we were told by managers of firm B that they had a hard time explaining to artists, managers and the like what they could offer. As it took time to build firm B's new competence — providing music consulting service to media producers — and make its reproduction reliable over a sequence of services, firm B was temporarily in a state of incompetence. This situation was brought about intentionally by a top-down planning of a group of managers, who had a long career in the music business, and who knew that the firm had failed to generate significant alternative income for its music investment in the past when it was still striving for hit creation.

The counteractions these managers initialized in their plan come close to what is referred to as "organizational unlearning" (Nystrom/Starbuck 1984; de Holan/Phillips 2004). Unlearning is regarded as erasing organizational memory so as to make way for the storage of new experiences and learning from them. The process of breaking a competence path, as we could observe in the case of firm B, is geared towards erasing the organizational potential for doing things in a certain way and thereby cutting the recursive reproduction of the firm's competences (as a specific potential for action). The path-breaking counteractions found in the case of firm B do not represent a competence in themselves. Just as unlearning does not imply new learning, the counteractions that turn the firm's competence into an incompetence do not produce a valuable output for the firm. Nevertheless, they shield the efforts of forming new business opportunities from the negative effects of a path-dependent reproduction of firm's traditional competences.

5.2 Managing through Temporary Incompetence as a Method of Refining Unlearning and Tolerating Uncertainty

This is easier said than done, as the path-induced competence is deeply inscribed in the firm's idea of how to create or capture value due to a historical process that has long been governed by positive feedback. It is hardly conceivable that this deep inscription of a path in the "organization body" (Koch 2011) can be rubbed out by an on-off, top-down management invention. That is why we found that the process of path breakage does not equate to a somewhat simple top-down planning and implementation process. As we could observe in firm B, the counteractions were and still are subject to refinement if the desired result of incompetence is not achieved. These refinements originate from various levels within the organization. For example, splitting up budget payouts to artists and promotion agencies to circumvent chart-oriented expenditure was introduced by the staff members of "new recordings" department and subsequently became part of firm B's general idea of how to finance record releases.

Refining unlearning where it is necessary, and preventing the organization from falling back to the familiar ideas and rules, requires tolerating the uncertainty such a temporary state of incompetence brings about for the whole organization. Even if the firm manages to successfully counteract competence path reproduction, this does not ensure the formation of a new competence itself, nor does it guarantee future success in the market process. Instead it produces a sort of "clean slate situation" (Pentland et al. 2010), where no "ready made" action-orienting rules and procedures are at hand, but still need to be formed and tested. It can be assumed that the longer this takes, the more attractive falling back into the old action pattern becomes.

As we could observe in the case of firm B, the whole firm accepted a high risk of failure. Although this risky situation was clearly supposed to be limited in its temporal extension, it was uncertain at the beginning how long it would take to establish new competences to guide organizational actions of reliable value creation. Therefore it did not surprise us that we found a comparably flat hierarchy in the "new organization" of firm B, giving members of the organization the possibility to immediately test ideas and new courses of action. Furthermore, former freelancers were preferred by the firm when recruiting new staff. These employees, especially, often referred to the situation of firm B as representing an opportunity rather than a risk. This observation of a comparably high degree of distributed entrepreneurship inside the firm points only to one facet that still awaits further investigation when it comes to the question of how to effectively break a competence path.

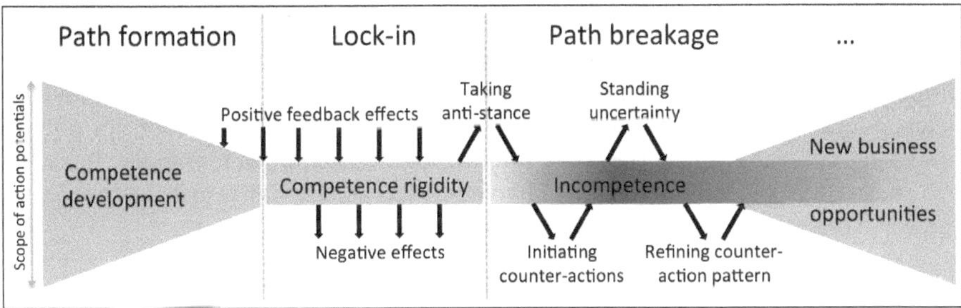

Figure 1: Process of competence path breakage

6. Conclusion

As argued above, breaking a competence path by turning a state of competence into temporary incompetence is of great relevance not only for record companies in the digital age. For us it seems worthwhile to further study and conceptualize such processes because clearly not all, but still many of the most successful firms can be expected to have formed their action potentials following a path-dependent process and sooner or later will be confronted with the necessity of breaking the lock-in.

For example, Microsoft has developed extraordinary competences in producing proprietary software favored by positive feedback effects. The more software they produced, the easier it became for them to build on existing code when producing new releases of operating systems and application software (cf. Vergne/Durand 2011). But when the users' software preferences (e.g. cloud-based) and/or the way software is produced (e.g. customer co-production), changes, adaptation to these trends could mean that Microsoft must stop the drivers of its competence development and reproduction. At the same time, stopping the drivers would mean deliberately transforming the firm's competence of accumulating and reusing proprietary code into an incompetence of doing so. The example of Microsoft indicates that there are plenty of cases that await study from the perspective of how to break competence paths.

This paper represents a first step in the direction of conceptualizing the process of competence path breakage. Our empirical case study results indicate that this is best done by conceptualizing the (strategic) process and building on what we know from research on organizational unlearning (Akgün et al. 2007). As such, competence path breaking is distinctive from that of forming new competences. Instead, the process entails preconditioning as well as accompanying the forming of new competences, as it means managing for a state of temporary incompetence. Analyzing this competence path breakage always implies investigating the competence path formed in the past. Only tracing the events and mechanisms that shaped the specific path of competence development allows the path-breaking counteractions to be identified and analytically separated from actions intended to activate the new competence. Our tentative conceptualization of the process of path breakage therefore echoes what Lewin (1947) described as two different methods of changing levels of organizational conduct: adding forces in the direction of desired change, and diminishing opposing forces. We propose that competence path breakage first requires radical "unfreezing", as a competence lock-in amounts to a deeply frozen organization. This calls for not only diminishing opposing forces (negative effects), but disabling them entirely. Inversely, this means turning the organizational competence upside down and for the firm to force and tolerate a (temporary) state of incompetence.

References

Adler, M. (1985): Stardom and Talent. In: The American Economic Review, 75(1): 208-212.

Akgün, A. E./Byrne, J. C./Lynn, G. S./Keskin, H. (2007): Organizational Unlearning as Changes in Beliefs and Routines in Organizations. In: Journal of Organizational Change Management, 20(6): 794-812.

Anand, N. (2006): Charting the Music Business: Billboard Magazine and the Development of the Commercial Music Field. In: Lampel, J/Shamsie, J./Lant, T. K. (Eds.): The Business of Culture: Strategic Perspectives on Entertainment and Media, Routledge: London: 139-154.

Anand, N./Peterson, R. A. (2000): When Market Information Constitutes Fields: Sensemaking of Markets in the Commercial Music Industry. In: Organization Science, 11(3): 270-284.

Arthur, W. B. (1989): Competing Technologies, Increasing Returns, and Lock-In by Historical Events. In: The Economic Journal, 99(394): 116-131.

Arthur, W. B. (1994): Increasing Returns and Path Dependence in the Economy, Ann Arbor: University of Michigan Press.

Barney, J. 1991: Firm Resources and Sustained Competitive Advantage. In: Journal of Management, 17(1): 99 -120,

BVMI (2011): Musikindustrie in Zahlen 2010, Berlin: Bundesverband Musikindustrie.

Burgelman, R. A. (2002): Strategy as Vector and the Inertia of Co-Evolutionary Lock-in. In: Administrative Science Quarterly, 47(2): 325-357.

Burgelman, R. A. (2008): Strategic Consequences of Co-Evolution Lock-In: Insights from a Longitudinal Process Study. In: SSRN eLibrary, http://papers.ssrn.com/sol3/papers.cfm?abstract_id=1314453, May 29, 2010.

Danneels, E. (2011): Trying to Become a Different Type of Company: Dynamic Capability at Smith Corona. In: Strategic Management Journal, 32(1): 1–31.

David, P. A. (1985): Clio and the Economics of QWERTY. In: The American Economic Review, 75(2): 332-337.

Dobusch, L./Kapeller, J. (2011): Striking New Paths: Theory and Method in Path Dependence Research, Presented at the 2nd International Conference on Path Dependence, Berlin.

Dosi, G. (1982): Technological Paradigms and Technological Trajectories. In: Research Policy, 11(3): 147-162.

Dowd, T. (2006): From 78s to MP3s: The Embedded Impact of Technology in the Market for Prerecorded Music. In: Lampel, J/Shamsie, J./Lant, T. K. (Eds.): The Business of Culture: Strategic Perspectives on Entertainment and Media, Routledge: London: 205-226.

Eisenhardt, K. M. (1989): Building Theories from Case Study Research. The Academy of Management Review, 14(4): 532-550.

Elberse, A. (2010): Bye-Bye Bundles: The Unbundling of Music in Digital Channels. In: Journal of Marketing, 74: 107–123.

Freiling, J./Gersch, M./Goeke, C. (2008): On the Path Towards a Competence-based Theory of the Firm. In: Organization Studies, 29(8-9): 1143-1164.

Garofalo, R. (1999): From Music Publishing to MP3: Music and Industry in the Twentieth Century. In: American Music, 17(3): 318-354.

Garud, R./Kumaraswamy, A./Karnøe, P. (2010): Path Dependence or Path Creation? In: Journal of Management Studies, 47(4): 760-774.

Gerring, J. (2007): Case Study Research: Principles and Practices, University Press: Cambridge.

Gersch, M./Goeke, C./Freiling, J. 2009. Empirische Herausforderungen (co-)evolutorischer Forschungskonzeptionen. Anstöße für eine Methodenreflexion im Rahmen der empirischen Kompetenzforschung. In: Jahrbuch Strategisches Kompetenz Management, 3: 104-135. München/Mering: Hampp.

Glaser, B. G./Strauss, A. L. (1967): The Discovery of Grounded Theory, New York: Aldine de Gruyter.

Helfat, C. E./Peteraf, M. A. (2003): The Dynamic Resource-Based View: Capability Lifecycles. In: Strategic Management Journal, 24(10): 997-1010.

de Holan, P. M./Phillips, N. (2004): Organizational Forgetting as Strategy. In: Strategic Organization, 2(4): 423 -433.

Inkpen, A./Choudhury, N. (1995): The Seeking of Strategy where it is not: Towards a Theory of Strategy Absence. In: Strategic Management Journal, 16(4): 313–323.

Koch, J. (2008): Strategic Paths and Media Management—A Path Dependency Analysis of the German Newspaper Branch of High Quality Journalism. In: Schmalenbach Business Review, (60): 50-73.

Koch, J. (2009): Innovation, organisationale Routinen und strategische Pfade. In: Zeitschrift für Management, 4(3): 189–208.

Koch, J. (2011): Inscribed Strategies: Exploring the Organizational Nature of Strategic Lock-in. In: Organization Studies, 32(3): 337 -363.

Langley, A. (1999): Strategies for Theorizing from Process Data. In: Academy of Management Review, 24(4): 691-710.

Leonard-Barton, D. (1992): Core Capabilities and Core Rigidities: A Paradox in Managing New Product Development. In: Strategic Management Journal, 13: 111-125.

Lewin, K. 1947. Quasi-Stationary Social Equilibria and the Problem of Permanent Change. In: Burke, W. W./Lake, D. G./Paine, J. W. (Eds.): Organization Change: A Comprehensive Reader, Hoboken: John Wiley & Sons: 73-78.

Miles, M. B./Huberman, A. M. (1994): Qualitative Data Analysis: An Expanded Sourcebook, London: Sage.

Nystrom, P. C./Starbuck, W. H. (1984): To Avoid Organizational Crises, Unlearn. In: Organizational Dynamics, 12(4): 53-65.

Page, S. E. (2006): Path Dependence. In: Quarterly Journal of Political Science, 1(1): 87–115.

Pentland, B. T./Feldman, M. S. (2005): Organizational Routines as a Unit of Analysis. In: Industrial Corporate Change, 14(5): 793-815.

Pentland, B. T./Feldman, M. S./Becker, M. C./Lui, P. (2010): The Temporal Foundations of Organizational Routines. Presented at the Helsinki Conference on the Micro-level Origins of Organizational Routines and Capabilities, Helsinki.

Pierson, P. (2000): Increasing Returns, Path Dependence, and the Study of Politics. In: The American Political Science Review, 94(2): 251-267.

Rosen, S. (1981): The Economics of Superstars. In: The American Economic Review, 71(5): 845-858.

Schreyögg, G./Kliesch, M. (2007): How Dynamic Can Organizational Capabilities Be? Towards a Dual-Process Model of Capability Dynamization. In: Strategic Management Journal, 28(9): 913-933,

Schreyögg, G./Sydow, Jörg. (2011): Organizational Path Dependence: A Process View. In: Organization Studies, 32(3): 321 -335.

Shapiro, C./Varian, H. R. (1999): Information Rules: a Strategic Guide to the Network Economy. In: Harvard Business Press: Cambridge.

Siggelkow, N. (2007): Persuasion with Case Studies. In: Academy of Management Journal, 50(1): 20-24.

Sydow, Jörg/Schreyögg, G./Koch, J. (2009): Organizational Path Dependence: Opening the Black Box. In: Academy of Management Review, 34(4): 689-709.

Teece, D. J. (2007): Explicating Dynamic Capabilities: the Nature and Microfoundations of (Sustainable) Enterprise Performance. In: Strategic Management Journal, 28(13): 1319–1350.

Teece, D. J. (2010): Business Models, Business Strategy and Innovation. In: Long Range Planning, 43(2-3): 172-194.

Teece, D. J./Pisano, G./Shuen, A. (1997): Dynamic Capabilities and Strategic Management. In: Strategic Management Journal, 18(7): 509-533.

Vergne, J.-P./Durand, R. (2010): The Missing Link Between the Theory and Empirics of Path Dependence: Conceptual Clarification, Testability Issue, and Methodological Implications. In: Journal of Management Studies, 47(4): 736-759.

Vergne, J.-P./Durand, R. (2011): The Path of Most Persistence: An Evolutionary Perspective on Path Dependence and Dynamic Capabilities. In: Organization Studies, 32(3): 365 -382.

Wikström, P. (2006): Reluctantly Virtual: Modelling Copyright Industry Dynamics, Karlstad: University Press.

Wikstrom, P. (2010): The Music Industry: Music in the Cloud, Polity Press: Cambridge.

Yin, R. K. (2009): Case Study Research: Design and Methods, Sage Publications: London.

Zollo, M./Winter, S. G. (2002): Deliberate Learning and the Evolution of Dynamic Capabilities. In: Organization Science, 13(3): 339-351.

Strategische Prozessdynamisierung durch betriebliches Flexibilitätscontrolling

Torsten Klein

Zusammenfassung

Ausgehend von zunehmender Dynamik und Instabilität von Märkten, auf denen sich Unternehmen im Wettbewerb behaupten müssen, sind Organisationen mit der Herausforderung zur flexiblen Gestaltung konfrontiert. Die dynamische Kompetenzforschung befasst sich dazu mit Ansätzen zur dynamischen Prozessgestaltung. Der vorliegende Beitrag untersucht dazu ergänzend, wie eine Organisation die zur Flexibilisierung notwendigen Ressourcen frühzeitig unter Berücksichtigung der ökonomischen Aspekte Kosten und Zeit sichern und geplant steuern kann. Dazu wird ein Konzept zur Erzeugung flexibler Ressourcenverfügbarkeit erstellt. Dies befasst sich vornehmlich mit externer und interner Positionierung von strategischen Reserveressourcen sowie der Nutzung inaktiver Ressourcenfunktionen. Die Überlegungen münden schließlich in einem dynamischen Ansatz des Ressourcencontrollings zur Klärung der Frage, wie ein Unternehmen Ressourcenflexibilität nachhaltig steuern kann.

Schlüsselwörter: Prozesse, Ressourcen, Flexibilität, organisationale Kompetenzen, Dynamisierung, Ressourcencontrolling, Unternehmenswandel, Marktvolatilität

Abstract

Modern market-driven mechanisms are different to the business context twenty or thirty years ago. Nowadays markets are often characterized by high volatility. Future is more unpredictable and offers economic markets a lot of possible directions to develop. Therefore companies are looking for efficient solutions to manage dynamic challenges and to defend or increase competitive advantages. Several fields of economic sciences have come up in the last recent decades trying to explain competitive advantages, especially in dynamic markets. For example, the last fifteen years were dominated by theories of dynamic capabilities in several contexts of organizational sciences. Researchers as well as companies try to dynamize internal processes and competencies. If we analyze organizational behavior we can note, that the resource base of a company is eminently important for gaining more flexibility. The organization can avert the danger of failure in a volatile market and even increase the adaption by raising the configuration flexibility of competencies. The specific resource availability is the foundation of energetic activities and generating competitive advantages. Additionally, we have to go adrift from the traditional perspective of resource theory. Instead, we have to be aware of the tremendous potential of slack resources that are retained internal and external the business. Therefore this paper investigates additionally to existing approaches of dynamization, how a business achieves necessary resources to build organizational flexibility. An adequate quantity and quality of resources has to be available at any time. Because of the incremental relevance of the organizational resource base for increasing strategic flexibility in an unpredictable environment, slack resources and additional resource functions are focused to increase resource flexibility. Internal and also external resources can be the solution for a strategic business model if the organization has the option to completely internalize and utilize these resources at any time. Additionally, a company can use inactive functions of resources like unused employee skills, that can be identified and activated if required. Thus three strategic sources of resource flexibility were identified: positioning internal and also external slack resources and identify inactive functions of already existing resources. The approach finally leads to a dynamic system of resource controlling. By this means the research question can be answered, how an organization can manage resource flexibility permanently in daily business.

Keywords: Processes, Resources, Flexibility, Organizational Competencies, Dynamization, Resource Controlling, Organizational Changes, Market Volatility

1. Einleitung

Die Kompetenzforschung befindet sich im Umbruch. Die Stabilisierungslogik organisationaler Kompetenzen wird den dynamischen Anforderungen ausgehend von volatilen Märkten nicht länger gerecht. Deshalb entstand eine Forderung nach Dynamisierung des Konzepts organisationaler Kompetenzen (bspw. Teece et al. 1997; Schreyögg/Kliesch 2006). Gemeinsam haben die meisten bislang erbrachten Ansätze, dass sie die Dynamisierungsanforderung aus der Perspektive der Mittelverwendung betrachten. Dabei wird im Wesentlichen der Einsatz von betrieblichen Ressourcen im Sinne von organisationalem Lernen diskutiert. Durch organisationales Lernen soll eine Anpassung der Kompetenzen an die dynamische Umwelt ermöglicht werden.

Diverse Studien verdeutlichen den hohen Wert dynamischer Kompetenzen für die Organisation als Treiber von Innovation und Entwicklung. (bspw. Ellonen et al. 2011). Die bestehenden Dynamisierungsvorschläge vernachlässigen dabei jedoch die Perspektive der strategischen Ressourcenbereitstellung (Cavusgil et al. 2007: 161). Um Ressourcen zur Dynamisierung einzusetzen, müssen zunächst Ressourcen verfügbar sein und strategisch positioniert werden (Ruiz-Moreno et al. 2008: 520; Su et al. 2009: 88). Der Beitrag erstellt ein Konzept flexibler Ressourcenverfügbarkeit unter Anwendung von Überschussressourcen und inaktiven Ressourcenfunktionen. Zusätzlich wird ein konzeptioneller Ansatz dargestellt, der beschreibt, wie es einer Organisation gelingen kann, Ressourcensicherung sowohl nachhaltig als auch gleichzeitig effizient zu gestalten: Eine generelle Herausforderung des Unternehmertums im Zwiespalt zwischen Wettbewerbsfähigkeit und Kosten.

Der nachhaltige Aufbau eines Pools an zusätzlichen Ressourcen (Cyert/March 1963: 36-38) könnte gegenüber der langwierigen externen Gewinnung von Ressourcen die schnellere, flexiblere und auch günstigere Alternative zur Bereitstellung neuer Ressourcen bieten (Zajac et al. 2000: 433; Mishina et al. 2004: 1182). Dieser Aspekt ist im Dynamisierungsprozess von organisationalen Kompetenzen allerdings bislang nicht ausreichend analysiert.

Im Fokus dieses eingereichten Beitrags steht die Forschungsfrage: Wie und mit welchen Elementen lässt sich unter der Prämisse organisationaler Dynamisierung ein zielgerichteter Prozess zur effizienten und nachhaltigen Ressourcensicherung konzeptionell gestalten und steuern?

2. Statische Denkbilder als überholungsbedürftige Auslaufmodelle

Die Diskussion um die Sinnhaftigkeit von dynamischen Kompetenzen verläuft kontrovers – weniger im Hinblick auf den theoretischen Erklärungsansatz (Teece et al. 1997; Eisenhardt/Martin 2000; Schreyögg/Kliesch 2006; Wang/Ahmed 2007; Ambrosini/Bowman 2009) als vielmehr in Bezug auf den Verwertungs- und Gestaltungszusammenhang: Wann und wie kann ein strategischer Entscheider eines Unternehmens eine Ressourcenausstattung konkret als dynamische Kompetenz planen und verwenden?

Organisationale Kompetenzen werden in der Literatur als Konfigurationen von Ressourcen definiert (Prahalad/Hamel 1990: 81-82; Black/Boal 1994: 134; Day 1994: 38). Deren statisches Konzept wird von Vertretern der dynamischen Kompetenzen kritisiert. Sukzessiv setzt sich die Auffassung durch, organisationale Kompetenzen anstatt als statische Bestandsgrößen zu verstehen, sie als dynamische Veränderungsprozesse zu konzipieren (Montealegre 2002: 516-517), wie auch Uotila et al. (2009) in ihrer Studie zeigen.

Die in den Wirtschaftswissenschaften vorhandenen Modelle des strategischen Managements basieren häufig auf starren Prämissen und festen Rahmenbedingungen (Jaikumar/Bohn 1992: 265; Chi et al. 2008: 62; Gould/Hogg 2008: 160; Payne et al. 2009: 422-423). Sie sind verhaftet in statischen Denkbildern zur Erklärung und Gestaltung organisationaler Strukturen. Die Aufbau- und Ablauforganisation eines Unternehmens wird beispielsweise oftmals in Form von inflexiblen Organigrammen visualisiert und optimiert (Schierenbeck 2003: 105).

Diese apodiktischen Denkbilder der Unternehmensführung fingieren eine Wirtschaftswelt geprägt durch Überschaubarkeit und Berechenbarkeit, von Eindimensionalität und Gradlinigkeit. Tatsächlich ist der Markt von Unternehmen zumeist keine starre Einbahnstraße umgeben von statisch-dogmatischen Rahmenbedingungen, die Sicherheit und Planbarkeit suggerieren (Ghemawat/Costa 1993: 59-61). Die wettbewerbliche Realität ist geprägt durch flexible und mutable Marktphänomene, die Instabilität und Unsicherheit erzeugen sowie Modifikation und Adaption von erfolgreichen Marktakteuren verlangen (Weimar 2002: 240-241; Otto/Simon 2008: 321; Hou/Chien 2010; 97-98).

Es bedarf einer mentalen Transition weg von statischen Denkmustern hin zu einem dynamischen Leitbild der strategischen Unternehmensführung (Graversen et al. 2005: 1508). Dabei dürfen Prozesse nicht länger als starre Routinen, und Strukturen nicht länger als feste Bestandsgrößen im Unternehmen betrachtet werden, sondern müssen als dynamisch-veränderliche Variablen begriffen werden (Sanchez/Mahoney 1996: 64-65; Schreyögg/Kliesch 2006: 456; Tallon 2008: 1-2). Neben einer veränderten, dynamisch geprägten Perspektive auf Routinen und Strukturen muss auch der Umgang mit diesen Elementen innerhalb der Unternehmen dynamisiert werden (Romme et al. 2010: 1291-1292). Da das System des Unternehmens im Sinne von Aufbau- und Ablauforganisation adaptionsfähig und in einer dynamischen Umwelt vor allem auch adaptionsbedürftig ist, müssen die betrieblichen Routinen und Strukturen flexibel gestaltet werden, damit eine Adaption des Organisationssystems an veränderte Marktbedingungen gelingen kann (Davis et al. 2009: 414).

Die Notwendigkeit zur Dynamisierung aufgrund einer volatilen Unternehmensumwelt ergibt sich auch im Bereich der organisationalen Kompetenzen. Die dynamische Gestaltung von organisationalen Kompetenzen wurde in der jüngeren Literatur zunehmend behandelt und entsprechende Lösungsansätze wurden diskutiert (bspw. Teece et al. 1997; Eisenhardt/Martin 2000; Schreyögg/Kliesch 2006; Wang/Ahmed 2007; Ambrosini/Bowman 2009). Ausgangspunkt für die Dynamisierungsforderung bei Kompetenzen von Unternehmen ist die Diskrepanz zwischen dem statischen Kompetenzkonstrukt auf der Seite der Organisation und dynamischer Wettbewerbsverläufe auf der Seite der Unternehmensumwelt (Zott 2003: 98). Das grundlegende klassische Kompetenzkonstrukt (bspw. Prahalad/Hamel 1990) ist in Statik gebettet. Die klassischen Ansätze sehen lediglich die Umweltdynamik als nennenswert, vernachlässigen jedoch die Einbeziehung der notwendigen organisationsinhärenten Flexibilität (bspw. Prahalad/Hamel 1990). Somit benennen sie bestenfalls die Marktdynamik als Ausgangspunkt für eine nähere Betrachtung der organisationalen Kompetenzen. Jedoch blockieren Sie in ihren Ansätzen im nächsten Schritt die Entfaltung der wettbewerbsnotwendigen Organisationsdynamik, indem sie dann wiederum Identifikation, Ausbau und Stabilisierung von Kompetenzen fokussieren (Schoemaker 1992). Sie setzen dadurch auf deren Beibehaltung als konstituierender Kern der Wettbewerbsfähigkeit und zielen damit auf langfristige Statik ab. Den klassischen Ansätzen fehlt damit die auf Kompetenzen und Ressourcen bezogene Dynamik als integraler Bestandteil (Stein/Klein 2010).

3. Organisationale Kompetenzen unter der „Dynamisierungslupe"

3.1 Ressourcenpotenziale als Ausgangspunkt zur Kompetenzdynamisierung

Als Ansatzpunkt zur Dynamisierung von organisationalen Kompetenzen, muss bei näherer Betrachtung das der Organisation zur Verfügung stehende Flexibilisierungspotenzial definiert werden (McKelvie/Davidsson 2009). Dazu bietet sich zunächst eine Fokussierung der drei Betrachtungsobjekte organisationale Ressourcen, organisationale Kompetenzen und dynamische organisationale Kompetenzen an.

Das Forschungsfeld der organisationalen Ressourcen betrachtet das wettbewerbsorientierte Verhalten eines Unternehmens unter Berücksichtigung der Potenziale, die der Organisation zur Verfügung stehen. Ausgehend von Ressourcen, über die das betrachtete Unternehmen verfügt, plant die Organisation das Verhalten auf dem Markt. Die zur Verfügung stehenden Ressourcen geben den Verhaltensspielraum für das Unternehmen vor (Penrose 1959: 24).

Der Bereich der Forschung im strategischen Management, in dem organisationale Kompetenzen untersucht werden, stellt hingegen die Fähigkeiten eines Unternehmens in den Mittelpunkt der Analyse. Ausgehend von der Bestimmung der organisationalen Kompetenz legt ein Unternehmen Strategien für das Verhalten im Wettbewerb fest (Selznick 1957: 47). Ähnlich wie im Forschungsfeld der organisationalen Ressourcen, bestimmen die internen Größen einer Organisation die Aktionen im Wettbewerb. Während bei den organisationalen Ressourcen Potenziale in Form von Produktionsfaktoren ausschlaggebend für das Marktverhalten sind, bilden im Forschungsfeld der organisationalen Kompetenzen die Fähigkeiten eines Unternehmens die Basis für die Verhaltensbestimmung auf dem Markt.

Dynamische organisationale Kompetenzen entsprechen vom Zielvorhaben her ebenfalls dem Konzept der organisationalen Kompetenzen. Aufbauend auf den Fähigkeiten einer Organisation soll die Wettbewerbsposition des betrachteten Unternehmens gesichert und bestenfalls ausgebaut werden. Der Unterschied zwischen dynamischen organisationalen Kompetenzen und den organisationalen Kompetenzen liegt in der konzeptionell zugrundeliegenden Dynamik (bspw. Teece et al. 1997; Eisenhardt/Martin 2000; Schreyögg/Kliesch-Eberl 2007).

Die Dynamik, welche in Ansätzen der dynamischen organisationalen Kompetenzen gefordert wird, benötigt veränderte Voraussetzungen und Logiken in der Kompetenzforschung. Während Ansätze zu organisationalen Ressourcen und organisationalen Kompetenzen auf statischen Annahmen und Betrachtungsweisen aufbauen, verlangt die gegenwärtige wirtschaftswissenschaftliche Forschungswelt Antworten auf Forschungsfragen, die auf einem Paradigma mit dynamischen Grundannahmen fußen. Die statischen Betrachtungen gelten nicht in einer Welt voller komplexer Dynamik, geprägt durch stetige Veränderungs- und Anpassungsprozesse (Schreyögg/Kliesch 2006: 455-456; Wang/Ahmed 2007: 35-39).

Da Kompetenzen einer Organisation als Zusammensetzung von Inputfaktoren mit dem Ergebnis eines wettbewerbsfähigen Ressourcenbündels betrachtet werden (bspw. Helfat/Peteraf 2003: 999), ist die Grundannahme gesetzt, dass jegliche Dynamisierungsbemühung bei der Ressourcenkonfiguration beginnen muss.

3.2 Kompetenzdynamisierung im strategischen Management

Durch ein strategisches Management von Ressourcenkonfigurationen kann eine Organisation ihre Position im Wettbewerb mit den Konkurrenten langfristig behaupten und ausbauen (Freiling 2001: 27). Neben der Fähigkeit zur marktgerechten und effizienten Kombination dieser Ressourcen muss die Organisation insbesondere über knappe und wettbewerbsentscheidende Ressourcen stets flexibel verfügen können (Barney 1991: 106).

Die Aufrechterhaltung einer in der Vergangenheit erfolgreichen Ressourcenkombination kann in einer neuen Situation mit geänderten Umweltzuständen zu Misserfolg führen. Es bedarf einer Anpassung der Ressourcenkombination an die veränderten Umweltzustände. Angesichts der Dynamik in der Wettbewerbsumwelt von Organisationen erfüllt der ressourcenbasierte Ansatz mit dem Konzept der organisationalen Kompetenz in seiner bestehenden Form die dynamischen Anforderungen nicht: So führen Schreyögg/Kliesch (2006: 456) bereits kritisch an, Kompetenzen seien von ihrer Grundkonstruktion her vorrangig Bestandsgrößen mit statischem Charakter und zeigen dadurch die Dynamisierungsschwierigkeit gezielt auf. Kompetenzen lassen sich als Fähigkeit einer Organisation beschreiben, Ressourcen effektiv in einem Wertschöpfungsprozess einzusetzen und das in der Organisation vorhandene Potenzial zu nutzen (Freiling 2001: 25).

Ressourcen erfolgreich im Sinne der marktgerechten Verwertung miteinander zu kombinieren, ist eine sich wiederholende Aufgabe der Organisation, bei der sich die Anforderungen aufgrund der Umweltveränderungen von Mal zu Mal unterscheiden. Der grundlegende, immer wiederkehrende Verlauf der Ressourcenkombination verfestigt sich durch Wiederholung und wird zu einer Routine des organisationalen Handelns (Winter 2003: 991+994). Die Routinisierung der Ressourcenkombination beschränkt die Fähigkeit der Organisation, die als organisationale Kompetenz bezeichnet wird, indem die Routine zu einem statischen Verhalten gegenüber eintretenden Umweltveränderungen führt (Schreyögg/Kliesch 2006: 460).

Teece et al. sowie Schreyögg/Kliesch beispielsweise fordern eine Dynamisierung des Konzeptes der organisationalen Kompetenz, bei der die Statik der organisationalen Kompetenz zugunsten der Dynamik aufgelöst werden soll (Teece et al. 1997; Schreyögg/Kliesch 2006). An die Stelle der statischen Bestandsgröße Kompetenz soll eine dynamische Kompetenz treten. Diese dynamische organisationale Kompetenz wird als Teil eines kontinuierlichen Veränderungsprozesses verstanden. Die Autoren führen an, es genüge nicht, aus der organisationalen Kompetenzen formell dynamische Veränderungsgrößen zu machen.

Die Folgerung von Teece et al. sowie Schreyögg/Kliesch ist das Postulat nach einer Umgestaltung des bestehenden Konzepts der organisationalen Kompetenzen. Die bisher als statisch betrachtete Grundlogik des Kompetenzansatzes muss um dynamische Elemente erweitert werden. Bislang ist es der Wissenschaft jedoch nicht gelungen, eine umfassende und weitsichtige Lösung für das Diskrepanzproblem zwischen der Statik der theoretischen Modelle und der Dynamik der tatsächlichen Unternehmensanforderungen zu schaffen. Die sich in der wissenschaftlichen Diskussion hervorhebenden Ansätze von bspw. Teece et al. (1997), Eisenhardt/Martin (2000), Wang/Ahmed (2007) oder Ambrosini et al. (2009) liefern keine ausreichenden Ergebnisse. Die Ansätze der Autoren greifen zu kurz, da sie nicht bis zum eigentlichen Kern von Kompetenzen, den Ressourcen, zurückgehen. Vielmehr sind die Beiträge darin verhaftet, die Ressourcenverfügbarkeit als gegeben vorauszusetzen. Sie konzentrieren sich stark auf die Prozessgestaltung in Form von kontextualem Lernen der Organisation und der Schaffung von innovationsfördernden Rahmenbedingungen innerhalb des Unternehmens. Dies sind sehr konstruktive Ansätze und bereichern die Dynamisierungsforschung in hohem Maße, lassen gleichwohl die Perspektive der Ressourcenverfügbarkeit außen vor. Es wird dabei aus einer sehr prozessgetriebenen Perspektive auf die Dynamisierung geblickt. Dabei wird nicht hinterfragt, woher das benötigte Ressourcenpotenzial in ausreichender Anzahl und Güte beschafft werden soll. Zusätzlich geht damit auch der kritische Faktor Zeit zur unmittelbaren Ressourcenverfügbarkeit in der Kerndiskussion verloren.

4. Strategische Ressourcenkonfiguration als Kern dynamischer Organisationen

4.1 Flexible Ressourcenverfügbarkeit

Während die klassische Dynamisierungsforschung bezüglich Kompetenzen vor allem die Ressourcenverwendung thematisiert (Teece et al. 1997; Eisenhardt/Martin 2000; Schreyögg/Kliesch 2006; Wang/Ahmed 2007; Ambrosini/Bowman 2009), konzentriert sich der vorliegende Beitrag auf die Gestaltung einer flexiblen Ressourcenausstattung, damit die Organisation überhaupt über das notwendige Potenzial zur dynamischen Veränderung von Ressourcenkonfigurationen verfügt. Dazu können die benötigten Ressourcen zum Einen aus der Unternehmensumwelt gewonnen werden (Eisenhardt/Martin 2000: 1107; Wang/Ahmed 2007: 35). Zum Anderen besteht jedoch die Möglichkeit – wie es der vorliegende Beitrag propagiert –, Überschussressourcen sowohl innerhalb des Unternehmens als auch außerhalb des Unternehmens gezielt aufzubauen. Der gezielte Aufbau von Überschussressourcen bietet der langwierigen externen Gewinnung von Ressourcen über die Faktormärkte die schnellere und flexiblere Alternative zur Bereitstellung neuer Ressourcen (Zajac et al. 2000: 433; Mishina et al. 2004: 1182).

Ausschlaggebend für Erfolg oder Misserfolg bei der Anpassung von Kompetenzen an eine dynamische Umwelt ist grundlegend die spezifische Ressourcenausstattung, durch die das Adaptionspotenzial bestimmt wird (Ghemawat/Costa 1993: 70-71; Álvarez/Meríno 2003). Mangelt es einer Organisation an einer umfangreichen und flexiblen Rückgriffsmöglichkeit auf Ressourcen, die zur wettbewerbsentscheidenden Überarbeitung von bestehenden Ressourcenkonfigurationen benötigt werden, fehlt es ihr an der integralen Dynamisierungsvoraussetzung, ohne die eine flexible Veränderung der Kompetenzen unmöglich ist (Zott 2003: 103). Deshalb rückt die dynamisch orientierte Ressourcenverfügbarkeit der Organisation in den Untersuchungsfokus (Burr 2002: 28; Sanchez 2004: 527; Sanchez 2008: 8).

Bestehende Dynamisierungsansätze betrachten die Ad-hoc-Akquisition von Ressourcen zum Zeitpunkt des Anpassungsbedarfs. Zur Veränderung der Kompetenzen sollen benötigte Ressourcen über den externen Faktormarkt beschafft werden, sobald sich die Organisation zur Adaption an die veränderte Umwelt entschieden hat (Eisenhardt/Martin 2000: 1107; Wang/Ahmed 2007: 35). Hingegen bleibt die strategische Vorsorge und Positionierung von Ressourcen mit dem Ziel der unmittelbaren und flexiblen Verfügbarkeit von wettbewerbsentscheidenden Ressourcen weitestgehend unberücksichtigt. Eine Organisation kann sich jedoch genau in diesem Punkt von den Konkurrenten unterscheiden und strategisch absetzen (Collis/Montgomery 1995: 120-122; Helfat/Peteraf 2003: 999). Dazu genügt es nicht, dass sich die Organisation schlicht das Ziel setzt, im Bedarfsfall benötigte Ressourcen über den Faktormarkt zu generieren.

Neben der Zufuhr und Entnahme einzelner Ressourcen, wie es Ansätze der dynamischen organisationalen Kompetenzen propagieren (Eisenhardt/Martin 2000: 1107-

1108; Wang/Ahmed 2007: 35) berücksichtigt das Konzept dynamischer Ressourcenkonfiguration die Erzielung flexibler Handlungsoptionen durch strategischen Aufbau und nachhaltige Pflege von Überschussressourcen. Denn zur wettbewerbstauglichen Dynamisierung der organisationalen Kompetenzen reicht es nicht aus, erst zum Bedarfszeitpunkt benötigte Ressourcen über den Faktormarkt zu beschaffen. In einem dynamischen Markt sind insbesondere Zeit- und Kostenvorteile die entscheidende Quelle für Wettbewerbsvorteile (Stalk/Hout 1990; Staehle 1991: 321). Zeitvorteile ergeben sich bei der Einbindung neuer Ressourcen in bestehende Konfigurationen, wenn das Unternehmen über einen strategischen Ressourcenpool verfügt. Daraus können unmittelbar und flexibel Ressourcen entnommen und zur Veränderung von organisationalen Kompetenzen eingesetzt werden. Kostenvorteile entstehen, da die Ressourcen bereits deutlich vor dem Dynamisierungszeitpunkt beschafft werden. Zu diesem Moment sind die Ressourcen auf dem Faktormarkt noch nicht knapp – streng definitorisch gesehen deshalb auch nicht als Ressourcen, sondern lediglich als Inputgüter zu bezeichnen (Gregori 1987: 1241-1242) – und somit zu günstigeren Preisen als bei der ad-hoc-Akquisition zu beziehen. Gemäß dem Ressourcenverständnis von Freiling et al. und auch von Burr könnte man bei der Argumentation für einen strategischen Ressourcenpool im Unternehmen noch einen Schritt weiter gehen. Denn die Autoren beschreiben, dass über den Faktormarkt generell nur Inputgüter beschafft werden können und diese erst durch den Veredelungsprozess im Unternehmen zu wertvollen Ressourcen heranreifen (Freiling et al. 2006: 47; Burr 2007: 99). Demnach spielt der Aufbau von Überschussressourcen eine noch bedeutendere Rolle für die Dynamisierung organisationaler Kompetenzen. Denn erst durch die frühzeitige Aufnahme von Inputgütern in den strategischen Ressourcenpool, können sich diese im Unternehmen zu wettbewerbsentscheidenden Faktoren im Unternehmen weiterentwickeln. Hingegen fehlt bei der ad-hoc-Akquisition zum Bedarfszeitpunkt die Gelegenheit zur Veredelung der Inputgüter. Aufgrund von Zeitnot würden im Fall der ad-hoc-Akquisition die erworbenen Inputgüter in ihrer Rohform zur Veränderung bestehender Ressourcenkonfigurationen eingesetzt und sie könnten dadurch nicht ihr volles Potenzial in der organisationalen Kompetenz einbringen.

Der Ansatz, mit strategischen Überschussressourcen die dynamischen Kompetenzen zu stärken, wird durch die Aussage von Staehle gestützt. Denn bereits 1991 weist er auf die integrale Relevanz von Überschussressourcen für die allgemeine Flexibilität einer Organisation hin (Staehle 1991: 315). Nach Staehle (1991) droht einer Organisation sogar völlige Inflexibilität bei einem Defizit an Überschussressourcen. Bezüglich des Konstrukts der dynamischen Kompetenzen konnte sich diese Ansicht, vermutlich mangels systematischer Berücksichtigung und Aufarbeitung der Wirkung von strategischen Überschussressourcen, bislang nicht etablieren.

An dieser Stelle kann festgehalten werden, dass es einer ausreichenden Ressourcensicherung als Basisinvestition für betriebliche Flexibilität bedarf, um dynamische Prozesse in einer Organisation abbilden zu können (Gilbert 2005: 757-758). Ressourcenverfügbarkeit und Prozessflexibilität sind eng miteinander verzahnt. Während die klassische Dynamisierungsforschung, wie oben darstellt, auf die Prozessgestaltung abzielt, ohne sich um das Ressourcenfundament zu kümmern, geht der vorliegende Beitrag entsprechend des korrekten betrieblichen Ablaufs vor und befasst sich zunächst mit der Ressourcenbasis. Dynamische Prozesse, die sich auf Seite der Ressourcenverwendung befinden, fördern zwar die Organisationsflexibilität, sind jedoch ohne entsprechend im Vorfeld erzeugte Ressourcenauswahl nutzlos. Dementsprechend ist vor allem der Ressourcengewinnung und damit der Ressourcenverfügbarkeit die Hauptaufmerksamkeit zu widmen. Dabei ergibt sich im ersten Schritt die Frage nach einer rein faktischen Logik: Aus welchen Elementen besteht ein dynamischer Pool zur Ressourcenverfügbarkeit? Im zweiten Schritt folgt die Frage nach einer Prozesslogik: Wie kann ein Unternehmen den dynamischen Pool zur Ressourcenflexibilität steuern?

Zunächst soll der ersten Frage nachgegangen werden, bevor die Prozesssicht durch ein dynamisches Quantitäts- und Qualitätscontrolling ergänzt wird.

4.2 Elemente der dynamischen Ressourcenkonfiguration

Zur Erhöhung der strategischen Flexibilität lässt sich konzeptionell unterscheiden zwischen internen und externen Überschussressourcen. Beide Überschussarten stehen einem Unternehmen als Alternativen zur herkömmlichen Ressourcenbeschaffung über die Faktormärkte für die flexible Konfigurationsgestaltung von organisationalen Kompetenzen zur Verfügung. Dadurch bietet sich der Organisation ein breiter Ressourcenpool, aus dem sie zur flexiblen Adaption an eine veränderte Umwelt schöpfen und somit proaktiv in einem dynamischen Markt agieren kann. Externe Überschussressourcen stellen dabei alle Reserven einer Organisation dar, die unter Wahrung des Zugriffsrechts außerhalb der Organisation bereitgehalten werden. Der Vorteil externer Überschussressourcen besteht besonders darin, dass sie außerhalb des Kostenbereichs der Organisation liegen und dennoch auf sie bei Bedarf zugegriffen werden kann, wie beispielsweise bei ungenutzten Krediten, entliehenen Mitarbeitern oder kurzfristig vermieteten Immobilien (Klein 2010: 183-191).

Neben der Analyse des Dynamisierungspotenzials von internen Überschussressourcen und der konzeptionellen Gestaltung eines Modells strategischer externer Reserven bietet sich weiterhin die Nutzbarmachung inaktiver Ressourcenfunktionen zur Kompetenzdynamisierung an. Die strategische Identifikation und Nutzung inaktiver Ressourcenfunktionen wie ungenutzten Mitarbeiterfähigkeiten oder Maschinenpotenzialen bietet weiteren konzeptionellen Mehrwert gegenüber den Ansätzen zu dynamischen organisationalen Kompetenzen. So betrachtet eine dynamische Ressourcenkonfiguration nicht lediglich die Dynamik innerhalb der Ressourcencluster, sondern beinhaltet darüber hinaus die flexible Gestaltung einzelner Ressourcen durch Einbeziehung der betrieblichen Ressourcenfunktionen. Das Dynamisierungspotenzial, das in Form von inaktiven Ressourcenfunktionen in den einzelnen Ressourcen steckt, wurde bislang in der bestehenden Diskussion zur Dynamisierung organisationaler Kompetenzen außer Acht gelassen. Die Flexibilisierung einzelner Ressourcen trägt zur Befreiung des Ansatzes der Kompetenzbildung von der ihr durch Routinisierung anheftenden Statik bei, da mit den Ressourcen – und im Speziellen mit den Ressourcenfunktionen – bereits die Ausgangsbasis für die durch Konfiguration entstehenden organisationalen Kompetenzen flexibilisiert wird. Inaktive Ressourcenfunktionen sind somit als ungenutzte Mitarbeiterfähigkeiten (Keller 2006: 872), Wissensvorräte, zusätzliche Maschinenfunktionen, Logistikkapazitäten etc. zu verstehen.

Somit ergeben sich zur Dynamisierung von Kompetenzen neben der klassischen Ressourcenbeschaffung über den Faktormarkt drei weitere Möglichkeiten, das benötigte Ressourcenpotenzial flexibel zur Verfügung zu stellen (s. Abb. 1): interne Überschussressourcen, externe Überschussressourcen und inaktive Ressourcenfunktionen. Die dadurch geschaffene strategische Flexibilität der Organisation kann eingesetzt werden, um Dynamisierungsherausforderungen zu bewältigen. Somit kann das Unternehmen flexibel und proaktiv in einem dynamischen Markt planen und handeln.

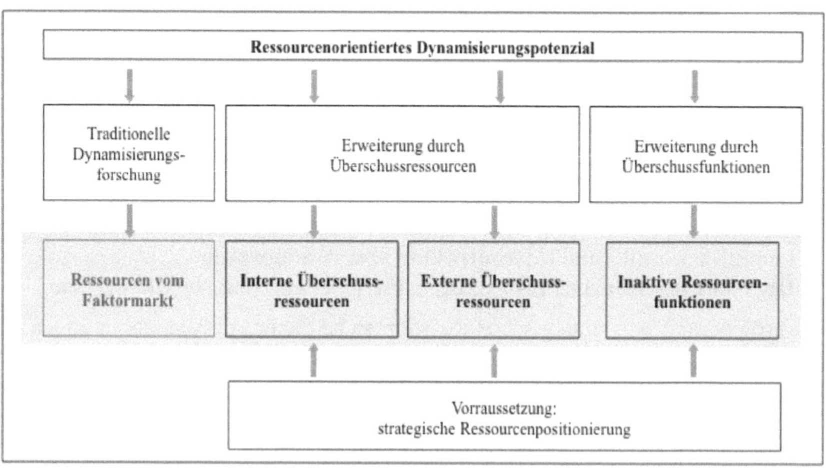

Abbildung 1: Ressourcenorientierte Dynamisierungspotenziale

Um die benötigte Ressourcenverfügbarkeit in Form von internen und externen Überschussressourcen sowie inaktiven Ressourcenfunktionen, die zur Dynamisierung organisationaler Kompetenzen eingesetzt werden sollen, gewährleisten zu können, bestehen für das Unternehmen drei mögliche strategische Vorgehensweisen (Klein 2010: 214):

1. Ad-hoc-Akquisition von Ressourcen über den Faktormarkt: Zur Dynamisierung erforderliche Ressourcen werden zum Bedarfszeitpunkt vom Unternehmen über den Faktormarkt beschafft. Dies ist die konventionelle Lösung, wie sie sich in der bisherigen Dynamisierungslogik gefestigt hat.

2. Aufbau interner strategischer Überschussressourcen: Die Organisation sichert sich die Zugriffsmöglichkeit auf wettbewerbsentscheidende Ressourcen bereits vor dem Adaptionszeitpunkt. Das Unternehmen kann sich schnell und flexibel der dynamischen Umwelt anpassen, ohne zunächst noch eine zeit- und kostenintensive Ressourcenakquisition durchführen zu müssen.
3. Aufbau externer strategischer Überschussressourcen: Strategisch wertvolle Ressourcen, die nicht zwingend innerhalb des Unternehmens gehalten werden müssen, werden unter Aufrechterhaltung einer Rückgriffsoption externalisiert. Dadurch kann die Organisation Aufrechterhaltungskosten von internen strategischen Überkapazitäten reduzieren und gleichzeitig trotzdem die Verfügbarkeit einer flexiblen Ressourcenausstattung beibehalten.

Für eine dynamisch-flexible Organisation gibt es kein Entweder-Oder zwischen Ad-hoc-(1) Akquisition, (2) Potenzialaufbau intern und (3) Potenzialaufbau extern. Stattdessen müssen diese drei Aspekte im Einklang zueinander gebracht werden. Die Aktualität des strategischen Ressourcenpools muss sichergestellt werden, damit die darin enthaltenen internen und externen Überschussressourcen sowie die inaktiven Ressourcenfunktionen stets den aktuellen Planungsanforderungen entsprechen (Weick/Sutcliffe 2007: 45; Cameron et al. 2008; Kirsch et al. 2009: 156-157). Wesentlicher Bestandteil dabei ist ein systematisches Quantitäts- und Qualitätscontrolling der fokussierten Überschussressourcen und Ressourcenfunktionen.

5. Quantitäts- und Qualitätscontrolling von strategischen Überschussressourcen als Prämisse für Effizienz und Nachhaltigkeit

Die Verfügbarkeit von strategischen Ressourcen ist die basale Voraussetzung, um aus Sicht des flexiblen Ressourceneinsatzes als Unternehmen flexibel agieren zu können. Dazu muss sich die Organisation auch besonders mit einer gestreuten Positionierung der Flexibilitätsreserven im internen organisationalen Bereich, im externen Umfeld oder durch Bereithaltung von inaktiven Ressourcenfunktionen befassen. Bis zu diesem Punkt stand vor allem Frage nach der den Elementen, aus denen sich der dynamische Pool zur Ressourcenverfügbarkeit zusammensetzt, im Fokus. Nun rückt die Frage nach einer Prozesslogik in den Mittelpunkt: Wie kann ein Unternehmen den dynamischen Pool zur Ressourcenflexibilität steuern?

Um nun einer Prozessorientierung zu folgen und damit das dynamische Ressourcenkonfigurationsmanagement lebendig werden zu lassen, folgt ein weiterer Baustein: Quantitäts- und Qualitätscontrolling strategischer Flexibilitätsressourcen und –funktionen. Dadurch wird der effiziente Einsatz von Überschussressourcen und inaktiven Ressourcenfunktionen gewährleistet (Baraldi/Strömsten 2009). Es wird aus der Kosten-Ertrag-Perspektive ein angemessenes quantitatives und qualitatives Maß zur Bereithaltung an strategischen Reservepotenzialen geregelt. Im Sinne einer dynamischen Lagersystematik werden ein- und ausgehende Überschussressourcen bewertet und der Gesamtbestand sowie der Bestand an Klassifizierungen fortlaufend ermittelt.

Somit kennt die Organisation stets die zur Dynamisierung zur Verfügung stehenden Ressourcen und kann diese schließlich zielgerichtet zur flexiblen Gestaltung von Organisationsprozessen verplanen und einsetzen (McKelvie/Davidsson 2009).

- Quantitätscontrolling von strategischen Überschussressourcen: Das Quantitätscontrolling regelt insbesondere das Kosten-Ertrag-Verhältnis der „eingelagerten" Überschussressourcen. Es wird dabei Art und Höhe der durch die Reserveressourcen verursachten Kosten sowie deren erwirtschaftete Ertrag festgehalten. Auf dieser Grundlage entsteht ein erstes Entscheidungskriterium bezüglich Für und Wider bestimmter Überschussressourcenarten und bezüglich des Umfangs des gewünschten Gesamtpools als Flexibilisierungsmasse im Unternehmen.
- Qualitätscontrolling von strategischen Überschussressourcen: Das Qualitätscontrolling dient der Bewertung des inhärenten Dynamisierungspotenzials der Reserveressourcen. Der spezifische qualitative Wert für die Organisation, der von den spezifischen Ressourcen ausgeht, ist das bestimmende Kriterium zur Entscheidung über die Zusammensetzung des Flexibilisierungspools.

Die Organisation sichert sich durch Quantitäts- und Qualitätscontrolling zum Einen die effiziente Nutzung des Pools an Überschussressourcen. Dazu wird sowohl das Kosten-Ertrag-Verhältnis der Aufrechterhaltung eines angemessenen Ressourcenpools betrachtet als auch die Werthaltigkeit bestimmter Ressourcen(-arten) berücksichtigt. Zum Anderen steigt durch Quantitäts- und Qualitätscontrolling die Nachhaltigkeit der dynamisch flexiblen Ressourcenbasis. Ausgehende Überschussressourcen werden erfasst, Umfang und Werthaltigkeit des Pools bewertet und Nachschub gezielt geplant. Es wird dadurch vermieden, dass das Depot an internen und externen Überschussressourcen sowie an inaktiven Ressourcenfunktionen lediglich in einer Einmalaktion getrieben von der Unternehmensführung gefüllt und anschließend vernachlässigt wird. Diese Gefahr bestünde, wenn die konstante marktgerechte Entwicklung (Hou/Chien 2010: 101-103) mangels Systematik und fehlender manifestierter Zuständigkeit fehlt. Das Quantitäts- und Qualitätscontrolling ermöglicht die Implementierung von Effizienz und Nachhaltigkeit bei der Pflege des Ressourcenpools in die operative Betriebsamkeit des Unternehmens.

Ein systematisches Quantitäts- und Qualitätscontrolling erfordert zunächst eine Klassifizierung der betreffenden Ressourcenarten, die eine Organisation als Flexibilisierungsmasse bereithält. Obergruppen für die Klassifizierung lassen sich unterteilen nach Innovationskapital, Sozialkapital, Markenkapital, Humankapital, Finanzkapital und Sachkapital (Hasenau 2009: 26-35+55).

- Innovationskapital umfasst die Organisationsmentalität bei Entwicklungen und Neuheiten, das schöpferische Potenzial sowie den Grad der Innovationsfreundlichkeit des Organisationsumfeldes.
- Sozialkapital bezeichnet die Faktoren Reputation der Organisation und Loyalität der Stakeholder.

- Markenkapital beinhaltet die Stärke der von der Organisation geführten Marken. Das Markenkapital ist eng mit der Reputation der Organisation verbunden, trennt jedoch Marke und Organisation mental voneinander.
- Humankapital bezeichnet das immaterielle Vermögen bestehend aus der Belegschaft der Organisation (Klein 2008; Stein 2008).
- Finanzkapital umfasst sowohl ungebundene liquide Mittel der Organisation als auch Budgetüberschüsse, respektive der Anteil des Ergebnisses oberhalb des zur Grundversorgung benötigten Kapitals sowie verfügbare Kredite und monetäre Anlagen.
- Sachkapital sind Vorratsbestände und unfertige Erzeugnisse sowie technische Überkapazitäten und ungenutzte Immobilien.

Anhand der Klassifizierung der Ressourcenarten nach den dargestellten Obergruppen gelingt der Organisation im Zusammenhang mit der richtigen Wahl des Controllinginstruments ein systematisches Ressourcenmanagement. Die zur Erzeugung von organisationaler Flexibilität notwendigen Überschussressourcen und inaktiven Ressourcenfunktionen lassen sich so nachhaltig und effizient im Unternehmen sowie in dessen Umfeld strategisch positionieren (Zaidi/Othman 2011: 231). Zur Identifizierung des geeigneten Controllinginstruments bestehen zwei wesentliche Kriterien. Zum Einen gibt die Klassifizierung der Ressourcenarten bereits einen Hinweis auf die passende Art des Quantitäts- und Qualitätscontrollings. So lassen sich beispielsweise Überschussressourcen der Kategorie Sachkapital meist durch entsprechende Dokumente wie spezifische Anlagenprotokolle quantitativ überwachen und qualitativ beispielsweise durch Ergebnisumlagen oder Wertgutachten ermitteln. Zum Anderen lässt sich bereits aus der Positionierung der Flexibilitätsreserve in Form von internen Überschussressourcen, externen Überschussressourcen oder inaktiven Ressourcenfunktionen erkennen, welches Controllinginstrument erfolgversprechend ist. Beispielsweise verlangen inaktive Ressourcenfunktionen in Form von ungenutzten Mitarbeiterfähigkeiten oftmals die Erhebung mittels Befragungen und Tests, wohingegen externe Überschussressourcen in Gestalt von Grundfertigkeiten von Leiharbeitern über die Dokumentation des Personalverleihers identifiziert werden können.

Um das Flexibilitätspotenzial einer Organisation abbilden zu können, bedarf es nach der Identifikation von Einzelressourcenarten nach beschriebener Klassifizierung nun der Kombination aus Quantitäts- und Qualitätscontrolling. Das Quantitätscontrolling lässt sich als Differenz aus Kosten und Ertrag der Bereitstellung des Ressourcenpools darstellen. Dadurch wird der Ertrag, der sich aus der Bereithaltung von Reserveressourcen ergibt, ermittelt. Intern gelagerte Flexibilisierungsressourcen verursachen tendenziell eher Kosten als extern positionierte Ressourcen. Während bei internen Ressourcen beispielsweise Lager- oder Aufrechterhaltungskosten anfallen, können externe Flexibilisierungsressourcen häufig einen Nutzen in Form eines Zusatzertrags für das Unternehmen liefern. So können beispielsweise entliehene Produktionskapazitäten durch Lohnarbeit Gewinn bringend eingesetzt werden.

$$BR = \sum_{i=1}^{n}(RA_i \cdot RN_i) - \sum_{i=1}^{n}(RA_i \cdot RK_i)$$

BR	Bereitstellungsertrag von Flexibilisierungsressourcen
IF	Identifikationskosten inaktiver Ressourcenfunktionen
DP	Dynamisierungspotenzial der Organisation
FW	Flexibilitätswert der Organisation
FQ	Flexibilitätsquote der Organisation
RA_i	Anzahl der Ressourcenart i
RN_i	Ressourcenhaltungsnutzen der Ressourcenart i
RK_i	Ressourcenhaltungskosten der Ressourcenart i
RFK_j	Identifikationskosten der Ressourcenfunktion j
RFA_j	Anzahl der Ressourcenfunktion j
DP_i	Dynamisierungspotential der Ressourcenart i
DP_j	Dynamisierungspotential der Ressourcenfunktion j

Inaktive Ressourcenfunktionen werden im Quantitätscontrolling ebenfalls aufgenommen. Sie sind in der Organisation bewusst oder auch unbewusst vorhanden. Das Unternehmen entscheidet zwar nicht über deren Aufbau oder Aufrechterhaltung, sondern lediglich über deren Identifikation und Einsatz. Inaktive Ressourcenfunktionen sind häufig zunächst latent vorhanden und müssen deshalb vom Unternehmen identifiziert und somit nutzbar gemacht werden.

$$IF = \sum_{j=1}^{m}(RFA_j \cdot RFK_j)$$

Das Qualitätscontrolling stellt das Dynamisierungspotenzial ausgehend von den Flexibilisierungsressourcen dar. Dabei werden sowohl interne und externe Ressourcen als auch inaktive Ressourcenfunktionen berücksichtigt, die der Organisation inhärentes Dynamisierungspotenzial bieten. Dabei wird das Dynamisierungspotenzial der einzelnen Ressourcen bzw. der Ressourcenfunktion dargestellt, indem das Unternehmen den Wert des Zusatzgeschäftes ermittelt, dass durch den Einsatz der Ressource bzw. der Ressourcenfunktion möglich würde.

$$DP = \sum_{i=1}^{n}(RA_i \cdot DP_i) + \sum_{j=1}^{m}(RFA_j \cdot DP_j)$$

Aus der Kombination von Quantitäts- und Qualitätscontrolling ergibt sich somit der Flexibilitätswert einer Organisation, der sich durch Reserveressourcen und -funktionen erzeugen lässt.

$$FW = \sum_{i=1}^{n}(RA_i \cdot DP_i) + \sum_{j=1}^{m}(RFA_j \cdot DP_j) + \sum_{i=1}^{n}(RA_i \cdot RN_i) - \sum_{i=1}^{n}(RA_i \cdot RK_i) - \sum_{j=1}^{m}(RFA_j \cdot RFK_j)$$

Die Flexibilitätsquote der Organisation wird durch die Relation des Flexibilitätswerts zur Ertragskraft des Unternehmens dargestellt.

$$FQ = \frac{FW}{EBIT}$$

Durch die Flexibilitätsquote kann eine Organisation die Entwicklung des Ressourcenpools, der zur Flexibilisierung des Unternehmens dient, nachhaltig gestalten, indem gemessen am operativen Erfolg die Intensität des dynamischen Ressourcenkonfigurationsmanagements ausgerichtet wird. Die Flexibilitätsquote kann des Weiteren als Benchmark zwischen Unternehmen als Spiegel der zukunftsorientierten Wettbewerbsvorteile genutzt werden.

6. Ergebnis

Anders als die bisherigen etablierten Ansätze zur Dynamisierungsdiskussion konzentriert sich dieser Beitrag auf die Gestaltung einer flexiblen Ressourcenausstattung, damit die Organisation überhaupt über das notwendige grundlegende Potenzial zur dynamischen Veränderung von Ressourcenkonfigurationen verfügt. Denn eine umfangreiche Ressourcenverfügbarkeit ist basale Voraussetzung zur Veränderung bestehender Ressourcenkonfigurationen mit dem Ziel der schnellen und flexiblen Adaption an eine volatile Unternehmensumwelt (Burr 2002: 28; Sanchez 2004: 527; Sanchez 2008: 8).

Wesentliche Bausteine sind dabei neben der klassischen Beschaffung von Ressourcen über den Faktormarkt auch die Einbeziehung der Potenziale ausgehend von internen und externen Überschussressourcen sowie von inaktiven Ressourcenfunktionen. Der Beitrag animiert das starre Denken rein in Ressourcenarten zugunsten von Ressourcenfunktionen abzulegen. Denn zur Dynamisierung von Ressourcenkonfigurationen – respektive von organisationalen Kompetenzen – ist nicht nur die Art der Ressource (McKelvie/Davidsson 2009) ausschlaggebend, sondern auch Funktion und Potenzial der Ressource in der Wertschöpfungskette von entscheidender Bedeutung.

Flexible Ressourcensicherung und betriebliches Flexibilitätscontrolling sind der integrale Treibstoff für den Motor der organisationalen Dynamisierung im Rennen um Flexibilität und Wettbewerbsfähigkeit. Für die strategische Prozessgestaltung liefern das Bewusstmachen der verborgenen Vielseitigkeit von Überschussressourcen und das immense Potenzial von inaktiven Ressourcenfunktionen wichtige Bausteine.

Literatur

Álvarez, V. S./Merino, T. G. (2003): The History of Organizational Renewal. Evolutionary Models of Spanish Savings and Loans Institutions. In: Organization Studies, 9: 1437-1461.

Ambrosini, V./Bowman, C. (2009): What Are Dynamic Capabilities and Are They a Useful Construct in Strategic Management?. In: International Journal of Management Reviews, 1: 29-49.

Ambrosini, V./Bowman, C./Collier, N. (2009): Dynamic Capabilities. An Exploration of How Firms Renew their Resource Base. In: British Journal of Management, S1: 9-24.

Baraldi, E./Strömsten, T. (2009): Controlling and Combining Resources in Networks – From Uppsala to Stanfort and back again: The Case of a Biotech Innovation. In: International Marketing Management, 5: 541-552.

Barney, J. B. (1991): Firm Resources and Sustained Competitive Advantage. In: Journal of Management, 1: 99-120.

Black, J. A./Boal, K. B. (1994): Strategic Resources. Traits, Configurations and Paths to Sustainable Competitive Advantage. In: Strategic Management Journal, 5: 131-148.

Burr, W. (2002): Service Engineering bei technischen Dienstleistungen. Eine ökonomische Analyse der Modularisierung, Leistungstiefengestaltung und Systembündelung, Gabler: Wiesbaden.

Burr, W. (2007): HRM aus ressourcen- und institutionenökonomischer Sicht. Ein Vergleich. In: Freiling, J./Gemünden, H. G. (Hrsg.): Jahrbuch Strategisches Kompetenz-Management. Dynamische Theorien der Kompetenzentstehung und Kompetenzverwertung im strategischen Kontext, Band 1, Hampp: München – Mering: 81-110.

Cameron, J./Nicholas, B./Silvester, K./Cronin, K. (2008): The Navigator Network. A New Zealand Futurewatch Case Study. In: Technology Analysis & Strategic Management, 3: 271-285.

Cavusgil, E./Seggie, S./Talay, M. (2007): Dynamic Capabilities View. Foundations and Research Agenda. In: Journal of Marketing Theory & Practice, 2: 159-166.

Chi, L./Holsapple, C./Srinivasan, C. (2008): Digital Systems, Partnership Networks and Competition. The Co-Evolution of IOS Use and Network Position as Antecedents of Competitive Actions. In: Journal of Organizational Computing and Electronic Commerce, 1: 61-94.

Collis, D. J./Montgomery, C. A. (1995): Competing on Resources. How Do You Create and Sustain a Profitable Strategy?. In: Harvard Business Review, 4: 118-128.

Cyert, R. M./March, J. G. (1963): A Behavioral Theory of the Firm, Englewood Cliffs, New Jersey: Prentice Hall.

Davis, J. P./Eisenhardt, K. M./Bingham, C. B. (2009): Optimal Structure, Market Dynamism and the Strategy of Simple Rules. In: Administrative Science Quarterly, 3: 413-452.

Day, G. S. (1994): The Capabilities of Market-Driven Organizations. In: Journal of Marketing, 4: 37-52.

Eisenhardt, K. M./Martin, J. A. (2000): Dynamic Capabilities. What Are They?. In: Strategic Management Journal, Sonderheft: 1105-1121.

Ellonen, H. K./Jantunen, A./Kuivalainen, O. (2001): The Role of Dynamic Capabilities in Developing Innovation-Related Capabilities. In: International Journal of Innovation Management, 3: 459-478.

Freiling, J. (2001): Resource-based View und ökonomische Theorie. Grundlagen und Positionierung des Ressourcenansatzes, DUV: Wiesbaden.

Freiling, J./Gersch, M./Goeke, C. (2006): Eine „Competence-Based Theory of the Firm" als marktprozesstheoretischer Ansatz. Erste disziplinäre Basisentscheidung eines evolutorischen Forschungsprogramms. In: Schreyögg, G./Conrad, P. (Hrsg.): Managementforschung 16. Management von Kompetenz, Gabler: Wiesbaden: 37-82.

Ghemawat, P./Costa, J. E. (1993): The Organizational Tension between Static and Dynamic Efficiency. In: Strategic Management Journal, S2: 59-73.

Gilbert, C. G. (2005): Unbundling the structure of inertia: Resource versus routine rigidity. In: Academy of Management Journal, 5: 741-763.

Gould, N./Hogg, M. K. (2008): Social Network Analysis and Consumption Dynamics. Research Review and Prospects. In: European Advances in Consumer Research – European Conference Proceedings: 160-165.

Graversen, E. K./Kalpazidou Schmidt, E./Langberg, K. (2005): Dynamic Research Environments. A Development Model. In: International Journal of Human Resource Management, 8: 1498-1511.

Gregori, T. R. De (1987): Resources are Not, They Become. An Institutional Theory. In: Journal of Economic Issues, 3: 1241-1263.

Hasenau, A. (2009): Identifikation betrieblicher Überschussressourcen in der Praxis. Eine empirische Untersuchung, Arbeitspapier an der Universität Siegen.

Helfat, C. E./Peteraf, M. A. (2003): The Dynamic Resource-Based View. Capability Lifecycles. In: Strategic Management Journal, 10: 997-1010.

Hou, J. J. /Chien, Y. T. (2010): The Effect of Market Knowledge Management Competence on Business Performance. A Dynamic Capabilities Perspective. In: International Journal of Electronic Business Management, 2. 96-109.

Jaikumar, R./Bohn, R. E. (1992): A Dynamic Approach to Operations Management. An Alternative to Static Optimization. In: International Journal of Production Economics, 3: 265-282.

Keller, P. (2006): Human-Resource-Management. Personal als Erfolgsfaktor. In: Zentes, J. (Hrsg.): Handbuch Handel. Strategien, Perspektiven, Internationaler Wettbewerb, Gabler: Wiesbaden: 852-872.

Kirsch, W./Seidl, D./Aaken, D. van (2009): Unternehmensführung. Eine evolutionäre Perspektive, Schäffer-Poeschel: Stuttgart.

Klein, T. (2008): Kampf um Talente. Das Kind ist (fast) in den Brunnen gefallen. In: HR Performance, 6: 44-47.

Klein, T. (2010): Dynamisches Ressourcenkonfigurationsmanagement: Eine funktionalorientierte Werterhaltung strategischer Kompetenzen, Peter Lang: Frankfurt a. M.

McKelvie, A./Davidsson, P. (2009): From Resource Base to Dynamic Capabilities. An Investigation of New Firms. In: British Journal of Management, S1: 63-80.

Mishina, Y./Pollock, T./Porac, J. (2004): Are More Resources Always Better for Growth? Resource Stickiness in Market and Product Expansion. In: Strategic Management Journal, 12: 1179-1197.

Montealegre, R. (2002): A Process Model of Capability Development. Lessons from the Electronic Commerce Strategy at Bolsa de Valores de Guayaquil. In: Organization Science, 5: 514-531.

Otto, P./Simon, M. (2008): Dynamic Perspectives on Social Characteristics and Sustainability in Online Community Networks. In: System Dynamics Review, 3: 321-347.

Payne, T. et al. (2009): Competitive Dynamics among Service SMEs. In: Journal of Small Business Management, 4: 421-442.

Penrose, E. T. (1959): The Theory of the Growth of the Firm, Basil Blackwell: Oxford.

Prahalad, C. K./Hamel, G. (1990): The Core Competence of the Corporation. In: Harvard Business Review, 3: 79-91.

Romme, A. G. L./Zollo, M./Berends, P. (2010): Dynamic Capabilities, Deliberate Learning and Environmental Dynamism: A Simulation Model. In: Industrial and Corporate Change, 4: 1271-1299.

Ruiz-Moreno, A. (2008): The Moderating Effect of Organizational Slack on the Relation between Perceptions of Support for Innovation and Organizational Climate. In: Personnel Review, 5: 509-525.

Sanchez, R: (2004): Understanding Competence-Based Management. Identifying and Managing Five Modes of Competence. In: Journal of Business Research, 5: 518-532.

Sanchez, R. (2008): A Scientific Critique of the Resource-Based View (RBV) in Strategy Theory with Competence-Based Remedies for the RBV's Conceptual Deficiencies and Logic Problems. In: Sanchez, R. (Hrsg.): A Focused Issue on Fundamental Issues in Competence Theory Development. Research in Competence-Based Management, Volume 4, Emerald Group: Bingley: 3-78.

Sanchez, R./Mahoney, J. T. (1996): Modularity, Flexibility and Knowledge Management in Product and Organization Design. In: Strategic Management Journal, Special Issue: 63-76.

Schierenbeck, H. (2003): Grundzüge der Betriebswirtschaftslehre, 16. Aufl., Oldenbourg: München – Wien.

Schoemaker, P. J. H. (1992): How to Link Strategic Vision to Core Capabilities. In: Sloan Management Review, 3: 67-81.

Schreyögg, G./Kliesch, M. (2006): Zur Dynamisierung Organisationaler Kompetenzen – „Dynamic Capabilities" als Lösungsansatz?. In: Zeitschrift für betriebswirtschaftliche Forschung, 6: 455-476.

Schreyögg, G./Kliesch-Eberl, M. (2007): How Dynamic Can Organizational Capabilities Be? Towards a Dual-Process Model of Capability Dynamization. In: Strategic Management Journal, 9: 913-933.

Selznick, P. (1957): Leadership in Administration. A Sociological Interpretation, Row, Peterson and Company: Illinois – New York.

Staehle, W. H. (1991): Redundanz, Slack und lose Kopplung in Organisationen. Eine Verschwendung von Ressourcen?. In: Staehle, W. H./Sydow, J. (Hrsg.): Managementforschung 1, de Gruyter: Berlin – New York: 313-345.

Stalk, G./Hout, T. M. (1990): Competing against Time. How Time-Based Competition is Reshaping Global Markets, Free Press: New York.

Stein, V. (2008): Aussagestarke Humankapitalbewertung. In: Personal, 10: 24-26.

Stein, V./Klein, T. (2010): Organizational Slack als Dynamisierungsquelle organisationaler Kompetenzen. In: Stephan, M./Kerber, W. (Hrsg.): Jahrbuch Strategisches Kompetenz-Management, Band 4, Hampp: München – Mering: 59-79.

Su, Z./Xie, E./Li, Y. (2009): Organizational Slack and Firm Performance during Institutional Transitions. In: Asia Pacific Journal of Management, 1: 75-91.

Tallon, P. P. (2008): Stuck in the Middle. Overcoming Strategic Complexity through IT Flexibility. In: Global Journal of Flexible Systems Management, 4: 1-9.

Teece, D. et al. (1997): Dynamic Capabilities and Strategic Management. In: Strategic Management Journal, 7: 509-533.

Uotila J./Maula, M./Keil, T./Zahra, S. A. (2009): Exploration, Exploitation and Financial Performance. Analysis of S&P 500 Corporations. In: Strategic Management Journal, 2: 221-231.

Wang, C. L./Ahmed, P. K. (2007): Dynamic Capabilities. A Review and Research Agenda. In: International Journal of Management Reviews, 1: 31-51.

Weick, K. E./Sutcliffe, K. M. (2007): Managing the Unexpected. Resilient Performance in an Age of Uncertainty, 2. Aufl., Jossey-Bass: San Francisco.

Weimar, R. (2002): Problem Solving in Organizations. In: Leidig, G./Mayer, T. (Hrsg.): Betriebswirtschaft und Mediengesellschaft im Wandel. Festschrift für Diethelm Schmidt und Lorenz Rottland, Bundesverband Druck und Medien: Wiesbaden: 239-252.

Winter, S. G. (2003): Understanding Dynamic Capabilities. In: Strategic Management Journal, 10: 991-995.

Zaidi, M. F. A./Othman, S. N. (2011): Understanding Dynamic Capability as an Ongoing Concept for Studying Technological Capability. In: International Journal of Business & Social Science, 6: 224-234.

Zajac, E./Kraatz, M./Bresser, R. (2000): Modeling the Dynamics of Strategic Fit. A Normative Approach to Strategic Change. In: Strategic Management Journal, 4: 429-453.

Zott, C. (2003): Dynamic Capabilities and the Emergence of Intraindustry Differential Firm Performance. Insights from a Simulation Study. In: Strategic Management Journal, 2: 97-125.

Reflexives Lernen durch Mitarbeiterbefragungen – Zwei Fallstudien in mittelständischen Industrieunternehmen

Tanja Schulze, Annett Schädlich und Silke Geithner

Zusammenfassung

Der langfristige Wettbewerbsvorteil eines Unternehmens liegt heute in der kontinuierlichen (Re-) konfiguration von Ressourcen (z.B. Barney 1991; Eisenhardt/Martin 2000) sowie in der flexiblen Anpassungs- und Veränderungsfähigkeit in einer zunehmend unsicheren Unternehmensumwelt (Teece et al. 1997). Die Entwicklung von Veränderungsfähigkeit kann dabei durch institutionalisierte Lerninstrumente, wie z.B. Mitarbeiterbefragungen (MAB), gefördert werden. Durch die adäquate Gestaltung eines solchen Instruments und vor allem der damit einhergehenden partizipativen Ergebnisverwertung ist es möglich, die bestehende Ressourcenbasis des Unternehmens zu hinterfragen und zu modifizieren sowie dynamische Fähigkeiten auszubauen. In kleinen- und mittleren Unternehmen (KMU) fehlen allerdings häufig geeignete Lerninstrumente, die zur erforderlichen Reflexion und Weiterentwicklung der Ressourcenausstattung sowie der organisationalen Prozesse beitragen. Im vorliegenden Beitrag wird daher diskutiert, unter welchen Voraussetzungen Mitarbeiterbefragungen einen Beitrag zum reflexiven Lernen in KMU leisten. In zwei mittelständischen Industrieunternehmen wurde mittels Aktionsforschung (Lewin 1946, 1947) eruiert, wie Mitarbeiterbefragungen als organisationales Lerninstrument zur Entwicklung der Unternehmen beitragen können. Es hat sich dabei gezeigt, dass die Nutzung des Potenzials einer MAB vor allem von spezifischen intra-organisationalen Kontextfaktoren abhängig ist.

Schlüsselwörter: Dynamische Fähigkeiten, Resource-Based View, Reflexives Lernen, Mitarbeiterbefragung, KMU, Fallstudie, Action Research

Abstract

Today the long-term competitive advantage of an organization lies in the ongoing (re)configuration of resources (e.g. Barney 1991; Eisenhardt/Martin 2000) as well as in the flexible adaptability and capability to change within an increasingly uncertain business environment (Teece et al. 1997). The development of these dynamic capabilities can be supported by institutionalized instruments, e.g. employee surveys. Through the appropriate design of such an instrument and the associated participatory exploitation of results it is possible to question the existing resource base and to modify it. However, in small and medium sized enterprises (SMEs) there is a lack of suitable instruments that contribute to a necessary reflection and development of resources and organizational processes. The present contribution examines how employee surveys can support reflexive learning processes in SMEs. In two SMEs the conditions of employee surveys as organizational learning tools that are essential for developing and change were determined through action research (Lewin 1946, 1947). It has been shown that the use of the potential of an employee survey depends on specific intra-organizational contextual factors.

Keywords: Dynamic Capabilities, Resource-Based View, Organizational Learning, Employee Survey, SME, Case Study, Action Research

1. Einleitung

Mitarbeiterbefragungen (MAB) sind bewährte Instrumente der Organisationsentwicklung und -führung (Bungard 1997; Borg 2002). In den überwiegenden Fällen werden diese in Unternehmen eingesetzt, um die Arbeitszufriedenheit der Beschäftigten zu erfassen und Maßnahmen zu deren Steigerung abzuleiten (z.B. Borg 2002). Vor allem aus der Unzufriedenheit der Mitarbeiter mit bestimmten Aspekten ihrer Arbeit bzw. dem Unternehmen lässt sich Lern- und Veränderungsbedarf identifizieren. Das Potenzial einer Mitarbeiterbefragung, kontinuierlich reflexives Lernen in Unternehmen zu initiieren und zu fördern, wird allerdings häufig unterschätzt; Nachfolgeprojekte werden nicht systematisch verfolgt oder versanden mit der Zeit. Das ist auch in einem von zwei in diesem Beitrag untersuchten mittelständischen *Fallunternehmen* des produzierenden Gewerbes der Fall: Der *Werkzeughersteller* (Fall-KMU A) führte 2009 eine Mitarbeiterbefragung mit dem Ziel durch, die Zufriedenheit der Beschäftigten mit dem Entgeltsystem zu erfassen und daraufhin dieses neu zu gestalten. Obwohl auf Grundlage der Befragungsergebnisse weitere „Problemfelder" aufgedeckt und sieben konkrete Projekte definiert wurden, konnten bis heute kaum nachhaltige Veränderungen festgestellt werden. Im Gegensatz dazu, wurden die Ergebnisse einer 2009 realisierten Mitarbeiterbefragung im zweiten Fallunternehmen, einem *Automobilzulieferer* (Fall-KMU B), systematisch genutzt, um Verbesserungsprojekte erfolgreich durchzuführen. Beide Fall-KMU waren 2008 bis 2011 Praxispartner in geförderten Forschungsprojekten an der TU Chemnitz zu Fragen der innovationsförderlichen Arbeitsgestaltung. In diesen Forschungsprojekten kam explizit ein *Action Research Ansatz* (Lewin 1946, 1947) zur Anwendung, um durch kombiniertes deduktives und induktives Vorgehen, Erkenntnisse über Rahmenbedingungen und Voraussetzungen organisationaler Lernprozesse zu generieren. In beiden Unternehmen wurden im Projektverlauf jenseits der praktischen Problemstellung, d.h. der Ermittlung der Arbeitszufriedenheit, weitere Lernthemen identifiziert, die weit über eine einfache Arbeitszufriedenheitsbewertung hinausgingen. Allerdings muss der Lernerfolg, d.h. die Bewältigung der Lernthemen, in den Unternehmen unterschiedlich bewertet werden, weil bei dem Automobilzulieferer eher lernförderliche Rahmenbedingungen vorherrschen, während bei dem Werkzeughersteller Bedingungen vorzufinden sind, die Lernen eher hemmen.

Die Fallunternehmen agieren in einem dynamischen Marktumfeld, in dem die Kundenanforderungen deutlich zunehmen (mehr Lieferflexibilität, d.h. kleinere Losgrößen in kürzeren Lieferabständen, kürzere Durchlaufzeiten, hohe Qualitätsanforderungen). Lernen und Veränderung sind für beide Unternehmen daher eine notwendige Voraussetzung ihrer Wettbewerbsfähigkeit. *Reflexives Lernen* ist im Sinne der Anpassung, Veränderung oder Entwicklung von Strukturen, Prozessen, Regeln oder Routinen für die Unternehmen unverzichtbar. Wissen und Kompetenzen sind kontinuierlich weiter zu entwickeln (Cascio 2003; Holman/Wood 2003; Schirmer et al. 2012). Folgt man hierzu dem Dynamic Capabilities View (Teece et al. 1997), so sind es die dynamischen Fähigkeiten, verstanden als „*the firm's ability to integrate, build, and reconfigure internal and external competences to address rapidly changing environment*" (ebd.: 516), die den nachhaltigen Unternehmenserfolg bestimmen. Durch dynamische Fähigkeiten wird die unternehmerische Ressourcenbasis bestehend aus Wissen, Strukturen, Regeln und Routinen angepasst und entwickelt (Schirmer/Ziesche 2010: 16). Unternehmen benötigen dazu *spezifische Methoden und Instrumente*, die eine dynamische Erneuerung der Ressourcenbasis im Sinne des reflexiven Lernens ermöglichen und fördern. Insbesondere in kleinen und mittleren Unternehmen fehlen aber häufig institutionalisierte Instrumente sowie Wissen und Kompetenzen, die zur erforderlichen Reflexion und Weiterentwicklung der Ressourcenausstattung sowie der organisationalen Prozesse beitragen (Wood/Joyce 2003; Schachner et al. 2006).

Die zu Grunde liegende Annahme für die in beiden Fallunternehmen umgesetzte Mitarbeiterbefragung war insofern die, dass ihre regelmäßige Durchführung und die partizipative Verwertung der Befragungsergebnisse maßgeblich zur Reflexion organisationaler Ressourcen und Prozesse beitragen (kann). Die Ergebnisse des Action Research Prozesses zeigten dabei, dass nachhaltige Entwicklungen und Veränderungen von bestimmten *intra-organisationalen Kontextfaktoren* in den Unternehmen, wie z.B. dem Verständnis von Partizipation und Führung oder der Unternehmenskultur abhängig sind. Diese kontextspezifischen Rahmenbedingungen des Instrumenteneinsatzes werden häufig vernachlässigt. Der Beitrag der Forschung liegt daher in der Diskussion, unter welchen Voraussetzungen Mitarbeiterbefragungen organisationales Lernen fördern. Im Fokus steht insbesondere die Frage, welche intra-organisationalen Kontextfaktoren reflexives Lernen beeinflussen.

Den Grundsätzen der Aktionsforschung (Lewin 1946, 1947; Maurer/Githin 2010) folgend, wurden in den untersuchten Fall-KMU Mitarbeiterbefragungen realisiert und durch qualitative Forschungsmethoden, wie teilnehmende Beobachtung, Gruppendiskussion und Workshops begleitet. Im Beitrag wird gezeigt, dass in beiden Fallunternehmen signifikante Unterschiede in Bezug auf die intra-organisationlen Kontextfaktoren bestehen, die beim Werkzeughersteller lernhinderlich und beim Automobilzulieferer lernförderlich ausgeprägt sind.

Zu Beginn des Beitrages werden die Kernaussagen in Bezug auf den Dynamic Capability-Approach und reflexivems Lernen skizziert. In diesem Kontext werden die Spezifika von KMU hinsichtlich Lernens beschrieben, um deren Bedarf an reflexions- und lernförderlichen Instrumenten aufzuzeigen. Anschließend wird die Mitarbeiterbefragung als Lerninstrument dargestellt. Danach werden die zwei KMU-Fallstudien vorgestellt und der Aktionsforschungsprozess beschrieben. Im Anschluss daran werden die empirischen Ergebnisse erläutert und fallvergleichend diskutiert.

2. Theoretisch-konzeptioneller Bezugsrahmen

Der Dynamic Capability[1]-Approach (DC-Ansatz) baut auf den Überlegungen des Resource-Based View (RBV) auf und gilt als dessen Weiterentwicklung. Dem RBV folgend, hängt der Wettbewerbserfolg eines Unternehmens von intern existierenden und potentiellen, unternehmensspezifischen Vermögenswerten ab (z.B. Penrose 1960; Wernerfelt 1984; Barney 1986, 1991). Das Interesse dieses Ansatzes gilt folglich der heterogenen und zeitlich stabilen Ressourcenausstattung eines Unternehmens, aus denen Wettbewerbsvorteile abgeleitet werden. Dies wird allerdings kritisiert, da der Erklärungsbeitrag des RBV in Bezug auf dynamische Umwelten aufgrund seiner statischen Ausrichtung an Grenzen stößt (Eisenhardt/Martin 2000: 1106). Langfristige Wettbewerbsvorteile sind über eine unveränderte Ressourcenbasis in einer turbulenten, durch Veränderung gekennzeichneten Umwelt nicht möglich (Teece et al. 1997; Eisenhartdt/Martin 2000; Wang/Ahmed 2007). Aktuell werden daher vor allem dynamische Interpretationen, wie der Dynamic Capability-Approach diskutiert (Teece et al. 1997). Als dynamisch bezeichnen Teece et al. (1997: 15) die Fähigkeiten, durch die das Unternehmen auf veränderte Umweltbedingungen reagieren kann. Danach müssen Ressourcen kontinuierlich beschafft, entwickelt und neu kombiniert werden, um erfolgswirksam zu werden (Piening 2011: 60). Unternehmen sind dadurch in der Lage, auf das sich ändernde Marktumfeld zu reagieren bzw. proaktiv zu agieren. Diese Veränderungen gehen gleichzeitig mit einer Neukonfiguration von existierenden Regeln und Routinen bzw. einer Etablierung neuer Regeln einher, d.h. organisationale Prozesse und Strukturen werden ebenso gestaltet (Baldegger/Julien 2011: 142 ff.).

Die (Re-)Kombination von unternehmensinternen Ressourcen erfolgt durch organisationale Lernprozesse (Zollo/Winter 2002: 340 f.; Zott 2003: 100; Zahra et al. 2006: 921 ff.); organisationales Lernen ist die Voraussetzung für Dynamic Capabilities (Eisenhardt/Martin 2000: 1114 ff.). In Anlehnung an das Begriffsverständnis des organisationalen Lernens von Argyris/Schön (z.B. 1978, 1999) ist Lernen ein iterativ, zirkulärer Prozess, der mit Feedback-Schleifen verknüpft ist. Selbstbeobachtung und Selbstkritik – Kernelement von Mitarbeiterbefragungen – spielen dabei eine wesentliche Rolle. Argyris/Schön (1999) spezifizieren Lernen auf drei sich aufbauenden Lernniveaus – Typ I: Single-Loop Lernen (Anpassungslernen), Typ II: Double-Loop Lernen (Reflexives Lernen) sowie Typ III: Deutero-Lernen (Lernen durch doppelte Reflexion). Die Autoren verstehen Anpassungslernen als die Korrektur der durch Abgleich von Handlungserwartungen (outcomes) mit vorher festgelegten Erwartungen (Planvorgaben) auftretenden Abweichungen. Lernen ist reflexiv, wenn diese Abweichungen unter Veränderung der bisherigen Überzeugungen, Verständnisse oder Managementphilosophie korrigiert werden. Sich schnell ändernde Umweltbedingungen erfordern gerade diesen Lerntyp, bei dem bisherige organisationale Werte, Normen und Routinen durch neue Interpretationsschemata hinterfragt werden. Der

---

[1] Dynamic Capability wird synonym bezeichnet als dynamische Fähigkeit oder abgekürzt als DC

Umgang mit der Selbstreflexion ist dabei ein wichtiger Indikator für die Lernfähigkeit eines Unternehmens. Durch Reflexionsprozesse und das Aufdecken von Lernhindernissen und Lernerleichterungen können im Unternehmen Lernprozesse institutionalisiert werden, die zur Etablierung einer Lernfähigkeit des Unternehmens führen. Dynamische Fähigkeiten können im Unternehmen dabei als Manifestationen von Lernen auf höchster Ebene aufgefasst werden (Argyris/ Schön 1978: 26 f.; Klimecki et al. 1991). Anzumerken ist, dass organisationales Lernen dabei nie ohne das Lernen der Organisationsmitglieder stattfindet. Das individuelle Lernen wird dabei von kollektiven Entscheidungs- und Delegationsregeln der Organisation bestimmt (Argyris/Schön 1978: 9). Die Anpassungs- und Veränderungsfähigkeit einer Organisation ist folglich das Ergebnis des partizipativen Zusammenspiels von motivierten Akteuren. Bisherige Erfahrungen zu nutzen, zu reflektieren und daraus unternehmensbezogene Schlussfolgerungen abzuleiten sowie neues Wissen zu entwickeln, sind die Fähigkeiten der Mitarbeiter.

Moldaschl (2004, 2006) verweist auf eine weitere wichtige Differenzierung, indem er den Begriff der institutionellen Reflexivität vom organisationalen Lernen abgrenzt. Er konstatiert, dass mit institutioneller Reflexivität Verfahren der Selbstbeobachtung und Selbstkritik beschrieben werden, die zu organisationalem Lernen führen können. Gemeint sind Managementkonzepte und organisationale Regelsysteme, die zur Revision bzw. Innovation bisheriger Sichtweisen und Praktiken beitragen (Moldaschl 2004: 9 ff.). Organisationale Lernprozesse gehen mit der Dekonstruktion, Anpassung sowie Adaption von Routinen und Regeln einher (ebd.: 12 f.). Notwendig sind dazu jedoch institutionalisierte Verfahren und Methoden, die etablierte Routinen, Regeln und Prozesse reflektieren. Solche Verfahren können beispielsweise Lessons-Learned im Rahmen des Projektmanagements, Kunden- oder auch Mitarbeiterbefragungen sein (Moldaschl 2006: 19; Schirmer et al. 2012: 27). Allerdings korrelieren die Lernfähigkeit eines Unternehmens und dessen Wettbewerbserfolg nicht mit der Anzahl institutionalisierter reflexiver Verfahren und Praktiken. Vielmehr spielt hier deren Gebrauch, d.h. die sinnvolle Einbettung im alltäglichen Handeln die wesentliche Rolle (Modaschl et al. 2011: 4). Insbesondere der *Kontext eines Unternehmens* bestimmt über die Anforderungen reflexiver Methoden und Instrumente. Fokussiert wird bisher vor allem der *Außenkontext*, das Unternehmensumfeld: Je dynamischer das Wettbewerbsumfeld ist, desto höher sind die Anforderungen an reflexiven Instrumenten. Herausgestellt werden muss dabei aufgrund der hier untersuchten Fallunternehmen, dass speziell der Gebrauch reflexiver Instrumente vom *intra-organisationalen Kontext* abhängig ist, der z.B. das Partizipationsverständnis oder den gelebten Führungsstil im Unternehmen widerspiegelt. Diese intra-organisationalen Kontextfaktoren wirken sich somit förderlich oder hemmend auf organisationales Lernen aus.

Bei den Fallunternehmen handelt es sich um KMU[2], die im Vergleich zu Großunternehmen Spezifika aufweisen, die für die organisationale Lern- und Veränderungsfähigkeit gleichermaßen Vor- und Nachteile bieten. KMU verfügen aufgrund der geringen Anzahl an organisatorischen Einheiten über flache Hierarchien, Kommunikationsvorteile und kürzere Entscheidungswege (Theile 1998: 36; Scharpe 1992: 21). Reflexionsprozesse und Lernen werden dadurch potenziell erleichtert und können zu einer höheren Lern- und damit Veränderungsfähigkeit führen (Jutzi et al. 2000: 18; Menzel 2009: 104). Darüber hinaus ist die hohe Flexibilität von KMU bei der Neukombination von Ressourcen und damit bei der Entwicklung von dynamischen Fähigkeiten von Vorteil. Infolge dessen sind KMU in der Lage, sich schnell anzupassen, auf Wandel zu reagieren, Strategien zu entwickeln und Innovationsprozesse anzustoßen (Baldegger/Julien 2011: 144 f.). KMU verfügen jedoch über eine geringere finanzielle Ressourcenausstattung. Für den Prozess des organisationalen Lernens bedeutet diese Ressourcenknappheit, dass Veränderungen meist erst dann umgesetzt werden, wenn sie sich als unbedingt notwendig erweisen (Jutzi et al. 2000: 135). Strategische Überlegungen in Bezug auf Veränderungen und Innovationen werden aufgrund des hohen Stellenwertes des operativen Tagesgeschäftes kaum angestellt (Kirner et al. 2006: 30). Veränderungen werden somit nicht systematisch geplant und sind meist reaktiv getrieben, statt aktiv betrieben (Bundesinstitutes für Berufsbildung 2008: 11). Hinzu kommt, dass in KMU häufig Methoden, institutionalisierte Instrumente, Wissen und Kompetenzen fehlen, die zur Reflexion und Weiterentwicklung ihrer Ressourcenausstattung und Praktiken beitragen (Wood/Joyce 2003; Schachner et al. 2006). Regelmäßig durchgeführte Mitarbeiterbefragungen können ein solches Instrument sein, um Reflexion und Lernen anzustoßen.

3. Mitarbeiterbefragungen als organisationales Lerninstrument

Mitarbeiterbefragungen sind bewährte Instrumente der Organisationsentwicklung und -führung (Borg 2002, 2003; Bungard 1997). Sie beinhalten das Potential, Veränderungsprozesse zu initiieren und zu steuern (Liebig 2006: 12; Jöns 1997: 15 ff.; Seidel 2008: 93). Die Befragung selbst stellt hierbei nur einen Teil des Veränderungsprozesses dar (Borg 2003: 27). Reflexionsprozesse werden dabei bereits durch die Fragen im Fragebogen und insbesondere durch die Rückmeldung der Befragungsergebnisse ausgelöst. Die Organisation verändert sich dadurch als soziale Einheit oder gerät zumindest in Bewegung (Bungard et al. 2007: 7).

Der Schwerpunkt einer MAB als Lerninstrument liegt in der gezielten Initiierung und Steuerung von Veränderungsprozessen in der Follow-up-Phase der Befragung (Bungard 2007: 8; Schirmer et al. 2012: 64). Neben dem aktiven Einbezug der Mitarbeiter

2 In diesem Beitrag wird bei der Bestimmung, was als KMU gilt, der Definition des Institutes für Mittelstandforschung (IfM) Bonn gefolgt. Danach werden solche Unternehmen als kleine und mittlere Unternehmen aufgefasst, die weniger als 500 Beschäftigte und weniger als 50 Millionen € Jahresumsatz aufweisen (IfM Bonn).

in den Gesamtprozess, sind eine differenziertere Ergebnisrückmeldung, ein oft zweistufiger Feedbackprozess (Führungskräfte, Mitarbeiter), die Ableitung und Umsetzung von Maßnahmen sowie eine Evaluation der Maßnahmen wesentliche Erfolgsfaktoren einer Mitarbeiterbefragung (Liebig 2006: 17; vgl. Abb. 1).

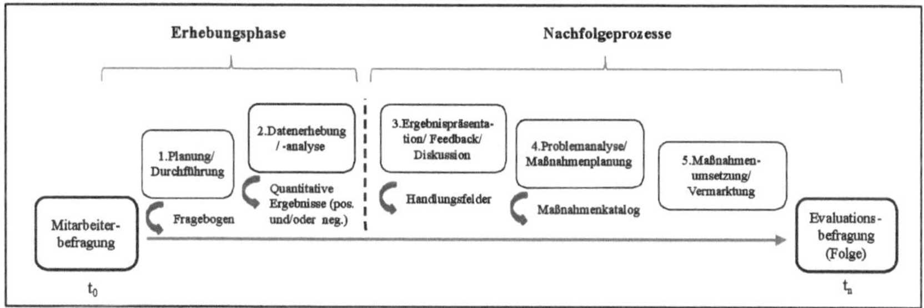

Abbildung 1: Prozesse einer Mitarbeiterbefragung in Anlehnung an Liebig (2006)

In der Vorlauf- und Erhebungsphase stehen die Ziel- und Themendefinition, das Projektmarketing zur Steigerung der Teilnahme an der Befragung sowie die Datenerhebung im Vordergrund. Der Schwerpunkt der Folgeprozesse liegt in der Diffusion der Ergebnisse und in der Auseinandersetzung mit diesen. Die gesammelten Daten werden den Mitarbeitern auf verschiedenen Hierarchieebenen zurückgespiegelt. Je konkreter und detaillierter die Analyse der Ergebnisse und deren Rückspiegelung ist, desto stärker ist die Identifizierung der Mitarbeiter mit den Ergebnissen als Voraussetzung von Veränderungsprozessen (Bungard et al. 2007: 15). Die Rückmeldung der Ergebnisse kann dabei allgemein bestätigende, nicht bestätigende und zu Fragen auffordernde Effekte erzielen (Miles et al. 1975: 378) und damit zur Entwicklung von Aktionsplänen für eine Veränderung der Praxis führen (Seidel 2008: 83). Für den Ausbau dynamischer Fähigkeiten und die Erneuerung der Ressourcenbasis sind insbesondere die Ableitung und Umsetzung von Maßnahmen in den Folgeprozessen zentral. Damit Mitarbeiterbefragungen allerdings tatsächlich zu konkreten Entwicklungen und Veränderungen führen, sind die intra-organisationalen Kontextfaktoren in Unternehmen als Rahmenbedingungen des Lernens zu betrachten. Dieser Zusammenhang wird nachfolgend anhand der zwei Fallunternehmen diskutiert.

4. Fallstudien

Bei den Fallstudien handelt es sich um mittelständische Unternehmen des produzierenden Gewerbes: Fallunternehmen A stellt *Werkzeuge für die Metall- und Steinbearbeitung* für einen anonymen Weltmarkt her; Fallunternehmen B ist ein *Automobilzulieferer*, der Motorenkomponenten für die internationale Automobilindustrie fertigt. Nachfolgende Tabelle 1 gibt einen Überblick über die Unternehmen:

Fall-KMU A „Werkzeughersteller“		**Fall-KMU B „Automobilzulieferer“**
nationaler Standort mit ca. 150 Mitarbeiter, zzgl. 10-30 Leiharbeiter	*Mitarbeiterzahl*	drei nationale und internationale Standorte mit zwischen 85-450 Mitarbeitern (Unternehmensgruppe), zzgl. Leiharbeiter je nach Auftragslage
Werkzeuge der Metall- und Steinbearbeitung; hohe Losgrößenzahl (große Varianz an Typen, Dimensionen, Qualitäten)	*Produkte*	Komponenten für Verbrennungsmotoren (Ventiltrieb) im PKW-/LKW-Motorenbau (variantenflexible Serienfertigung)
anonymer Weltmarkt: Herstellung unter Eigen- und Fremdlabel; Exportquote ca. 90 %	*Markt*	internationale Automobilindustrie; weltweite Technologieführerschaft durch patentiertes Verfahren zur Komponentenherstellung
schnell ändernde Kundenanforderungen, flexible Anpassung an veränderte Markterfordernisse erfordert adäquate interne organisationale Prozesse	*Herausforderungen*	Marktdynamik erfordert (technologische) Innovationen, Kundenanforderungen sind kostengünstige Produkte in hoher Qualität, Lieferflexibilität, Zuverlässigkeit

Tabelle 1: Überblick über die Fallunternehmen

Der *Werkzeughersteller*, dessen Arbeitsstrukturen bisher weitgehend tayloristisch geprägt waren, befindet sich derzeit in einem tiefgreifenden Veränderungsprozess, der hauptsächlich von sich schnell ändernden Kundenanforderungen getrieben ist. Die Kunden wollen insbesondere eine hohe terminliche Lieferflexibilität und kürzere Durchlaufzeiten, d.h. kleinere Losgrößen in kürzeren Lieferabständen. Zukünftig gewinnt daher die flexible Anpassung an sich veränderte Marktanforderungen sowie das proaktive Agieren, bei Maximierung des Kundennutzens noch mehr an Bedeutung. Die sich ändernden Markanforderungen stellen auch für den *Automobilzulieferer* eine große Herausforderung dar, weil seine Kunden immer kostengünstigere Produkte bei zunehmenden Qualitätsanforderungen wünschen. In der Automobilzulieferindustrie tragen weiterhin der technologische Fortschritt, der internationale Konkurrenzdruck und der damit einhergehende Kosten- und Rationalisierungsdruck wesentlich zur Branchendynamik bei (Blöcker et al. 2009). Permanente Innovationen in der Automobilzulieferindustrie, die für die Kunden einen Mehrwert bedeuten, sind entscheidend für den Wettbewerb (Geithner 2011). Beide Fallunternehmen sind damit konfrontiert, die unternehmensinternen Abläufe und Strukturen zu hinterfragen und zu gestalten. Lern- und Entwicklungsprozesse sind von hoher Bedeutung.

4.1 Forschungsdesign: Mitarbeiterbefragung und Aktionsforschung

Als Form der Beschreibung des aktuellen Zustandes sowie des Aufzeigens von Veränderungsbedarf wurde in beiden Unternehmen eine Mitarbeiterbefragung durchgeführt. Anlass der Befragungen war aus *Sicht der Unternehmen* zunächst die Erfassung der Arbeitszufriedenheit. Aus der unterschiedlichen Ausprägung der Zufriedenheit mit verschiedenen Bedingungen im Unternehmen sollte jeweils konkreter Handlungsbedarf abgeleitet werden. Konzeptionelle Grundlage für die Fragebogenkonzeptionen bildete jeweils der Leistungs-Zufriedenheits-Motor (LZ-Motor) von Borg (2001), der als valides Modell zur Erfassung der Arbeitszufriedenheit gilt. Der LZ-Motor[3] berücksichtigt explizit die organisationalen Voraussetzungen und Bedingungen der Arbeitszufriedenheit und verbindet die Perspektive der Mitarbeiter mit der des Unternehmens. Aufbauend auf dem LZ-Motor wurde mit den beiden Unternehmen ein Fragebogen entwickelt, der u.a. die Dimensionen Arbeitsbedingungen, Kommunikation und Zusammenarbeit, Einstellung zum Unternehmen, Weiterbildung und Entwicklungsmöglichkeiten sowie ein offenes Kommentarfeld enthält. Der Fragebogen ist eine adäquate Grundlage, um Strukturen und Vorgänge innerhalb des Unternehmens transparent zu machen und Verbesserungspotentiale aufzuzeigen.

Aus *Forschungsperspektive* stand neben der eigentlichen Erfassung der Arbeitszufriedenheit der gesamte Lern- und Veränderungsprozess im Fokus, der durch eine Mitarbeiterbefragung ausgelöst wird bzw. werden kann. Von besonderer Bedeutung sind hierbei die Prozesse im Anschluss der Befragung, d.h. der Umgang mit den Ergebnissen sowie die Umsetzung von Nachfolgeprojekten. In beiden Fallunternehmen wurden die Durchführung und die Nachfolgeprozesse der MAB dem *Action Research Ansatz* (Lewin 1946, 1947) folgend von einem Forscherteam begleitet und evaluiert. Der Action Research Ansatz zielt darauf ab, Praxis und Wissenschaft so zu verknüpfen, dass einerseits praxisrelevante Lösungen für Probleme umgesetzt werden und andererseits Theorienentwicklung als Reflexion auf Praxis stattfindet. Ausgangspunkt sind zumeist konkrete Probleme der Praxis (French/Bell 1973). In iterativen Prozessen von Forschen und Handeln werden neue Kenntnisse über das zu untersuchende soziale System entwickelt. Prozesse der (wissenschaftlichen) Reflexion auf Praxis und Theorie(weiter)entwicklung sowie der Gestaltung von Praxis wechseln sich gegenseitig ab. Die Forscher nehmen über einen längeren Zeitraum begleitend an diesem Prozess teil und versuchen, Veränderungs- und Entwicklungsprozesse voranzu-

[3] Der LZ-Motor basiert auf verschiedenen Motivationstheorien (Porter/Lawler 1968; Pinder 1984; Heckhausen 1989; Schuler 1991; Mealiea/Latham 1996;) und schließt praxisbewährte Zusammenhänge des Leistungsmanagements (Stewart 1986) sowie zahlreiche psychologische Gesetze sowie die etablierten Verursachungszusammenhänge aus den Bereichen der Zielsetzungs- und Feedbacktheorien (Borg 1997: 2) ein. Die Wahl des LZ-Motors als konzeptionelles Modell für die Fragebogenkonstruktion erleichtert die Interpretation der Ergebnisse, sichert die Relevanz der Befragungsthemen und die fördert die Identifikation von Handlungsbedarfen (Bungard et al. 2007: 28). Für die praktische Fragebogenkonstruktion war es dabei wichtig, zu jedem Kriterium des LZ-Motors Fragen zu platzieren, um Wirkungszusammenhänge und Rückkopplungsschleifen erkennen zu können.

treiben, indem sie auswertend an der Einschätzung der Forschungsergebnisse beteiligt sind.

Das Forscherteam übernahm in beiden Fallunternehmen die Konzeption des Fragebogens sowie die Auswertung der erhobenen Daten. Anschließend wurden die Ergebnisse zielgruppenspezifisch (Geschäftsführung und oberes Management, Belegschaft, Betriebsrat) zurückgespiegelt, um Nachfolgeprojekte und konkrete Veränderungsmaßnahmen zu definieren. Im Fall-KMU A, dem *Werkzeughersteller*, wurden die Ergebnisse im Rahmen von Workshops diskutiert und priorisiert. Diese Workshops wurden von einem Forscher moderiert und von zwei weiteren beobachtet. Die protokollierten Beobachtungsergebnisse wurden ausgewertet. Parallel wurden durch das Forscherteam Prozess- und Arbeitsabläufe analysiert und dokumentiert, um ein umfassendes Unternehmensbild zu generieren. Eine Gesamtauswertung wurde mit dem Geschäftsführer diskutiert. Im weiteren Verlauf begleitete das Forscherteam die Umsetzung der abgeleiteten Maßnahmen aus der Befragung. Prozessbegleitend fanden problemzentrierte Interviews (Witzel 1982) mit Personen des mittleren Managements sowie dem Geschäftsführer statt. Die Auswertung und Ergebnisrückmeldung der MAB im Fallunternehmen B, dem *Automobilzulieferer*, verlief ähnlich wie beim Werkzeughersteller. Auch hier wurden verschiedene Präsentationen und Workshops durchgeführt, in denen die Ergebnisse diskutiert, Entwicklungspotentiale identifiziert sowie Folgeprojekte definiert wurden. Die Workshops wurden ebenfalls durch die Forscher beobachtet, protokolliert und fotodokumentiert. Des Weiteren wurden sowohl die Workshopteilnehmer als auch andere Personen in regelmäßigen Abständen interviewt, um die Entwicklungsfortschritte der Nachfolgeprojekte einzuschätzen.

Der zugrunde liegende Leitfaden für die halb-standardisierten Experteninterviews in beiden Fallunternehmen basiert auf den theoretisch-konzeptionellen Überlegungen zum reflexiven Lernen. Ziel war, die intra-organisationalen Kontextfaktoren des Lernens zu identifizieren. Diese Faktoren wurden v.a. induktiv im Rahmen der Auswertung der Interviews sowie der Beobachtungsprotokolle anhand der strukturierenden qualitativen Inhaltsanalyse nach Mayring (2008) herausgearbeitet. Darüber hinaus war die Bewertung der Nachhaltigkeit angestoßener Veränderungsprojekte von besonderem Interesse.

4.2 Ergebnisse Werkzeughersteller

An der Mitarbeiterbefragung beim Werkzeughersteller haben 127 Mitarbeiter teilgenommen (inklusive Leiharbeiter). Dies entspricht einer Rücklaufquote von 71,1 Prozent. Insgesamt sind die Befragten mit dem Unternehmen und ihrer Arbeit zufrieden. Die Mitarbeiter haben eine hohe Bindung an das Unternehmen; sie identifizieren sich sowohl mit dem Unternehmen als auch mit den Produkten. Die Beschäftigten verfügen darüber hinaus über eine hohe Qualitätsorientierung. Sie sind motiviert und engagiert, gegenüber Veränderungen aufgeschlossen und bereit, diese mitzutragen. Kritisiert wurde allerdings die Zusammenarbeit im Unternehmen, die innerbetriebliche

Kommunikation und Information, die Weiterbildungs-/ Entwicklungsmöglichkeiten sowie das bestehende Entlohnungssystem.

Der Geschäftsführung war es wichtig, alle Unternehmensbereiche und deren Mitarbeiter über die aus der Befragung resultierenden Ergebnisse zu informieren und diese weiter zu verfolgen. Im Unternehmen wurden neben einer bereichsübergreifenden Informationsveranstaltung sowie einer Betriebsversammlung, bereichsspezifische Ergebnis- und Auswertungsworkshops durchgeführt, in deren Zuge intensive Gespräche mit den Abteilungsleitern stattfanden. Die Feedback- und Reflexionsschleifen sollten die weitere Analyse und Interpretation der Ergebnisse unterstützen. In den bereichsspezifischen Workshops mit Bereichsleiter und Geschäftsführer wurden die jeweils relevanten Ergebnisse im Vergleich zum Gesamtunternehmen vorgestellt, bewertet und diskutiert. Anschließend wurden bereichsspezifische Mitarbeiter-Workshops durchgeführt, um eine Interpretation der Ergebnisse aus Mitarbeitersicht zu erhalten.

Auf Grundlage der Diskussion in den Workshops wurden insgesamt sieben Nachfolgeprojekte definiert, die sowohl operative als auch längerfristige, strategische Maßnahmen enthalten. Dazu zählen beispielsweise die Reform des bestehenden Entlohnungsmodells, die Neuaufsetzung des kontinuierlichen Verbesserungsprozesses im Unternehmen sowie Maßnahmen zur Entwicklung der Führungskompetenzen als auch zur Verbesserung der unternehmensinternen Kommunikation. Dem Ziel, die Mitarbeiter an der Zukunftsgestaltung des Unternehmens zu beteiligen, wurde Rechnung getragen, indem Mitarbeiter und Betriebsrat in fünf der sieben Projekte mitarbeiten konnten. Die Mitarbeiter konnten sich für eine Projektgruppe bewerben und wurden im Führungskreis im Beisein des Betriebsrates ausgewählt.

Darüber hinaus forderte die Geschäftsführung eine monatliche Information aus den Projekten, die am Schwarzen Brett ausgehängt wurde, um über den Umsetzungsfortschritt in den Projekten zu informieren. Die angestoßenen Veränderungsprojekte sollen nicht wie bisher „im Sand verlaufen“. Daher wird die Mitarbeiterbefragung in regelmäßigen Abständen wiederholt, um den Umsetzungsstand der Maßnahmen zu evaluieren.

4.3 Ergebnisse Automobilzulieferer

Die Mitarbeiterbefragung beim Automobilzulieferer wurde papierbasiert an drei Standorten der Unternehmensgruppe durchgeführt. 425 Beschäftigte (Rücklaufquote 62 Prozent) haben insgesamt an der Befragung teilgenommen, wobei die Rücklaufquote zwischen den drei Standorten unterschiedlich war (50, 80 und 84 Prozent). Zur Wahrung der Anonymität und Vertraulichkeit wurden die Fragebögen extern durch das Forscherteam ausgewertet. Insgesamt kann die Arbeitszufriedenheit der Beschäftigten als hoch eingeschätzt werden, wobei es standortspezifisch Unterschiede gab. Gezeigt hat sich, dass die Beschäftigten über ein ausgeprägtes Qualitätsverständnis der hergestellten Produkte verfügen und sich mit dem Unternehmen identifizieren. Darüber hinaus sind die Beschäftigten mit dem Verhältnis zu den Kollegen und der betrieblichen Gesundheitsförderung am meisten zufrieden. Kritisiert wurden vor allem die leistungsgerechte Bezahlung sowie die beruflichen Weiterbildungsmöglichkeiten. Außerdem wurden in allen drei Standorten die Informationsflüsse innerhalb und zwischen den Abteilungen sowie standortübergreifend bemängelt.

Zur Analyse der Ergebnisse wurden verschiedene Nachfolgeprozesse initiiert. Dazu gehörten eine detaillierte Ergebnisrückmeldung in Form von standortbezogenen Ergebnisberichten und deren Veröffentlichung im Intranet und der Mitarbeiterzeitung sowie Präsentationen, Feedbackzirkel, mehrere eintägige Reflexionsworkshops an allen drei Standorten und ein übergreifender Strategie-Workshop. In den Workshops, an denen jeweils die Standortgeschäftsführung, Personalleitung, Beschäftigte sowie die Arbeitnehmervertretung teilnahmen, wurden die Ergebnisse der Befragungen bewertet und gemeinsam diskutiert, um Maßnahmen abzuleiten sowie Aktionslisten zur Umsetzung zu erstellen. Um den standortübergreifenden Austausch, der ein kritisches Ergebnis der Mitarbeiterbefragung war, sicherzustellen, nahmen jeweils zwei Standort-Vertreter an allen Workshops teil.

Wie im Fall des Werkzeugherstellers können die Ergebnisse der Workshops in operative und strategische Maßnahmen unterteilt werden. Zu letzteren gehören beispielsweise die Analyse und Reorganisation des standortübergreifenden Forschungs- und Entwicklungsprozesses oder die konzeptionelle Überarbeitung des Verbesserungsmanagements. Operative Maßnahmen betreffen die Reduktion der Geräuschbelastung in der Produktion sowie die Luft- und Temperatursituation. Die Maßnahmen können weiterhin in standortspezifisch und standortübergreifend unterschieden werden. Standortübergreifend ist die Entwicklung eines Strategiepapiers, welches die Standortstrategien und Kompetenzen festlegt und kommuniziert. Dabei soll auch die mittelfristige Personalentwicklungsstrategie reformuliert und das bestehende Arbeits- und Entlohnungsmodell analysiert werden. Standortübergreifende Maßnahmen zielen weiterhin auf die Entwicklung einer unternehmensweiten Kommunikationskultur sowie die Verbesserung der Zusammenarbeit ab. Es ist geplant, die Mitarbeiterbefragung regelmäßig durchzuführen, wobei auch die Umsetzung der abgeleiteten Veränderungsmaßnahmen evaluiert werden soll.

In beiden Fallunternehmen verliefen die Erhebungs- und Auswertungsphasen der MAB nahezu identisch und fehlerfrei. Deutliche Differenzen zeigten sich allerdings in Bezug auf die Nachfolgeprozesse, d.h. die nachhaltige Umsetzung der definierten Veränderungsprojekte. Ursachen hierfür liegen v.a. in der unterschiedlichen Ausprägung der *intra-organisationalen Kontextfaktoren*, die Lernen eher begünstigen (Automobilzulieferer) oder hemmen (Werkzeughersteller). Dies wird nachfolgend diskutiert.

5. Diskussion der intra-organisationalen Kontextfaktoren

Die in Tabelle 2 zusammengefassten intra-organisationalen Kontextfaktoren haben sich als relevante Einflussfaktoren des Lernens in den Fallunternehmen erwiesen.

Diese sind (1) das Verständnis von Partizipation, (2) das Verständnis von Führung, (3) Projektmanagement, (4) externe Kooperation, (5) Anlass und Verständnis des Instruments Mitarbeiterbefragung sowie die (6) Unternehmenskultur. Diese Faktoren wurden induktiv aus der Auswertung der Beobachtungsprotokolle der Workshops, der teilnehmenden Beobachtung während des gesamten Prozesses sowie den Interviews herausgefiltert.

Fall-KMU A, der *Werkzeughersteller*, ist funktional und tayloristisch geprägt und eher auf Reaktion, denn auf Aktion bedacht. Die Information und Kommunikation im Unternehmen erfolgt unsystematisch; die Partizipationsmöglichkeiten der Beschäftigten sind eher gering. Der kontinuierliche Verbesserungsprozess (KVP) als eine Form der institutionalisierten Partizipation wird als *„Leiche"* (Führungskraft Produktion, Werkzeughersteller) charakterisiert. Das Verhältnis zwischen der Geschäftsführung und dem Betriebsrat ist von Misstrauen gekennzeichnet; eine deutliche Spaltung zwischen Management und Belegschaft ist erkennbar. Der Verlauf der Nachfolgeprozesse der MAB ließ eine beginnende Zunahme der Partizipation der Beschäftigten erkennen. Entscheidungsprozesse sind allerdings wenig transparent. Darüber hinaus hat sich im gesamten Prozess gezeigt, dass die Entscheidungen durch das Top-Management getroffen werden und Kooperation insgesamt eher wenig ausgeprägt ist.

Partizipation ist im Fall-KMU B, dem *Automobilzulieferer*, wesentlich stärker ausgeprägt. Dies ist u.a. im kooperativen Führungsstil des Geschäftsführers begründet, der darauf achtet, die Führungskräfte in Entscheidungsprozesse sowie Mitarbeiter in Veränderungsprozesse einzubeziehen. Auf Mitwirkung, Mitbestimmung und ein freundschaftliches Arbeitsklima wird großer Wert gelegt. Die Beschäftigten nutzen häufig das betriebliche Vorschlagswesen, auch wenn sie die relativ langen Bearbeitungszeiten ihrer Vorschläge bemängeln. An den Nachfolgeprozessen der MAB nahmen neben der Bereichsleitung auch die Arbeitnehmervertretung sowie Werker teil. Die Führungskräfte verstehen es, Prozesse bzw. Projekte zu planen und zu koordinieren. Instrumente des Projektmanagements sind, vor allem bedingt durch die Projektarbeit in der Forschungs- und Entwicklungsabteilung, vorhanden und werden auch genutzt. Kontinuität und Erfolgskontrolle (Projektreporting in Teamleitersitzung, Intranet) spielen eine große Rolle. Nichtsdestotrotz besteht Entwicklungsbedarf in den Führungsfähigkeiten, insbesondere bei Führungskräften in der Produktion (z.B. Schichtleiter, Vorarbeiter) sowie in der übergreifenden ganzheitlichen Projektsteuerung in Bezug auf die Entwicklung des Unternehmens. Häufig überlagern Tagesprobleme die Projektarbeit.

Beide Unternehmen führten die Mitarbeiterbefragung unter Begleitung eines externen Forscherteams durch, welche die Konzeption der Fragebögen, die Datenauswertung sowie die Ergebnispräsentationen und Reflexionsworkshops gestalteten. Die Rolle der Forscher lag in den Reflexionsworkshops vor allem darin, kritische Denkanstöße zu liefen und die Beteiligten zu Selbstreflexion und -kritik aufzufordern. Darüber hinaus wurden die Forscher als Impulsgeber und externe Wissensquelle genutzt. Insbesondere Fall-KMU B bezieht das Forscherteam in den Folgeprozess und die Umsetzung der definierten Maßnahmen und Projekte mit ein.

Intra-organisationale Kontextfaktoren	Fall-KMU A: Werkzeughersteller	Fall-KMU B: Automobilzulieferer
1. Verständnis von Partizipation	• tayloristische Arbeits- und funktionale Organisationsstrukturen prägen das Verständnis von Partizipation im Unternehmen, d.h. Partizipation (materiell und inmateriell) ist kaum vorhanden. • Zunahme der Partizipation im Verlauf der Nachfolgeprozesse der MAB	• organisationale Prozesse im Unternehmen sind geprägt von Mitwirkung, Mitbestimmung und Einbeziehung von Mitarbeitern • im Unternehmen herrscht ein kollektives, freundschaftliches Arbeitsklima
2. Verständnis von Führung	• Führungskräfte weisen Defizite in Führungskompetenzen auf • es fehlt an Transparenz bei Entscheidungsprozessen • kontinuierliche Verbesserungsprozess ist gescheitert: wird weder vorgelebt, noch ist es bei den Führungskräften anerkannt	• Geschäftsführer pflegt einen kooperativen Führungsstil • Bereichsleiter übernehmen zunehmend planende, koordinierende und kontrollierende Tätigkeiten → ausgeprägte kooperative Führungskultur • Führungsdefizite eher im Bereich der Produktion (z.B. Schichtleiter, Vorarbeiter)
3. Projektmanagement	• Projekte werden nicht als bereichsübergreifender Prozess, sondern als funktional differenzierte Aufgabe gesehen • bisherige Erfahrungen bestehen eher darin, dass *„Projekte versanden"*, d.h. sie besitzen keine Nachhaltigkeit • fehlende ganzheitliche Projektsteuerung	• es erfolgt eine kontinuierliche Projektverfolgung mit dem Ziel die Projekte erfolgreich abzuschließen • die Ergebnisse der Befragung wurden gezielt kommuniziert und verbreitet • die einzelnen Projekte und deren Bearbeitungsstand wurden konsequent verfolgt • die übergreifende Projektsteuerung ist ausbaufähig
4. Externe Kooperation	• Einbezug externer Forscher, die die MAB wissenschaftlich begleiten und evaluieren sowie Impulse in den Nachfolgeprozessen setzen (Aktionsforschung) • tragen dazu bei, dass die Ergebnisse kritisch reflektiert werden und die Mitarbeiter in den Reflexionsworkshops eine Position der Selbstreflexion/Selbstkritik einnehmen	
	• Forscher sind in die Nachfolgeprojekte nur punktuell eingebunden	• Forscher sind in die Nachfolgeprojekte eingebunden und werden als externe Wissensquellen genutzt
5. Anlass/ Verständnis des Instruments Mitarbeiterbefragung	• Anlass: Entwicklung eines neuen Entlohnungsmodells (stärkere Beteiligung der Mitarbeiter) • ein Hauptziel: Evaluation der Zufriedenheit der Mitarbeiter am Beispiel des Entlohnungsmodells • Auswertung der MAB zeigte Probleme auf, die die Geschäftsführung so nicht erwartet hatte (Problemverschiebung) • Problembewusstsein wurde bei der Geschäftsführung tendenziell erhöht	• MAB wird im Unternehmen als Instrument zur Reflexion und zum Anstoß von Veränderungen eingesetzt • Anlass war die eher unzufriedenen Ergebnisse der MAB im Jahr 2008 • die MAB wurde bewusst im Krisenjahr 2009 durchgeführt, um das aktuelle Stimmungsbild der Belegschaft zu erhalten und Veränderungsprozesse anzustoßen
6. Unternehmenskultur	• Unternehmenskultur ist veränderungsresistent, d.h. man fällt schnell in alte Muster zurück, Veränderungsprojekte versanden (*„Geschichte des Scheiterns"*) • sehr reaktives Unternehmen • geringe Offenheit gegenüber Neuem und gegenüber Fehlern	• Unternehmenskultur ist geprägt von Partizipation • aufgrund der Technologieführerschaft und des hohen Wettbewerbsdruck ist das Unternehmen stark auf Innovation, Lernen und Entwicklung ausgerichtet (Lernkultur)

Tabelle 2: Erfolgskritische intra-organisationale Kontextfaktoren in den Fall-KMU

Beide KMU hatten bereits Erfahrungen mit Mitarbeiterbefragungen. Im KMU A wurde vor einigen Jahren eine MAB durchgeführt, die als allgemeine Meinungsumfrage angelegt war. Eine Nachhaltigkeit war jedoch nicht gegeben. Die 2010 durchgeführte Befragung sollte vordergründig die Zufriedenheit der Mitarbeiter mit dem Entlohnungsmodell evaluieren. Die Integration weiterer Themenkomplexe war vor allem durch die Zusammenarbeit mit dem Forscherteam möglich. Die Auswertung der MAB ergab daher eine Reihe an zu bearbeitenden Themen (z.B. die Neugestaltung des KVP), die in sieben Nachfolgeprojekten bearbeitet wurde. Aus der guten Rücklaufquote von über 71 Prozent lässt sich schlussfolgern, dass die Beschäftigten hohes Interesse an Veränderungen haben. Allerdings wurde bzw. wird seitens der Unternehmensführung das Potential und die Bedeutung der Nachfolgeaktivitäten unterschätzt. Die Ergebnisse der MAB und die Diskussionen bei der Ergebnispräsentation zeigen, dass die Beschäftigten andere Probleme sehen als die Geschäftsführung. Dadurch wurde zwar einerseits das Bewusstsein für andere Problemlagen geschaffen. Andererseits besteht nach wie vor eine hohe Gefahr, dass die Projekte versanden, was sich wiederum negativ auf die Motivation und Veränderungsbereitschaft der Beschäftigten auswirken kann.

Der Automobilzulieferer versteht eine MAB als wichtiges Instrument zur Reflexion. Die Ergebnisse der MAB aus dem Jahr 2008 waren wenig zufriedenstellend, insbesondere im Bereich Einarbeitung, Qualitätsmanagement, Weiterbildung oder auch Entlohnung. Daraufhin wurden verschiedene, eher kurzfristige Maßnahmen umgesetzt. Mit der 2009 vom Forscherteam durchgeführten Befragung sollte explizit hinterfragt werden, inwieweit eine positive Entwicklung festzustellen ist. Diskutiert wurde auf oberer Führungsebene weiterhin, ob die MAB aufgrund der weltweiten wirtschaftlichen Krisensituation 2009 verschoben werden sollte. Es wurde sich allerdings bewusst dafür entschieden, die MAB in der angespannten Situation durchzuführen: „*Wir wollen ja gerade herausfinden, was nicht gut läuft.*“, konstatiert der Personalleiter. Insgesamt wird die MAB als wichtiges Reflexions- und Veränderungsinstrument wahrgenommen und soll zukünftig regelmäßig, d.h. zweijährig, durchgeführt werden.

Der Forschungsprozess zeigte schließlich, dass die vorhandene Unternehmenskultur ein elementarer Faktor in Bezug auf Lernen und Entwicklung ist. Die Kultur beim Werkzeughersteller ist von einer hohen Beharrungstendenz geprägt und kann als veränderungsresistent charakterisiert werden. Sowohl die Beobachtungseindrücke als auch Aussagen von Interviewpartnern bestätigen, dass schnell in alte Muster zurückgefallen wird und die Mehrzahl der Veränderungsprojekte versanden. Ein Befragter spricht sogar von einer „*Geschichte des Scheiterns*“. Insgesamt herrscht nur eine geringe Offenheit gegenüber Neuem und gegenüber Fehlern. Dies ist auch historisch bedingt, weil die bisher gefertigten Produkte im Vergleich zum Automobilzulieferer weniger anspruchsvoll sind und das Unternehmen weniger darauf angewiesen war, technologischen Fortschritt zu erzielen. Allerdings haben die Befragten in den Interviews mehrfach darauf hingewiesen, dass die Anforderungen der Kunden vor allem hinsichtlich der Lieferflexibilität stark zugenommen haben und dies die Anpassung von Strukturen und Prozessen im Unternehmen erfordert. Im Unterschied dazu kann die Unternehmenskultur beim Automobilzulieferer als Lernkultur bezeichnet werden. Die Themen Innovation, Lernen und Entwicklung spielen von je her eine sehr große Rolle, u.a. bedingt durch das Ziel, die Technologieführerschaft zu erhalten. Das Unternehmen ist ein veränderungsbereites Unternehmen, welches Wandel und Anpassung sehr offen gegenüber steht.

Im Vergleich der beiden Fallunternehmen hat sich gezeigt, dass die nachhaltige Umsetzung von Veränderungs- und Entwicklungsmaßnahmen aufgrund einer Mitarbeiterbefragung maßgeblich von den vorherrschenden intra-organisationalen Rahmenbedingungen in den Unternehmen abhängen. Die Ausprägung der in Tabelle 2 dargestellten Aspekte ist beim Automobilzulieferer wesentlich günstiger für einen nachhaltigen Veränderungsprozess. Durch die intensive Auseinandersetzung mit den Ergebnissen der MAB wurde in diesem Unternehmen reflexives Lernen (Double-Loop-Lernen) gefördert, welches zu verschiedenen Veränderungsprojekten führte. Darüber hinaus fördert die Institutionalisierung des Instrumentes in beiden Fällen ein Lernen durch doppelte Reflexion (Deutero-Lernen), in dessen Rahmen auch ein Hinterfragen der MAB möglich wird.

Die Ausprägung der o.g. intra-organisationalen Kontextfaktoren beim Werkzeughersteller lassen jedoch vermuten, dass das Potential des Instrumentes Mitarbeiterbefragung als Reflexions- und Lerninstrument bisher noch unzureichend ausgenutzt wird. Es besteht die Gefahr, dass die gesetzten Entwicklungsimpulse versanden und zukünftige Befragungen von den Beschäftigten weniger akzeptiert und genutzt werden. Bisher ist das Unternehmen häufig in alte Muster zurückgefallen (Beharrungstendenz) und hat sich Entwicklungsprozessen verschlossen. Lernen würde in diesem Fall nur als Anpassungslernen (single-loop Lernen) (Agyris/Schön 1999) stattfinden, indem innerhalb eines vorhandenen und bekannten Handlungsrepertoires agiert wird. Fehler werden zwar erkannt und abgestellt, jedoch defensive Routinen und veränderungsfeindliche Verhaltensmuster nicht geändert. Inwieweit dies Auswirkungen auf die Wettbewerbsfähigkeit des Unternehmens hat, kann abschließend nicht bewertet werden. Es ist jedoch anzunehmen, dass die dynamische Umweltentwicklung und die zunehmenden Flexibilitätsanforderungen der Kunden des Werkzeugherstellers einen grundlegenden Veränderungsprozess notwendig machen. Wichtige Ansatzpunkte liegen dabei in den identifizierten Problemfeldern aus der durchgeführten MAB, die nachhaltig weiter verfolgt werden sollten. Dies erfordert allerdings auch eine grundlegende Reflexion der bisherigen Führungs- und Unternehmenskultur, der Partizipationsmöglichkeiten der Mitarbeiter sowie des praktizierten Projektmanagements, also Double-Loop Lernen und Deutero Lernen. Abbildung 2 fasst die Erkenntnisse zusammen und verbindet den theoretisch-konzeptionellen Bezugsrahmen mit den Ergebnissen der Untersuchung:

Es kann davon ausgegangen werden, dass dynamische Fähigkeiten in einer sich ständig verändernden Unternehmensumwelt die kontinuierliche (Re-)kon-figuration organisationaler Prozesse, Strukturen und Strategien ermöglichen. Dynamische Fähigkeiten sind dabei sowohl Voraussetzung als auch Ergebnis reflexiven Lernens. Reflexives Lernen kann durch Instrumente und Methoden, wie z.B. Mitarbeiterbefragungen gefördert werden. Der Gebrauch und Nutzen der Instrumente hängt dabei maßgeblich vom organisationalen Kontext ab, der sich in einen spezifischen Partizipations- und Führungsverständnis oder Unternehmenskultur zeigt. Diese intra-organisationalen Kontextfaktoren wirken, wie in den Fallunternehmen deutlich wurde, lernförderlich oder lernbehindernd.

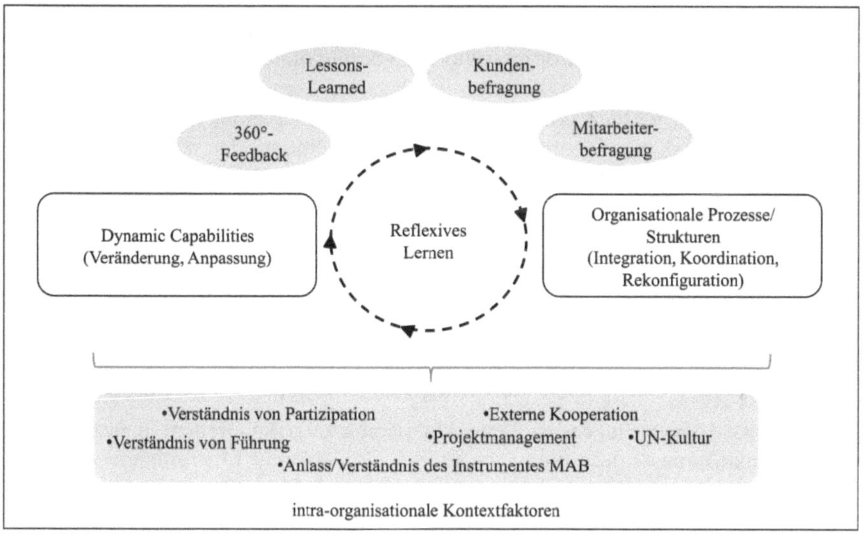

Abbildung 2: Reflexives Lernen im Zusammenhang intra-organisationaler Kontextfaktoren

6. Fazit und Ausblick

Mitarbeiterbefragungen kommen als Instrument des Veränderungsmanagements in Unternehmen zum Einsatz und zielen explizit auf Wandel und Anpassung ab. Als handhabbares Werkzeug, insbesondere für KMU, können in einer MAB alle Mitarbeiter in allen Hierarchieebenen erreicht werden. Verständlichkeit, Bekanntheit des Instrumentes und oft auch die Anforderung, eine Befragung im Rahmen einer ISO-Zertifizierung durchzuführen, sind Gründe für den Einsatz von Mitarbeiterbefragungen in der betrieblichen Praxis. Durch Feedback der Befragungsergebnisse sowie durch eine partizipative Ergebnisdiskussion in Form von Reflexionsworkshops, werden Folgeprozesse initiiert, die zu Veränderungen in den Strukturen und Prozessen des Unternehmens führen und damit einen Beitrag zur Erneuerung und Entwicklung der Ressourcenbasis leisten (können). Es werden Daten erhoben, die Grundlage einer umfassenden Organisationsentwicklung sein können, weil Defizite identifiziert und Verbesserungspotentiale abgeleitet werden (Comelli 1997; Liebig 2006). Lernprozesse und Wandel sind die Folge.

Intention dieses Beitrages war es nicht, die konkreten Ergebnisse einer Mitarbeiterbefragung zu erschließen, sondern anhand des Action Research Ansatzes den kompletten Interventions- und Veränderungsprozess zu betrachten. Die statistisch, quantitative Auswertung der eigentlichen Befragung rückt somit in den Hintergrund; der Umgang mit den Ergebnissen ist entscheidender. Die nachhaltige Wirkung einer Mitarbeiterbefragung wird folglich durch sich anschließende Nachfolgeprozesse bestimmt. Erst wenn die von einer MAB ausgehenden Veränderungsimpulse in konkrete Entwicklungen überführt werden, können Prozesse, Strukturen und Ressourcen verändert werden. Dies ist, wie die Erfahrungen in den beiden betrachteten Fallunternehmen zeigen, von bestimmten intra-organisationalen Kontextfaktoren abhängig. Die Identifikation dieser Bedingungen und deren Einfluss auf Lernen war Forschungsziel. Als relevante Faktoren wurden das Verständnis von Partizipation, das Verständnis von Führung, das Projektmanagement, die externe Kooperation, den Anlass und das Verständnis des Instruments Mitarbeiterbefragung sowie die Unternehmenskultur identifiziert. Es ist zu vermuten, dass es weitere Faktoren gibt, die auf Lernen und Entwicklung einwirken. Darüber hinaus ist anzunehmen, dass eine bestimmte Ausprägung dieser Bedingungen generell einen fördernden oder hemmenden Einfluss auf Lernen bzw. den Erfolg von Instrumenten und Methoden hat. Dies gilt es, zukünftig in weiteren Falluntersuchungen bzw. größeren quantitativen Erhebungen zu erforschen. Bei letzteren liegt die Herausforderung v.a. in der adäquaten Operationalisierung der Kontextfaktoren. Hierzu lieferte die vorliegende Untersuchung erste Impulse.

Die Ergebnisse der vorliegenden Aktionsforschung zeigen außerdem in Bezug auf die KMU-Thematik, dass diese nicht per se ihre Größen- und Flexibilitätsvorteile oder flachen Hierarchien hinsichtlich Lernen nutzen. Im Fall des Werkzeugherstellers hat sich z.B. bestätigt, dass die in KMU häufige Dominanz der oberen Führungsebene, die top-down Initiierung und Umsetzung von Veränderungsprojekten, die von einer Mitarbeiterbefragung ausgehenden Veränderungspotenziale nur unzureichend zur Entfaltung bringen.

Durch den hohen Druck des Tagesgeschäfts sowie die oftmals geringe personelle und finanzielle Kapazität besteht in KMU die Tendenz, Veränderungen und Entwicklungen nicht aktiv und vorausschauend zu gestalten, sondern erst dann darauf zu reagieren, wenn der Handlungsdruck unausweichlich ist (Jutzi et al. 2000: 135). Dies hat sich insbesondere im Fallunternehmen A, dem Werkzeughersteller, gezeigt. Die regelmäßige Durchführung von Mitarbeiterbefragungen könnte diesem Reaktionismus entgegenwirken und kontinuierliche Reflexion und Lernen fördern. Positiv wirkt sich dabei aus, dass ein einmal entwickeltes Erhebungsinstrument sowie standardisierte Formen der Datenauswertung und etablierte Nachfolgeprozesse den Aufwand der Durchführung einer MAB in einem überschaubaren Maß halten. Voraussetzung ist allerdings, dass diese als organisationales Interventions- und Veränderungsinstrument akzeptiert wird. Dies schließt ein, dass vom Management auch nicht erwartete Ergebnisse und Probleme ernst genommen werden. Ein Kulturwandel kann durch den proaktiven Umgang damit positiv beeinflusst werden. Dies setzt allerdings wiederum voraus, dass die Bedeutung der Nachfolgeprozesse nicht verloren geht, wie dies bisher beim Werkzeughersteller üblich war. Notwendig ist hierzu, wie beim Automobilzulieferer auch, ein ganzheitliches und systemisches Veränderungsmanagement, welches eine MAB als ein Veränderungsinstrument neben weiteren begreift. Gerade in diesem übergreifenden Veränderungsmanagement besteht in beiden Fallunternehmen Verbesserungsbedarf.

Das Fazit des Beitrages ist daher, dass eine Mitarbeiterbefragung Instrument potentieller organisationaler Entwicklung ist. Die Wirkung in Bezug auf reflexives Lernen ist allerdings von den vorherrschenden Rahmenbedingungen im Unternehmen abhängig. Eine Mitarbeiterbefragung trägt – wie im Fall des Automobilzulieferers – zur Unternehmensentwicklung bei, wenn Partizipation gelebt wird, ein kooperativer Führungsstil herrscht, Lernen als wichtig erachtet wird, das Unternehmen bereit zur Selbstreflexion ist sowie Impulse von außen als externe Wissensquellen nutzt. Die partizipative Ergebnisreflexion und Weiterverfolgung relevanter Themen stärkt die Lern-, Veränderungs- und Anpassungsfähigkeit des Unternehmens.

Im Fall des Werkzeugherstellers leistete die Mitarbeiterbefragung ebenfalls einen Beitrag. Dieser liegt vor allem in der Irritation der Erwartungen des oberen Managements und im Aufzeigen von Handlungsbedarfen. Jutzi et al. (2000: 176 ff.) folgend diente in diesem Fall die MAB als Instrument, welches Lernprozesse anstößt und ein bisher eher erstarrtes und lernresistentes System stört. Veränderungen in der Wahrnehmung von Problemlagen sowie die Entwicklung der Interaktion innerhalb des Unternehmens wurden angeregt. Außerdem wurden Handlungsroutinen hinterfragt und Angebote zu deren Veränderung eingebracht. Inwieweit dies einen nachhaltigen Nutzen hat, hängt maßgeblich von der Fortführung der Nachfolgeprojekte sowie der Gestaltung und Veränderungen der Rahmenbedingungen ab – es besteht die Notwendigkeit eines grundlegenden Wandels. Abschließend kann konstatiert werden, dass der vorliegende Beitrag primär die Notwendigkeit eines institutionalisierten Arrangements an Instrumenten und Werkzeugen zur Steigerung der Reflexivität in Organisationen, respektive in kleinen und mittelständischen Unternehmen aufzeigt. Das heißt, eine kontinuierliche Entwicklung der vorhandenen unternehmensspezifischen Ressourcenbasis kann durch MABs gefördert werden, sofern das Instrument innerhalb eines Unternehmens entsprechend institutionalisiert ist. Dabei ist es von entscheidender Bedeutung, nicht nur das Instrument Mitarbeiterbefragung als solches zu betrachten, sondern stets auch die vorherrschenden Kontextfaktoren zu reflektieren und zu gestalten. Diese organisationalen und strukturellen Voraussetzungen des Lernens sind auch stärker in die konzeptionellen Überlegungen des Dynamic-Capabilities Ansatzes zu integrieren.

Die Grenzen der vorliegenden Forschung liegen in der Generalisierung der gewonnenen Ergebnisse auf Grund des qualitativen Action Research Ansatzes (zwei Fallstudien). Zur Absicherung und weiteren Diskussion der Ergebnisse sind daher weitere Falluntersuchungen bzw. eine größere quantitative Erhebung notwendig. In diesem Zusammenhang könnten Mitarbeiterbefragungen und ihre Reflexions- und Lernpotentiale mit anderen Lern- und Veränderungsinstrumenten, wie z.B. Open Space, Lessons-Learned, Kundenbefragung gegenübergestellt werden.

Literatur

Argyris, C./Schön, D.A. (1978): Organizational Learning: A Theory of Action Perspective, Reading, Mass., u.a.: Addison-Wesley.

Argyris, C./Schön, D.A. (1999): Die lernende Organisation. Grundlagen, Methode, Praxis. Klett-Cotta-Verlag: Stuttgart.

Baldegger, R./Julien, P. (2011): Regionales Unternehmertum. Ein disziplinärer Ansatz, Gabler: Wiesbaden.

Barney, J.B. (1986): Strategic Factor Markets: Expectations, Luck, and Business Strategy. In: Management Science, Vol. 32, pp. 1231-1241.

Barney, J.B. (1991): Firm Resources and Sustained Competitive Advantage. In: Journal of Management, Vol. 17, pp. 99-120.

Blöcker, A./Jürgens, U./Meißner, H.-R. (2009): Innovationsnetzwerke und Clusterpolitik in europäischen Automobilregionen. Impuls für Beschäftigung. LIT: Münster.

Borg, I. (1997): Der LZ-Motor. Human Resources Consulting: München.

Borg, I. (2002): Mitarbeiterbefragungen – kompakt, Hogrefe: Göttingen.

Borg, I. (2003): Führungsinstrument Mitarbeiterbefragung. Theorien, Tools und Praxiserfahrungen, 3. Aufl., Hogrefe: Göttingen.

Bundesinstitutes für Berufsbildung (2008): Berufsbildung in Wissenschaft und Praxis, 37. Jahrgang H20155, 2/2008.

Bungard, W./Jöns, I. (1997): Mitarbeiterbefragung. Ein Instrument des Innovations- und Qualitätsmanagements, Beltz: Weinheim.

Bungard, W./Müller, K./Niethammer, C. (2007): Mitarbeiterbefragung – was dann...? Springer-Verlag: Heidelberg.

Cascio, W.F. (2003): Changes in workers, work, and organizations. In: Borman, W.C./Ilgen, D.R./Klimoski, R.J. (Eds.): Handbook of psychology. Industrial and organizational psychology, Vol. 12, Wiley: Hoboken, New Jersey, pp. 401-422.

Comelli, G. (1997): Mitarbeiterbefragungen und Organisationsentwicklungsprozesse. In: Bungard, W./Jöns, I. (Hrsg.): Mitarbeiterbefragung. Ein Instrument des Innovations- und Qualitätsmanagements. Weinheim.

Eisenhardt, K.M./Martin, J.A. (2000): Dynamic Capabilities: What Are They? In: Strategic Management Journal 21 (10-11), pp. 1105-1121.

French, W.L./Bell, C.H. (1973): Organisationsentwicklung, Bern/Stuttgart.

Geithner, S. (2011): Innovationsfähigkeit durch Organisationsentwicklung und Personalentwicklung!? – Arbeit, Entwicklung und Innovation aus Perspektive der kultur-historischen Tätigkeitstheorien. In: Barthel, E./Hanft, A./Hasebrook, J. (Hrsg.): Integriertes Kompetenzmanagement. Innovationsstrategien als Aufgabe der Personal- und Organisationsentwicklung. Waxmann: Münster, S. 221-250.

Heckhausen, H. (1989). Motivation und Handeln, 2. Aufl., Springer: Berlin.

Holman, D./Wood, S. (2003): The new workplace: An introduction. In: Holman, D. (Eds.): The new workplace: A guide to the human impact of modern working practices., Wiley: Chichester, West Sussex.

Institut für Mittelstandsforschung (IfM): KMU-Definition des IfM Bonn. [online: http://www.ifm-bonn.org/index.php?id=89, 31.08.2011].

Jöns, I. (1997): Formen und Funktionen von Mitarbeiterbefragungen. In: Bungard, W./Jöns, I. (Hrsg.): Mitarbeiterbefragungen. Ein Instrument des Innovations- und Qualitätsmanagements, Beltz: Weinheim, S. 15–31.

Jutzi, K./Delbrouck, I./Müller, H. (2000): Lernen kleine Unternehmen anders? Rainer Hampp: München, Mering.

Kirner, E./Som, O./Dreher, C./Wiesenmaier, V. (2006): Innovation in KMU: Der ganzheitliche Innovationsansatz und die Bedeutung von Innovationsroutinen für den Innovationsprozess, Frauenhofer ISI: Karlsruhe.

Klimecki, R./Probst, G./Eberl, P. (1991): Systementwicklung als Managementproblem. In: Staehle, W.H./Sydow, J. (Hrsg.): Managementforschung I, de Gruyter, Berlin, New York, S. 103-162.

Kraut, A. (1996): Organizational Surveys. Tools for Assessment and Change, Jossey-Bass: San Francisco.

Lewin, K. (1946): Action research and minority problems. In: Journal of Social Issues, 2, pp. 34-46.

Lewin, K. (1947): Feedback problems of social diagnosis and action. Part II-B of frontiers in group dynamics. In: Human Relations, 1, pp. 147-153.

Liebig, C. (2006): Mitarbeiterbefragungen als Interventionsinstrument. Untersuchung ihrer Effektivität anhand des Kriteriums Arbeitszufriedenheit. DUV: Wiesbaden.

Maurer, M./Githin, R.P. (2010): Toward a reframing of action research for human resource and organization development: Moving beyond problem solving and toward dialogue. In: Action Research 8(3), pp. 267-292.

Mayring, P. (2008): Qualitative Inhaltsanalyse. Grundlagen und Techniken. Beltz: Weinheim.

Mealiea, L.W./Latham, G.P. (1996): Skills for managerial success. Chicago, IL: Irwin.

Menzel, D. (2009): Wechselwirkungen zwischen Strategie- und Lernfähigkeit von kleinen und mittelständischen Unternehmen. Konzeptionelle Betrachtung und empirische Analyse. Rainer Hampp: München, Mering.

Miles, M./Hornstein, H./Callahan, D./Calden, P./Schiavo, R. (1975): Feedback von Befragungsergebnissen. Theorie und Bewertung. In: Bennis, W. (Hrsg.): Änderung des Sozialverhaltens. Stuttgart.

Moldaschl, M. (2004): Institutionelle Reflexivität. In: Papers und Preprints des Lehrstuhls Innovationsforschung und nachhaltiges Ressourcenmanagement (BWL IX) der Technischen Universität Chemnitz 1/2004. http://www.qucosa.de/fileadmin/data/qucosa/documents/5494/data/MM_Institutionelle.pdf

Moldaschl, M. (2006): Innovationsfähigkeit, Zukunftsfähigkeit, Dynamic Capabilities. Moderne Fähigkeitsmystik und eine Alternative. In: Conrad, P./Schreyögg, G. (Hrsg.): Managementforschung 16, Management von Kompetenz. Gabler: Wiesbaden. S. 1-36.

Moldaschl, M./Hallensleben, T./Jain, A. K./Manger, D. (2011): Innovationsfähigkeit. Empirische Befunde zur Rolle reflexiver Verfahren. In: Papers und Preprints des Lehrstuhls Innovationsforschung und nachhaltiges Ressourcenmanagement (BWL IX) der Technischen Universität Chemnitz 2/2011. http://www.tu-chemnitz.de/wirtschaft/bwl9/publikationen/lehrstuhlpapiere/WP_2011_2_Befunde.pdf

Piening, E.P. (2011): Prozessdynamiken der Implementierung von Innovationen. Gabler: Wiesbaden.

Pinder, C.C. (1984): Work motivation. Glenview, IL: Scott Foresman.

Porter, L.W./Lawler, E.E. (1968): Managerial Attitudes and Performance. Chicago, IL: Irwin.

Schachner, M./Speckbacher, G./Wentges, P. (2006): Steuerung mittelständischer Unternehmen: Größeneffekte und Einfluss der Eigentums- und Führungsstruktur. In: Zeitschrift für Betriebswirtschaft, 76(6), S. 589-614.

Scharpe, J. (1992): Strategisches Management im Mittelstand: Probleme der Implementierung und Ansätze zur Lösung, Eul: Bergisch Gladbach.

Schirmer, F./Ziesche, K. (2010): Dynamic Capabilities: Das Dilemma von Stabilität und Dynamik aus organisationspolitischer Perspektive. In: Barthel, E./Hanft, A./Hasebrook, J. (Hrsg.): Integriertes Kompetenzmanagement im Spannungsfeld von Innovation und Routine. Waxmann: Münster, New York, München, Berlin. S. 14-41.

Schirmer, F./Knödler, D./Tasto, M. (2012): Innovationsfähigkeit durch Reflexivität - Neue Perspektiven auf Praktiken des Change Management. Gabler: Wiesbaden.

Schuler, H. (1991): Der Funktionskreis 'Leistungsförderung' - eine Skizze. In: Schuler, H. (Hrsg.): Beurteilung und Förderung beruflicher Leistung, Verlag für angewandte Psychologie: Stuttgart, S. 171-189.

Seidel, S. (2008): Befragung als systemische Intervention in der Organisationsentwicklung: Organisationslernen vor dem Hintergrund von Daten. Dissertation, Dortmund. [online: https://eldorado.tu-dortmund.de/bitstream/2003/25832/2/Dissertation.pdf, 30.08.2011].

Stewart, D. (1986): The power of people skills. Wiley: New York.

Teece, D.J./Pisano, G./Shuen, A. (1997): Dynamic Capabilities and Strategic Management. In: Strategic Management Journal, 18. Jg., Nr. 7, pp. 509-533.

Theile, K. (1998): Ganzheitliches Management: ein Konzept für Klein- und Mittelunternehmen. Paul Haupt: Bern.

Wang, C.L./Ahmed, P.K. (2007): Dynamic capabilities: A review and research agenda. In: International Journal of Management Reviews, 9. Jg. 2000, Vol. 1, pp. 31-51.

Wernerfelt, B. (1984): A resource-based view of the firm. In: Strategic Management Journal, Vol. 5, pp. 171-180.

Witzel, A. (1982): Verfahren der qualitativen Sozialforschung. Überblick und Alternativen. Campus Verlag, Frankfurt a.M.

Wood, A./Joyce, P. (2003): Owner-Managers and the Practice of Strategic Management. In: International Small Business Journal, 21(2), pp. 181-195.

Zahra, S.A./Sapienza, H.J./Davidson, P. (2006): Entrepreneurship and Dynamic Capabilities: A Review, Model and Research Agenda. In: Journal of Management Studies 43 (4), pp. 917-955.

Zollo, M./Winter, S. (2002): Deliberate Learning and the Evolution of Dynamic Capabilities. In: Organization Science 13 (3), pp. 339-351.

Zott, C. (2003): Dynamic Capabilities and the Emergence of Intraindustry Differential Firm Performance: Insights from a Simulation Study. In: Strategic Management Journal 24 (2), pp. 97-125.

Gestaltung des Wandels mit struktureller und kontextueller Ambidextrie am Beispiel eines Technologieführers in der Automobilzulieferbranche

Birgit Renzl, Martin Rost und Jürgen Kaschube

Zusammenfassung

Der Beitrag untersucht ein Automobilzulieferunternehmen, das einerseits mit den tiefgreifenden Veränderungen in der Automobilzulieferindustrie konfrontiert ist, wie beispielsweise neuen Antriebsformen und veränderter Mobilität, und andererseits einen internen Strukturwandel vollzieht. Ziel des Veränderungsprozesses ist, eine dynamische Wandlungsfähigkeit im Unternehmen aufzubauen und Ambidextrie als Balance zwischen Nutzung des existierenden Wissens (Exploitation) und Schaffung neuen Wissens (Exploration) herzustellen. Die Fallstudie zeigt, wie neben der strukturellen auch die kontextuelle Ambidextrie durch gezielte Maßnahmen unterstützt werden kann und welche Anforderungen die Ambidextrie an Führungskräfte und Mitarbeiter stellt. Bei der strukturellen Ambidextrie ist die Verknüpfung über das Top-Management-Team nicht ausreichend und bedarf weiterer Maßnahmen im Bereich der Personalentwicklung und der Netzwerkbildung. Kontextuelle Ambidextrie erfordert ein „Ambidextrous Mindset“, das sich in einer entsprechenden Unternehmenskultur entwickelt und durch einen adäquaten Führungsstil gefördert wird. Maßnahmen im Bereich des Kompetenzmanagements und der Personalentwicklung sind notwendig, um die Anforderungen, die kontextuelle Ambidextrie an Handeln, Kompetenzen und Verantwortungsübernahme der Mitarbeiter stellt, auch bewältigen zu können.

Schlüsselwörter: strukturelle und kontextuelle Ambidextrie, Dynamic Capabilities, Automobilzulieferindustrie, Kompetenzmanagement

Abstract

In order to deal with external and internal change organizations are challenged to simultaneously explore new capabilities and to exploit existing ones; a capability that has been named “Ambidexterity”. Research distinguishes between structural and contextual ambidexterity. Organizational ambidexterity, however, is always based on individual competencies of organizational members. Yet the link between organizational means aimed at achieving ambidexterity and the individual competencies of the employees have remained imprecise. To tackle this link, we conducted a case study at a German based organization in the automotive industry. In our paper, we demonstrate how the theory of ambidexterity can be combined with issues of Human Resource Management, Competence Management and new theories on work performance. Thereby, we shed light on the link between individual competencies and means aimed at achieving structural and contextual ambidexterity. The case study shows that besides integration by the top management team it is necessary to involve human resource development and foster networks in order to achieve structural ambidexterity. Contextual ambidexterity instead is based on an ambidextrous mindset which can be fostered through organizational culture and leadership. Competence Management and human resource development are necessary in order to cope with the requirements of contextual ambidexterity.

Keywords: Structural and Contextual Ambidexterity, Dynamic Capabilities, Automotive Industry, Competence Management

1. Einleitung

Die Automobilzulieferindustrie ist mit tiefgreifenden Veränderungen konfrontiert. Insbesondere gesteigerte Mobilität und die Entwicklung neuer Antriebstechnologien stellen große Herausforderungen dar. Um diese Herausforderungen zu bewältigen, müssen Automobilzulieferunternehmen ihre Wandlungsfähigkeit unter Beweis stellen, indem sie einerseits durch Ambidextrie (Beidhändigkeit) (Duncan 1976; Tushman/O'Reilly 1996; Gibson/Birkinshaw 2004; O'Reilly/Tushman 2004) ihre bestehenden Kernkompetenzen nutzen und andererseits neue zukunftsfähige Technologien entwickeln (Prahalad/Hamel 1990: 162).

In diesem Beitrag wird untersucht, wie ein Unternehmen aus der Automobilzulieferindustrie den Wandel gestaltet. Das Besondere an diesem Wandel ist, dass sich einerseits die externen Umweltbedingungen der Automobilzulieferbranche verändern und andererseits ein unternehmensinterner Strukturwandel zu bewältigen ist. Die gegenwärtigen Kernkompetenzen des Technologieführers müssen an die zukünftigen Erfordernisse der Branche herangeführt und die internen Strukturen entsprechend modifiziert werden. Ziel dieses Veränderungsprozesses ist eine dynamische Wandlungsfähigkeit im Sinne von Dynamic Capabilities (Teece et al. 1997) im Unternehmen aufzubauen und wettbewerbsfähig zu bleiben. Aus der Perspektive der Dynamic Capabilities sind Unternehmen dann wettbewerbsfähig, wenn sie nicht nur die vorhandenen Ressourcenbestände nutzen, sondern auch so flexibel sind, dass sie auf Veränderungen im Umfeld mit neuen Entwicklungen entsprechend reagieren können und damit langfristig erfolgreich sind.

Das Konzept der Dynamic Capabilities wurde seit der Veröffentlichung der Arbeiten von Teece, Pisano und Shuen im Jahr 1997 viel diskutiert und zieht nach wie vor die Aufmerksamkeit der Managementforschung auf sich (Easterby-Smith et al. 2009). Das Problem dabei ist, dass die Diskussion meist abgehoben auf einer konzeptionellen Ebene und der aggregierten Untersuchungseinheit eines Unternehmens oder einer Organisationseinheit stattfindet. Aber auch organisationale Fähigkeiten sind an Individuen gekoppelt, das heißt Fähigkeiten und Kompetenzen können nicht losgelöst von den einzelnen Individuen betrachtet werden. Diesem Aspekt widmet sich der vorliegende Beitrag und versucht, die aggregierte Ebene einer Organisationseinheit mit der individuellen Ebene der Mitarbeiter und Führungskräfte zu verbinden. Es wird untersucht, wie dynamische Wandlungsfähigkeit mit struktureller und kontextueller Ambidextrie gefördert werden kann. Dazu werden Maßnahmen und Instrumente aus dem Human Resource Management und der Leadership-Forschung herangezogen. Es wird analysiert, wie auf der Grundlage des Konzepts der organisationalen Ambidextrie die bestehenden Kompetenzen genutzt und gleichzeitig neue Kompetenzen entwickelt werden können. Die zentralen Forschungsfragen dabei sind: Wie können Wandelprozesse, die sowohl extern als auch intern angeregt werden, von Organisationen bewältigt werden? Wie können strukturelle und kontextuelle Ambidextrie im Unternehmen gefördert werden?

Im folgenden Abschnitt werden die konzeptionellen Grundlagen der organisationalen Ambidextrie und die beiden Ausprägungen der strukturellen und kontextuellen Ambidextrie dargestellt. Im Anschluss daran wird das untersuchte Unternehmen kurz vorgestellt und die in der Fallstudie verwendete Forschungsmethodik erläutert. Es wird analysiert, welche Maßnahmen und Instrumente verwendet werden, um strukturelle und kontextuelle Ambidextrie zu fördern und welche Anforderungen daraus für Führungskräfte und Mitarbeiter resultieren. Abschließend werden die wichtigsten Punkte nochmals zusammengefasst und die Ergebnisse der Fallstudie diskutiert.

2. Organisationale Ambidextrie

Der Begriff der organisationalen Ambidextrie wurde in der Managementforschung von Duncan (1976) geprägt, der die Notwendigkeit dualer Strukturen im Zuge des Innovationsprozesses sah. Die eigentliche Diskussion wurde von March (1991) bzw. Levinthal/March (1993) in Gang gesetzt, als sie auf die Gefahr einer einseitigen Betonung des explorativen bzw. exploitativen Lernens hinwiesen. Es gilt eine Balance zwischen ausreichend Exploitation und Exploration zu finden. Die langfristige Überlebensfähigkeit eines Unternehmens hängt davon ab, ob sich Unternehmen „engage in enough exploitation to ensure the organization's current viability and [...] engage in enough exploration to ensure future viability" (Levinthal/March 1993: 105). Eine mögliche Ausbalancierung zwischen Exploitation und Exploration wurde aus unterschiedlichen Perspektiven betrachtet, beispielsweise aus Sicht des Organisationalen Lernens, des Innovationsmanagements, des Strategischen Managements und aus Sicht der Organisationsgestaltung (Raisch/Birkinshaw 2008). In der Regel werden diese Prozesse stark mit Blick auf das Top-Management-Team (TMT) untersucht (Lubatkin et al. 2006). Deutlich weniger rückten bisher die konkreten Kompetenz- und Verhaltensanforderungen an Führungskräfte und Mitarbeiter sowie an das Human Ressource Management in den Vordergrund.

Das Konzept der organisationalen Ambidextrie als solches hat sich in der Managementforschung etabliert (vgl. Stephan/Kerber 2010). In der Diskussion steht nach wie vor, wie Exploration und Exploitation zusammenhängen und wie diese beiden Prozesse exakt voneinander unterschieden werden können (Adler et al. 1999; Raisch et al. 2009). Empirische Studien zeigen einerseits, dass Exploitation nach und nach Exploration verdrängt (Abernathy 1978; Levinthal/March 1993; Benner/Tushman 2002). Andererseits liefern Autoren Argumente dafür, dass Exploitation aber auch als Grundlage für Exploration dient bzw. diese sogar fördern kann (z.B.: Nelson/Winter 1982; Adler et al. 1999; Zollo 2002; Feldman 2003). Brunner et al. (2010) bezeichnen diese beiden unterschiedlichen Zugänge als zwei unterschiedliche Denkschulen, die *Conflict School* und die *Complement School*, die das Verhältnis zwischen den beiden Lernmodi bzw. wie Exploitation und Exploration zusammenhängen unterschiedlich verstehen (Brunner et al. 2010; Hobus/Busch 2011). Im Folgenden werden die beiden unterschiedlichen Formen von Ambidextrie, erstens, die strukturelle Ambidextrie aus der *Conflict School* und zweitens, die kontextuelle Ambidextrie aus der *Complement School*, vorgestellt.

2.1 Strukturelle Ambidextrie

Im Rahmen der strukturellen Ambidextrie werden duale Strukturen geschaffen, um dem Konflikt der Aktivitäten der Exploration und Exploitation entgegenzuwirken (Konlechner/Güttel 2009). Strukturelle Ambidextrie wird durch strukturelle Abgrenzung der beiden Lernprozesse erzielt, z.B. im Bereich neuer Technologien werden eigene Subeinheiten in Form von Forschungs- und Entwicklungsabteilungen geschaffen, die im (strukturell) abgegrenzten Rahmen Lernerfahrungen sammeln.

Strukturelle Ambidextrie kommt laut Brunner et al. (2010) aus der Tradition der *Conflict School* (Abernathy 1978; Levinthal/March 1993; Benner/Tushman 2002), die von einem grundsätzlichen Trade-off zwischen Exploitation und Exploration ausgeht (dichotomer Ansatz). Während Exploitation auf berechenbaren Routinen beruht, wird im Rahmen von Exploration-Aktivitäten versucht, eben diese Routinen zu durchbrechen und neue Wege zu finden (Hobus/Busch 2011). Daraus resultiert der prinzipielle Widerspruch, der eine gleichzeitige Verfolgung beider Lernmodi ausschließt. So werden beispielsweise die Aufgaben einer Forschungs- und Entwicklungsabteilung, getrennt von der Produktionsabteilung, in einer abgegrenzten Organisationseinheit durchgeführt. In der Forschungs- und Entwicklungsabteilung wird neues Wissen erforscht und entkoppelt, in der Produktionsabteilung wird vorhandenes Wissen effizient umgesetzt. Die Grundlage dafür liefert die Kontingenztheorie (mechanische versus organische Strukturen) mit der obersten Führungsebene, die eine integrative Vision entwirft, die Ressourcen verteilt und die exploitativen und explorativen Aktivitäten zusammenführt (Hobus/Busch 2011). Dazu bedarf es neben einer klaren Vision vor allem der Fähigkeit zur Kooperation und zum ständigen Informationsaustausch auf der Ebene der Unternehmensführung (siehe dazu auch das Konzept der *behavioral integration* bei Lubatkin et al. 2006).

2.2 Kontextuelle Ambidextrie

Kontextuelle Ambidextrie geht im Unterschied zu struktureller Ambidextrie davon aus, dass die beiden unterschiedlichen Lernmodi innerhalb einer Abteilung oder sogar in einer Person zu vereinen sind, z.B. in einer Produktentwicklung, die eine Moderationsfunktion zwischen Forschung und Entwicklung (F&E), Produktion und technischem Vertrieb übernimmt. Kontextuelle Ambidextrie erfordert ein ähnliches Mindset, gegenseitiges Einfühlungsvermögen und entsteht auf der Basis des *organisationalen Kontexts*, der kulturellen Werte und Normen. Demzufolge müssten *behavioral integration* (Lubatkin et al. 2006) und ein *Ambidextrous Mindset* nicht nur auf der Ebene des TMTs gelebt werden, sie wären vielmehr für einen großem Teil der Führungskräfte und auch einen nicht unerheblichen Teil der Fachkräfte zentrale Anforderungen. Diese Mitarbeitergruppen sollten in der Lage sein, Prozesse der Exploration und Exploitation parallel in ihrem Aufgabenbereich zu bewältigen.

Dem Konzept der kontextuellen Ambidextrie liegt ein dialektischer Ansatz zugrunde, der von einer gegenseitigen Ergänzung (Orthogonalität) von Exploitation und Exploration ausgeht. Brunner et al. (2010) sprechen von der *Complement School*, die diesem Ansatz zugrunde liegt, einem sowohl-als auch-Ansatz, mit Parallelen zu Konzepten wie Intrapreneurship, Empowerment, Mitunternehmertum oder Total Quality Management (Hobus/Busch 2011). Das Top Management greift lediglich steuernd ein, zumeist indirekt über die Unternehmenskultur und die Gestaltung des Kontextes. Das Unternehmen strebt inkrementelles und radikales Lernen an. In einer Organisationseinheit müssen einerseits Kompetenzen aufgebaut und andererseits die Kompetenzen gleichzeitig auch verwertet werden. Wissens- und forschungsintensive Unternehmen dienen als Beispiele für Organisationen mit einem hohen Anteil kontextueller Ambidextrie. Die Mitarbeiter dieser Unternehmen leben gewissermaßen in beiden Welten. Sie müssen regelmäßig beiden Arten von Aufgaben (Innovation versus Replikation) bewältigen (Konlechner/Güttel 2009). Daraus resultieren vielfältige Spannungen und Konflikte, die mit entsprechenden Rahmenbedingungen abgefedert werden müssen, z.B. Arbeit in flexiblen Projektteams, Zielvereinbarungsprozesse, um den nötigen Freiraum zu gewähren etc. Eine besondere Bedeutung kommt dabei einem gemeinsamen Bezugsrahmen zu, der auf einer breit im Unternehmen verankerten Unternehmenskultur basiert.

Auf der Ebene der Führungskräfte und Mitarbeiter führt dies zu erhöhten Anforderungen. Zunächst muss der Führungsstil, der eine solche Flexibilität des Handelns fördern soll, gleichermaßen von Flexibilität geprägt sein. Zieht man moderne Ansätze der Führungsstilforschung heran, so findet Exploration ihre Entsprechung im Stil der transformationalen Führung (Bass/Avolio 1994), die darauf setzt, Mitarbeiter in einem ständigen Lernmodus der Entwicklung eigener Kompetenzen zu halten (vgl. dazu auch Leadership im Wissenszeitalter bei Müller et al. 2007). Führungskräfte müssen in diesem Sinne ihre Mitarbeiter durch ihr eigenes Vorbild zum Mitdenken anregen, sie durch Zuwendung und intellektuelle Stimulierung „transformieren" und im Interesse der Organisation zur persönlichen Entwicklung motivieren (vgl. dazu auch die Leadership Company bei Hinterhuber/Stadler 2006). Mitarbeiter fordern dann Routinen heraus und arbeiten kontinuierlich an Verbesserungsprozessen zum Nutzen der Organisation. Während diese Art des Führungshandelns in den letzten Jahren beinahe zu einem Idealbild moderner Führung stilisiert wurde (Neuberger 2002), erscheint sie weniger geeignet, um Prozesse der Exploitation sicherzustellen. Hierzu scheint es eher förderlich, Mitarbeiter über klare Ziele und Belohnungen zur Erbringung kontinuierlicher Leistungen zu motivieren und eine Fokussierung auf die Alltagserfordernisse der Tätigkeit zu unterstützen. Dieses Führungsverhalten entspricht im Kern austauschtheoretischen Ansätzen wie dem Leader-Member-Exchange (Graen/Uhl-Bien 1995) oder der transaktionalen Führung (Bass/Avolio 1994). Eine Integration dieser beiden Führungsstile stellt sowohl hohe Anforderungen an die Führungskräfte selbst, die in Abhängigkeit von den Anforderungen der Situation ihre

Mitarbeiter zu extrem unterschiedlichen Formen der Aufgabenerfüllung motivieren müssen, als auch an die Mitarbeiter selbst, die ein breites Verhaltensspektrum beherrschen sollen.

Zusätzlich zu hoch entwickelten allgemeinen Kompetenzen (sozialen, personalen, Aktivitäts-, Handlungs-, Fach- und Methodenkompetenzen) müssen sie im Besitz sogenannter Metakompetenzen sein, um in diesem Kontext hohe Leistungsbeiträge zu erbringen. Metakompetenzen (Briscoe/Hall 1999) ermöglichen es Personen, durch Lern- und Anpassungsfähigkeit (adaptability) sowie Selbstreflexionsfähigkeit (self-awareness) ihre eigene Kompetenzbasis selbstständig weiterzuentwickeln (Briscoe/Hall 1999; Dimitrova 2009). Der Besitz von Metakompetenzen ermöglicht es, den Wechsel der Anforderungen sowie die damit verbundene Verantwortung im Rahmen der eigenen Tätigkeit aktiv zu bewältigen, die sonst schnell als Last, Bedrohung oder Überforderung wahrgenommen wird (Preisendörfer 1985).

Sowohl die Aufgabe der Exploration als auch die der Balance zwischen Exploration und Exploitation stellen vielfältige Anforderungen an die Mitarbeiter, da sich die geforderte Leistung deutlich über verantwortungsbewusste Pflichterfüllung hinausbewegt. In der Organisationspsychologie wurde dieser Unschärfe des Leistungsbegriffes zunächst mit einer Differenzierung in *task performance* und *contextual performance* (Motowidlo/Van Scotter 1994) Rechnung getragen. Mit Bezug zu Exploration und Exploitation lässt sich diese Ausweitung der geforderten beruflichen Leistung mit dem Begriff der Eigenverantwortung (Kaschube/Koch 2005; Kaschube 2006) umschreiben. Eigenverantwortung als Leistung besteht aus den Komponenten „allgemeine Verantwortungsübernahme", „Eigeninitiative", „Risikobereitschaft" und „Unkonventionalität" und beschreibt die Aufgabe, mit wechselnden Anforderungen, die – wenn überhaupt – oft erst im Prozess definiert werden, umzugehen. Wo früher Stellenbeschreibungen mit klar formulierten Aufgaben dominierten, ist es heute nicht selten Aufgabe der Mitarbeiter, ihren eigenen Tätigkeitsbereich situativ angemessen im Interesse der Organisation zu definieren, da Organisationen in schnellen Veränderungsprozessen diese Aufgabe nicht mehr erfüllen können. Dies betrifft sowohl die Auswahl der geeigneten Tätigkeiten („Welche Aufgabe ist zu erfüllen? Was hat Priorität?") als auch die Art der Ausführung („Welche Regelungen/Vorgaben sind auf eine Situation anzuwenden?"). In Prozessen der Exploration, die nicht per Definition auf ausgewählte Mitarbeiter der Forschung und Entwicklung (F&E) beschränkt werden, müssen Organisationsmitglieder selbstständig entscheiden, auf welche Aufgabenfelder sie ihre Ressourcen konzentrieren und wie viel Initiative sie zeigen. Da Prozesse der Exploration das gedankliche und manchmal auch reale unkonventionelle Brechen vorgegebener Regeln der Organisation beinhaltet, müssen Mitarbeiter sich dem Risiko der Entscheidung stellen, welche Regeln in Frage gestellt werden dürfen oder müssen und welche zwingend zu beachten sind; gleichzeitig müssen sie eine prinzipielle Bereitschaft mitbringen, notwendige Regeln im Sinne der Organisation anzuerkennen und sich ihnen bei Bedarf verantwortungsbewusst zu fügen, z.B. um routinisierte Prozesse der Exploitation ungehindert laufen zu lassen. Diese Entscheidung stellt selbst Führungskräfte vor deutliche Probleme: in Dilemmasituationen tendieren sie offensichtlich eher dazu, Explorationsprozesse und damit die Chance auf Innovationen zu Gunsten von Exploitation zurückzustellen (Kaschube/Gasteiger 2005).

3. Ambidextriefördernde Maßnahmen bei einem Automobilzulieferunternehmen

Anfangs beschäftigte sich die Literatur hauptsächlich damit, wie die unterschiedlichen Elemente der Ambidextrie zusammenwirken. Erst in den letzten Jahren verlagerte sich das Interesse zunehmend darauf, wie Unternehmen zu organisationaler Ambidextrie gelangen (Adler et al. 1999; Siggelkow/Levinthal 2003; Wollersheim 2011). Die Frage, wie Ambidextrie gefördert werden kann, wird in der nachfolgenden Fallstudie, differenziert nach struktureller und kontextueller Ambidextrie, untersucht. Der erste Abschnitt beschreibt das untersuchte Unternehmen und die methodische Vorgehensweise. Im Anschluss daran werden die in diesem Unternehmen eingesetzten strukturfördernden und kontextfördernden Maßnahmen und Instrumente präsentiert.

3.1 Unternehmensbeschreibung und Methodik

Die folgende Fallstudie untersucht organisationale Ambidextrie in einem Unternehmen der Automobilzulieferbranche mit Stammsitz in Deutschland. Der enorme Preisdruck und die standardisierten Qualitätsanforderungen erfordern effiziente Prozesse. Gleichzeitig unterliegt die Automobilzulieferbranche einem hohen Innovations- und Wandlungsdruck. Um die Umsatzeinbußen aufgrund neuer Antriebstechnologien auszugleichen, sind Neuproduktentwicklungen im untersuchten Unternehmen dringend notwendig. Das untersuchte Unternehmen ist folglich gezwungen, den Konflikt zwischen Exploitation und Exploration zu bewältigen. Dafür werden sowohl strukturfördernde als auch kontextfördernde Maßnahmen zur Entwicklung organisationaler Ambidextrie eingesetzt, die nach einer kurzen Vorstellung des Unternehmens präsentiert werden.

Das Unternehmen beschäftigt weltweit etwa 3000 Mitarbeiter und macht als Weltmarktführer in seinem Bereich einen jährlichen Umsatz von über 500 Millionen Euro. Mehr als die Hälfte der Mitarbeiter und des Umsatzes entfallen auf das Stammwerk. Dieses ist zusammen mit drei Tochterunternehmen in Deutschland, drei in Schwellenländern, einem in Osteuropa und einem in den USA in einer Holding angesiedelt, die zunehmend Zentralfunktionen übernimmt. Die Entwicklung von einem mittelständischen Automobilzulieferunternehmen zu einem weltweit tätigen Unternehmen begann Ende der achtziger Jahre mit der Gründung eines Tochterunternehmens in den USA. In den neunziger Jahren wurden weitere Tochterunternehmen in Deutschland gegründet, die insbesondere der Erweiterung der technologischen Basis und des Produktspektrums dienten. Die Gründungen zusätzlicher Tochterunternehmen außerhalb

Deutschlands erfolgten zwischen 1999 und 2009 und dienten dazu, die Automobilbauer mit Produktionsstätten vor Ort bei ihrer Internationalisierungsstrategie zu begleiten und die bestehenden Technologien des Stammwerkes effizient in großen Stückzahlen nutzen zu können. Im Rahmen des Wachstumsprozesses verteilten sich die Prozesse der Exploitation und der Exploration zunehmend auf verschiedene Standorte und Abteilungen.

Die Strukturen und Prozesse im Unternehmen sind traditionell durch die Produktion geprägt. Um dem enormen Preisdruck in der Automobilzulieferbranche zu entgehen, entwickelte das Unternehmen schon früh neue Produkte und Technologien. In diese Entwicklungen waren nicht nur die F&E und die Produktentwicklung eingebunden, sondern häufig auch Führungs- und Fachkräfte unterschiedlicher Bereiche (insbesondere auch der Produktion), die sich experimentierfreudig zeigten. Diese Innovationskraft des Unternehmens nahm durch den beschriebenen Wachstumsprozess ab. In der gegenwärtigen Situation sucht das Unternehmen nach einer Möglichkeit, die Vorteile einer spezialisierten Produktion und F&E einerseits und andererseits das Explorationspotenzial der Führungskräfte und Mitarbeiter aus allen Bereichen zu nutzen und gleichzeitig die Effizienz der Prozesse nicht außer Acht zu lassen.

Das Unternehmen wurde traditionell von Mitgliedern der Gründerfamilie geführt. Das Ausscheiden des geschäftsführenden Hauptgesellschafters aus der Unternehmensleitung führte zu einem Umbruch im TMT. Gemeinsame Werte, die zwischen Familienmitgliedern und langjährigen Mitarbeitern selbstverständlich geworden waren, mussten nun reflektiert und kodifiziert werden.

Die vorliegende Fallstudie soll die Möglichkeiten der Förderung von struktureller und kontextueller Ambidextrie umfassend analysieren, beschreiben und erklären (Eisenhardt 1989; Bortz/Döring 2002; Heimerl 2007). Im Rahmen dieser Fallstudie wurden unterschiedliche Datenerhebungsmethoden kombiniert (Eisenhardt 1989: 534). Es wurden zunächst in einer Sekundäranalyse interne Dokumente, die Selbstdarstellung des Unternehmens auf der Homepage und Presseberichte untersucht sowie zwei Workshops mit Vertretern der Personalabteilung durchgeführt. Die Workshops dienten dazu, den Ablauf des Forschungsvorhabens abzustimmen, ein umfassenderes Bild vom laufenden Veränderungsprozess zu gewinnen und zusätzliche Informationen, insbesondere über die verschiedenen Mitarbeitergruppen zu generieren. Darauf aufbauend wurden sieben halbstrukturierte Expertengespräche mit dem TMT, d.h. mit der Geschäftsleitung und den Leitern der Produktentwicklung, des technischen Vertriebes, der internen Beratung und der Personalabteilung geführt. Das befragte TMT verfügt über den besten Überblick über interne Entscheidungsprozesse, Märkte, Wettbewerber, Kunden, Technologien oder die verschiedenen Mitarbeitergruppen. Der Inhalt der Expertengespräche bezog sich auf die Historie des Unternehmens, die relative Wettbewerbsstärke und die Entwicklung von Kernkompetenzen sowie konkrete Ansatzpunkte für Veränderungsfähigkeit und für die Förderung von organisationaler Ambidextrie.

Um die Voraussetzungen für Ambidextrie auf Mitarbeiterebene zu analysieren, wurden 35 Führungskräfte in einer Delphi-Studie befragt. Dabei handelt es sich um eine Befragungsform, bei der Experten in der Regel schriftlich befragt werden (Ammon 2009). In der ersten Befragungsrunde erhielten die Befragten einen Fragebogen, die zweite wurde in Form von Expertengesprächen durchgeführt. Die Teilnehmer wählten im Fragebogen aus einem Kompetenzkatalog, der auf der Grundlage des Kompetenzatlasses (Heyse/Erpenbeck 2004; Heyse 2010) zusammengestellt wurde, die für die Arbeit in ihrem Bereich notwendigen Kompetenzen aus und wurden zu ihrem Beziehungsnetzwerk befragt. Nach zwei Monaten wurden den Führungskräften die Ergebnisse aus der ersten Befragung zusammen mit der Untersuchung zu den organisationalen Kompetenzen vorgelegt und sie wurden gebeten, zwischen diesen Verbindungen herzustellen sowie Ansatzpunkte für die Förderung und Entwicklung der einzelnen individuellen Kompetenzen in den Bereichen zu erläutern. Die ausgewählten Führungskräfte wurden dabei als „Experten" angesehen, da sie die tatsächlichen Anforderungen aufgrund ihrer täglichen Arbeit gut beschreiben konnten und zu erwarten war, dass bei ihnen im Rahmen von Mitarbeiterbeurteilungen diesbezüglich schon Reflexionsprozesse stattgefunden hatten. Aus diesen transkribierten Interviews wurden über 400 Situationen zusammengestellt, zusammengefasst und anschließend im Sinne einer strukturierenden Inhaltsanalyse (Mayring) herausgearbeitet, ob die genannten Kompetenzen bei Aufgaben eingesetzt wurden, die den Lernmodi Exploration und Exploitation zuzurechnen waren, oder nur allgemein eine hohe Bedeutung für die Arbeit im Unternehmen hatten. Nachfolgend werden die Ergebnisse, untergliedert in strukturfördernde und kontextfördernde Maßnahmen, zur Entwicklung organisationaler Ambidextrie dargestellt.

3.2 Strukturfördernde Maßnahmen

Organisationsstruktur

Die Gestaltungsmöglichkeiten im Bereich der Organisationsstruktur können auf zwei grundlegende Strukturkonzepte reduziert werden: räumliche Trennung und parallele Strukturen (Raisch/Birkinshaw 2008: 389). Die *räumliche Trennung* erfolgt durch die Schaffung von spezialisierten Einheiten, die entweder in der Exploration (z.B. Forschungs- und Entwicklungsabteilungen) oder in der Exploitation (z.B. Produktionsabteilungen) exzellent sind. Organisationseinheiten mit dem Fokus auf Exploration sind in der Regel kleinere dezentrale Einheiten mit flexibel gestalteten Prozessen, während jene mit Fokus auf Exploitation größer und zentral gesteuert sind, mit relativ stark festgelegten Verfahrensabläufen (Tushman/O'Reilly 1996; Benner/Tushman 2002).

Der Einsatz von *Parallelstrukturen* erlaubt je nach Erfordernissen zwischen verschiedenen Strukturtypen zu wechseln. Die Primärstruktur wird für Routineaufgaben verwendet. Parallel dazu gibt es eine Sekundärstruktur (z.B. Projektteam oder Netzwerke), die die Schwächen der Primärstruktur ausgleicht und für Nicht-Routinearbeiten und innovative Aufgaben verwendet wird. Die Sekundärstruktur ergänzt die Primärstruktur, um Effizienz und Flexibilität zu gewährleisten (Adler et al. 1999).

In der Literatur wird diskutiert, wie stark und auf welche Weise die getrennten Einheiten integriert werden müssen (O'Reilly/Tushman 2004; Hobus/Busch 2011). Im vorliegenden Fall wurde eine relativ starke Integration auf verschiedenen Ebenen verwirklicht. Das untersuchte Unternehmen verfügt über ein breites Spektrum an Technologien zur Bearbeitung von Stahl, die, je nach Kundenanforderung, sehr flexibel kombiniert werden können. Aufgrund der zunehmenden Bedeutung neuer Werkstoffe wurde begonnen, in einem abgetrennten kleinen Tochterunternehmen mit diesen zu arbeiten. Das zweite deutsche Tochterunternehmen wurde gegründet, um die Wertschöpfungskette zu verlängern und eigene Halbfertigprodukte unter Einsatz neuer Technologien weiterverarbeiten zu können. Das Stammwerk blieb bei seinen bisherigen Technologien, entwickelte diese fort und setzte sie in effizienten Prozessen um. Dadurch wurde, ähnlich wie von der Mercedes-Benz AG Ende der 1990er-Jahre bei der Einführung des „Smart", (Konlechner/Güttel 2009) eine Möglichkeit gefunden, dem Konflikt zwischen der effizienten Nutzung vorhandenen Wissens (Exploitation) und dem Aufbau von neuem Wissen in neuen Bereichen (Exploration) auf Ebene des Gesamtunternehmens strukturell zu begegnen. Strukturelle Ambidextrie innerhalb des Stammwerkes wurde im Laufe der Entwicklungsgeschichte verwirklicht, indem zunächst eine Abteilung „Produktentwicklung" von den Produktionsabteilungen getrennt und immer weiter ausgebaut wurde, und anschließend eine Unterabteilung F&E geschaffen wurde, die auch unabhängig von den bestehenden Technologien forschen konnte (siehe dazu Hobus/Busch 2011). In der Literatur wird diskutiert, wie stark die einzelnen Einheiten integriert werden müssen. Eine Extremposition nimmt dabei Christensen (1998) ein, der für eine strikte Trennung plädiert, um bahnbrechende Innovationen zu ermöglichen. Im Gegensatz dazu stehen Strukturen mit vielen straff organisierten Subeinheiten, die wiederum relativ lose miteinander verbunden sind (O'Reilly/Tushman 2004). Die strategische Integration erfolgt über die Koordination des Top Managements, das als „Knowledge Broker" und Übersetzer zwischen den unterschiedlichen Welten fungiert (vgl. auch Hobus/Busch 2011) und über eine von allen geteilte Unternehmensvision.

Verknüpfungen durch das Top-Management-Team

Um die Vorteile der gemeinsamen Nutzung von Ressourcen und Wissen innerhalb eines Unternehmens realisieren zu können, müssen Organisationseinheiten, die Exploration betreiben, mit jenen, die ihren Fokus in der Exploitation haben, verknüpft werden. Diese Funktion wird zumeist dem TMT zugeschrieben (O'Reilly/Tushman 2007; Hobus/Busch 2011). In der vorliegenden Fallstudie kam dem Geschäftsführer des Familienunternehmens innerhalb des TMT eine herausragende Stellung zu, indem die Informationen aus allen Tochterunternehmen bei ihm zusammenflossen. Zudem war er in alle größeren Projekte im Unternehmen direkt oder indirekt eingebunden. Er organisierte nicht nur den Austausch von Wissen im TMT, sondern band auch

Abteilungsleiter, Teamleiter und Meister mit ein und förderte den Wissensaustausch unter diesen.

Durch die starke Präsenz des Geschäftsführers im Unternehmen trug dieser maßgeblich zur Bildung gemeinsamer Visionen, Werte und eines „Wir"-Gefühls bei. Um diese gemeinsamen Werte auch in Phasen starken Wachstums und bei der durch die Internationalisierung bedingten zunehmenden räumlichen Distanz zwischen den Tochterunternehmen zu erhalten, wurde ein Leitbild formuliert, in dessen Zentrum die innovative technologische Orientierung, die Gemeinsamkeiten innerhalb der Unternehmensgruppe und eine menschliche Leistungskultur standen. Durch diese Orientierungsleitlinien sollte nach Aussagen von Mitgliedern des TMT u.a. auch sichergestellt werden, dass in den in Schwellenländern angesiedelten Tochterunternehmen mit Fokus auf Exploitation keine Arbeitsbedingungen Einzug hielten, die mit den Werten des Unternehmens nicht zu vereinbaren waren und dadurch dessen Unternehmenskultur beschädigten. Trotz der starken Gemeinsamkeiten innerhalb der Unternehmensgruppe konnten in der Untersuchung zwischen den Abteilungen und Werken deutliche Unterschiede festgestellt werden. Dadurch blieb Raum für die im Rahmen der strukturellen Ambidextrie notwendigen Subkulturen und deren notwendige Spezialisierung (Gilbert 2006; Konlechner/Güttel 2009). In der folgenden Abbildung 1 werden die Bereiche, die bei der Verknüpfung von Exploitation und Exploration zu struktureller Ambidextrie maßgeblich sind, dargestellt.

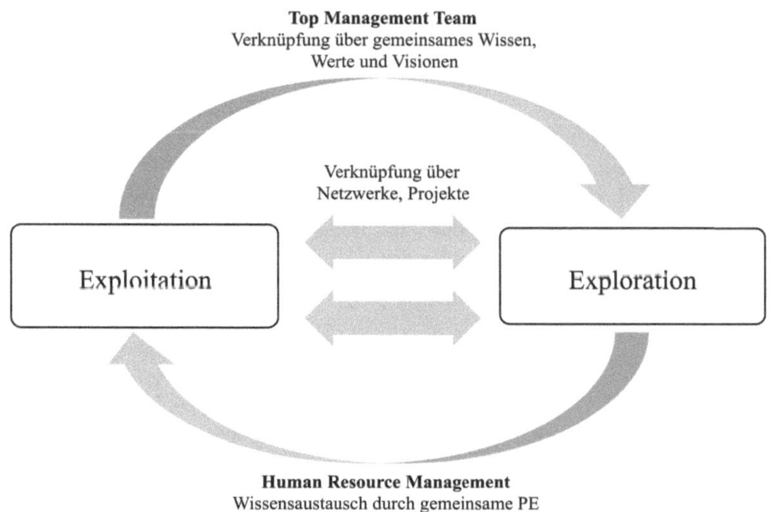

Abbildung 1: Strukturelle Ambidextrie durch Verknüpfung von Exploitation und Exploration

Verknüpfungen durch Human Resource Management

Während der starken Wachstumsphase ab 1990 wurde der administrative Bereich ausdifferenziert und professionelle Serviceeinheiten wie ein gemeinsames Rechnungswesen, Informationstechnologie (IT) und Human Resources (HR) unter einer Holding angesiedelt, um den einzelnen Tochterunternehmen Dienstleistungen anbieten zu können und so die Verknüpfung sowohl auf Ebene der Tochterunternehmen, als auch der Abteilungen zu fördern. HR kann zu diesem Empfinden von Gemeinsamkeiten im Unternehmen beispielsweise durch eine weltweite Personalentwicklung beitragen. Führungskräfte aus Tochterunternehmen oder Abteilungen mit Fokus auf Exploitation (z.B. die Produktion) lernen so gemeinsam mit Einheiten mit Fokus auf Exploration und entwickeln ihr Führungsverhalten und ihre Persönlichkeit fort. Eine weitere identifizierte Möglichkeit ist eine auf Ambidextrie ausgerichtete Laufbahnentwicklung. So begannen einige Ingenieure teilweise nach der Promotion ihre Laufbahn in der Abteilung F&E, wechselten anschließend im Sinne einer funktionalen Laufbahnbewegung (Schein, 1995) in die kundenorientierte Produktentwicklung, um in den weiteren Karriereschritten größere Einheiten in der Produktion, im Qualitätsmanagement oder ausländische Tochterunternehmen zu übernehmen. Dadurch entstanden intensive Netzwerke zwischen den unterschiedlichen Organisationseinheiten.

Verknüpfungen durch Netzwerke und Projekte

Im Rahmen einer Netzwerkanalyse konnte die Abteilung Produktentwicklung als ein zentraler Knotenpunkt mit Verbindungen im gesamten Unternehmen identifiziert werden. Sie bildete folglich zusätzlich zum in der Literatur diskutierten TMT (Konlechner/Güttel 2009) einen weiteren Bereich der Verknüpfung und Wissensverteilung. Einerseits entwickelten die Mitarbeiter dieser Abteilung selbst neue Produkte und Technologien und arbeiteten eng mit der Abteilung F&E zusammen, andererseits waren deren Mitarbeiter aber auch zentrale Ansprechpartner für Abteilungen wie Produktion, Konstruktion, technischer Vertrieb und externe Kunden. Außerdem fand ein intensiver Austausch zwischen den Abteilungen der Produktentwicklung in den einzelnen Tochterunternehmen statt, der die Verbindung des Einsatzes alter und neuer Technologien zu neuen Produkten förderte.

3.2 *Kontextfördernde Maßnahmen*

Mit zunehmender Komplexität stößt die Integration der unterschiedlichen Strukturkonzepte an ihre Grenzen. So zeigt sich auch beim untersuchten Unternehmen, dass sich in der Phase des Unternehmenswachstums bei gleichzeitig steigendem Veränderungsdruck durch die Marktbedingungen die Anzeichen mehrten, dass einige der strukturellen Maßnahmen nicht ausreichten, um Ambidextrie im gewünschten Maße zu fördern. Insbesondere war zu beobachten:

- mangelnder Austausch zwischen Abteilungen mit Exploration und Exploitation;
- ein gefühlter Mangel an Wertschätzung in den Bereichen der Exploitation;
- fehlende Informationen über strategisch wichtige Prozesse außerhalb des Stammwerkes;
- eine Führungskultur, die die Entwicklung von Mitarbeitern nicht förderte;
- ein Mangel an „gelebten" Werten des Unternehmens im mittleren Management;
- Informationen nicht schnell genug das TMT erreichten;
- Mangel an qualifizierten Mitarbeitern, die einen Wechsel von Abteilungen mit Schwerpunkt auf Exploitation hin zu Abteilungen mit Exploration und umgekehrt vollziehen wollten.

In Summe wurde von der Unternehmensspitze erkannt, dass die bisherigen strukturellen Maßnahmen nicht ausreichten und dass langfristig die Wettbewerbs- und Entwicklungsfähigkeit des Unternehmens gefährdet erschien. Kontextuelle Ambidextrie entsteht auf der Grundlage einer gemeinsamen Wertebasis und einer Unternehmenskultur, die als integrativer Bezugsrahmen dient (Raisch/Birkinshaw 2008; Güttel/Konlechner 2009: 168). Mit Kontext sind die Systeme, Prozesse und Einstellungen gemeint, die das Verhalten der Individuen in Organisationen beeinflussen (Burgelman 1983b; Burgelman 1983a; Denison 1990; Goshal/Bartlett 1994). Die Herausforderung besteht nun darin, die internen Rahmenbedingungen so zu gestalten, dass die Balance zwischen explorativen und exploitativen Aktivitäten kontinuierlich gewährleistet ist. Im untersuchten Unternehmen wurden Maßnahmen im Bereich Unternehmenskultur und Führung und im Bereich Personal- und Kompetenzmanagement ergriffen, die den geschilderten Problemen entgegenwirken sollen. Diese Maßnahmen, die auf eine Förderung kontextueller Ambidextrie abzielen, werden im Folgenden geschildert.

Unternehmenskultur und Führung

Kontextuelle Ambidextrie bedarf einer Unternehmenskultur, die Lernen fördert und sowohl durch hohe Leistungsanreize und Disziplin, als auch durch gegenseitige Unterstützung, Vertrauen und eine ausgeprägte Lern- und Fehlerkultur geprägt ist, in der sich Mitarbeiter weiterentwickeln können. Das Fehlen der sozialen Komponenten führt zu hoher Fluktuation und erschwert damit die Bildung von kontextueller Ambidextrie (Birkinshaw/Gibson 2004: 51). Dies findet sich auch in den Ergebnissen der Fallstudie wieder. Die gemeinsam gelebten Werte und das Leitbild beinhalteten in besonderer Weise die Themen menschliche Leistungskultur, Kooperation und Loyalität. Das untersuchte Unternehmen zeichnete sich durch eine lange durchschnittliche Unternehmenszugehörigkeit aus. Dies begünstigte auch die angesprochene Vernetzung, die Laufbahnentwicklung und die Entstehung gemeinsamer Werte. Um diese Elemente der Kultur lebendig zu halten, wurde zunächst eine Initiative gestartet, in der die bisherigen Werte noch einmal explizit kommuniziert wurden und zusätzlich auf übergreifende Prozesse, in denen Exploration und Exploitation gemeinsam von hoher Bedeutung sind, verwiesen wurde. Diese Prozesse werden in ihrer strategischen Bedeutung schrittweise an alle Mitarbeiter kommuniziert.

Zusätzlich wird auf der Ebene des Führungsstils explizit auf eine Verknüpfung von Elementen transformationaler und transaktionaler Führung hingearbeitet, um sowohl Prozesse der Exploration als auch der Exploitation fördern zu können. Dafür werden Verhaltensrichtlinien für Führungskräfte entwickelt, die zukünftig bei Auswahlverfahren, in Trainings und in Führungsfeedbacks vermittelt und überprüft werden sollen. Aus Ergebnissen der Mitarbeiterbefragung wurde abgeleitet, in welchen Abteilungen bisher besonders große Defizite erkennbar waren, um mittelfristig Ansatzpunkte für Schulungsmaßnahmen zu finden. Zusätzlich sollen Entwicklungsprogramme für junge Führungskräfte und Mentoren Systeme initiiert werden.

Personal- und Kompetenzmanagement

Die Abteilung Human Resources (HR) übernimmt zusätzlich zu den Führungskräften eine zentrale Funktion bei der Gestaltung einer lernförderlichen Unternehmenskultur und der Entwicklung von Mitarbeitern. Daher wurde zur Unterstützung kontextueller Ambidextrie ein Kompetenzmodell erarbeitet, in dem neben allgemeinen Kompetenzen speziell Wert auf solche Kompetenzen wie z.B. Meta-Kompetenzen und die Fähigkeit zur Eigenverantwortung gelegt wird, die beide Lernmodi sowie ein *Ambidextrous Mindset* fördern und in Arbeitsbereichen, in denen sowohl Exploration als auch Exploitation betrieben werden soll, von hoher Bedeutung für die berufliche Leistung sind.

Die Personalabteilung sollte die für Exploitation und Exploration notwendigen individuellen Kompetenzen in einem sogenannten *Multiple-Job Kompetenzmodell* (Mansfield 1996) abbilden, das für alle Unternehmensbereiche und Stellen gilt. Je nach dem, ob eine Stelle in einem Bereich angeordnet ist, in dem der Fokus auf Exploitation, Exploration oder auf beidem liegt, werden im Kompetenz-Soll-Profil die entsprechenden Kompetenzen mit unterschiedlich hoher Ausprägung gefordert. Führungskräfte sollten generell ein *Ambidextrous Mindset* haben und trotz einer möglichen Spezialisierung auf Exploitation oder Exploitation und den damit verbundenen förderlichen Führungsstilen ausreichend hohe Kompetenzausprägungen für Exploitation und Exploration haben, um kontextuelle Ambidextrie fördern zu können. Durch die zunehmende Überlagerung der Organisationsstrukturen durch Projektstrukturen sind zunehmend auch Mitarbeiter aus Bereichen mit Fokus auf Exploitation in kontextuelle Ambidextrie eingebunden und müssen entsprechend geführt werden.

Die aktuelle Wahrnehmung der notwendigen Kompetenzen wurde mittels Experteninterviews in Bereichen mit kontextueller Ambidextrie (insbesondere der Produktentwicklung) sowie in Abteilungen mit entweder hoher Explorations- oder Exploitationsfunktion durchgeführt. Die Kompetenzbeschreibungen besitzen einen gemeinsamen Kern, weisen aber auch deutliche Unterschiede auf. In der folgenden Abbildung 2 wird die Bedeutung, die die einzelnen individuellen Kompetenzen für die Bereiche der Exploitation und Exploration haben, dargestellt.

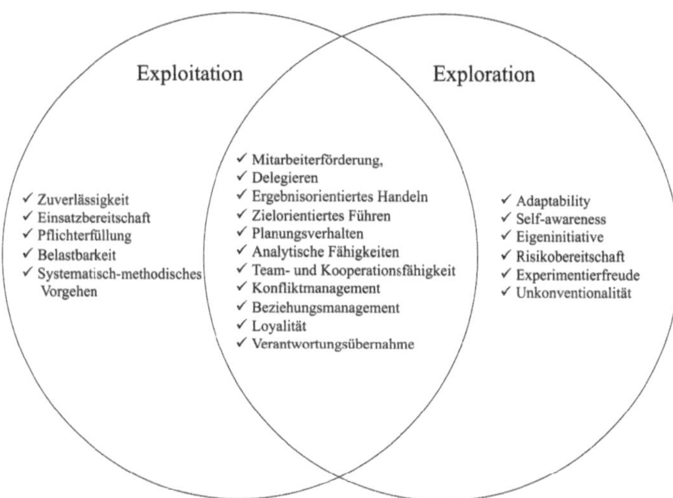

Abbildung 2: Individuelle Kompetenzanforderungen für Exploitation und Exploration

Um an den relativ hoch standardisierten Prozessen in Abteilungen mit Fokus auf Exploitation (Tushman/O'Reilly 1996; Benner/Tushman 2002) teilzunehmen, erscheinen Zuverlässigkeit, Pflichterfüllung, Belastbarkeit, Einsatzbereitschaft und systematisch-methodisches Vorgehen von hoher Bedeutung zu sein. Kompetenzen wie Mitarbeiterförderung, Delegation, ergebnisorientiertes Handeln, zielorientiertes Führen, Planungsverhalten, analytische Fähigkeiten und Team- und Kooperationsfähigkeit scheinen Exploitations- wie auch Explorationsprozesse zu unterstützen, aber auf unterschiedliche Weise. Analytische Fähigkeiten dienen in Exploitationsprozessen dazu, Fehler zu finden und Prozesse effizienter zu machen. Im Kontext von Exploration und kontextueller Ambidextrie sind sie hilfreich, um sich über die eigene Position klar zu werden, zu wissen, ob es notwendig ist, in eine neue Richtung zu gehen und Möglichkeiten oder Gelegenheiten in der Ressourcenbasis des Unternehmens oder im Markt aufzuspüren. Teamfähigkeit und Kooperationsbereitschaft sind wichtige Bedingungen für die Verknüpfung von Abteilungen mit Fokus auf Exploitation und solchen mit Fokus auf Exploration. Mitarbeiter benötigen Sensibilität und sollten in der Lage sein zu verstehen, was in anderen Abteilungen mit unterschiedlicher Kultur und anderem Aufgabenhintergrund wichtig ist. Dafür sind auch Konfliktfähigkeit und Beziehungsmanagement von besonderer Bedeutung. Diese Kompetenzen können auch helfen, wenn Mitarbeiter zwischen Abteilungen mit Fokus auf Exploitation und Exploration im Laufe ihrer Karriere wechseln. Ein System aus Delegation, zielorientierter Führung und vorausschauender Planung hilft Führungskräften und Mitarbeitern an strukturierten Prozessen und Routinen teilzunehmen, Ziele aus Abteilungen mit unterschiedlichen Lernmodi zu integrieren und zusammen zu arbeiten. Außerdem sind diese Kompetenzen notwendig, um Projekte für beide Lernmodi zu realisieren.

Die zwei Metakompetenzen *Adaptability* und *Self-awareness* (Briscoe/Hall 1999; Dimitrova 2009) sind wichtig für beide Lernmodi, wenn auch unverzichtbar für Prozesse der Exploration. *Self-awareness* wurde als eine zentrale Kompetenz angesehen, um zukünftigen Herausforderungen auf der individuellen und der organisationalen Ebene zu begegnen, wie beispielsweise neue Technologien und Wissen in der Umwelt wahrzunehmen. Damit ist sie auch sehr wichtig, um die Dynamic Capability *Absorptive Capacity* (Zahra/George 2002) zu unterstützen. Durch diese Reflexion in Bezug auf die Person selbst und ihr Arbeitsumfeld können Routinen aufgebrochen werden. „Adaptability“ dient dazu, die für die neuen Bereiche notwendigen individuellen Kompetenzen zu erwerben. Diese Metakompetenzen können insbesondere durch die Übertragung anspruchsvoller Aufgaben entwickelt werden, bei denen Mitarbeiter die Grenzen ihres bisherigen Aufgabenfeldes überschreiten und dabei durch intensive Feedbackprozesse (z.B. in Form von Mitarbeitergesprächen, Mentoring und Coaching) begleitet werden.

Eigenverantwortliches Handeln (EVH vgl. Kaschube 2006) wird als generelle Bereitschaft zur Verantwortungsübernahme ebenfalls für beide Bereiche mit hoher Ausprägung benötigt, während die weiteren Dimensionen der Eigenverantwortung (Risikobereitschaft, Unkonventionalität und Eigeninitiative) stärker auf Exploration bezogen werden. Risikobereitschaft und Unkonventionalität benötigen Personen, um Routinen aufzubrechen, neue Wege zu beschreiten, etwas auszuprobieren und mit Konflikten umzugehen. Eigeninitiative richtet sich hingegen hauptsächlich auf die eigenständige Aufnahme von Wissen und Zielbestimmung auch in unklaren Situationen. Generell wird die Übernahme von Eigenverantwortung in allen Bereichen als grundlegende Kompetenz mit unterschiedlich starker Ausprägung wahrgenommen. In der Produktentwicklung wird EVH als selbstverständliche Anforderung an Mitarbeiter angesehen, da nur so Neues entstehen könne. Die starke Einbindung in Prozesse wie den technischen Vertrieb oder den Kontakt zu Konstruktion und Produktion stellt jedoch auch bei deren Mitarbeitern sicher, dass Exploitation nicht aus dem Blickfeld gerät. Exploitationsprozesse sind im untersuchten Unternehmen so stark von Standards und Routinen, wie regelmäßigen Abstimmungsprozessen und einem primär an Exploitationszielen orientierten Vergütungssystem bestimmt, dass das unkontrollierte Eingehen von Risiken von einzelnen Mitarbeitern unwahrscheinlich erscheint. Unterstützt werden kann diese Balance zudem durch eine Teamzusammensetzung, die eine Zusammenarbeit von Mitarbeitern mit einer eher vorsichtigen Herangehensweise und Mitarbeitern mit hoher Risikobereitschaft fördert. Eigenverantwortliches Handeln scheint folglich ein Verhalten zu sein, dass in produktionsorientierten Unternehmen gefördert werden kann, um die Lernraten im Bereich der Exploration zu erhöhen und die Unsicherheit, die Explorationsprozesse mit sich bringen, zu reduzieren, ohne die Effizienz der Prozesse zur Nutzung der bestehenden Kernkompetenzen zu gefährden. Die Förderung von Eigenverantwortung der Mitarbeiter wurde von den Befragten als zentrale Führungsaufgabe gesehen: Führungskräfte sollten einerseits eine Vertrauenskultur schaffen und Eigenverantwortung fördern und gleichzeitig mit den Mitarbeitern ein gemeinsames Verständnis darüber entwickeln, in welchen Situationen Absprachen aufgrund des hohen Risikos für den Bereich oder das Unternehmen unerlässlich sind. Zusammen mit dem Beurteilungs- und Vergütungssystemen zeigte sich damit auch in der Fallstudie, dass für die Entwicklung von EVH eine Kombination von transaktionalem und transformationalem Führungsstil förderlich ist (Kaschube 2006).

Mitarbeiter von Bereichen, in denen kontextuelle Ambidextrie vorliegt, müssen alle diese genannten Anforderungen erfüllen und benötigen folglich ein sehr breites Kompetenzprofil (Birkinshaw/Gibson 2004), um in den beiden „Welten" (Konlechner/Güttel 2009: 48) Exploration und Exploitation hohe Leistungsbeiträge erbringen zu können.

Im Bereich der Personalentwicklung soll dies durch Potenzialanalysen und Laufbahnplanungen unterstützt werden. Nach dem Laufbahnmodell von Schein (1995) verlaufen laufbahnbezogene Bewegungen neben Wechseln in der Hierarchie entweder funktional oder von der Peripherie hin zu Bereichen mit einer intensiveren Zusammenarbeit mit den Entscheidungsgremien der Organisation. Zur Verbesserungen der Voraussetzungen für kontextuelle Ambidextrie sollten vor allem funktionale Wechsel zwischen Bereichen mit Fokus auf Exploration und solchen auf Exploitation angeregt werden, um somit eine breite Kompetenzentwicklung im Prozess der Arbeit und das Entstehen eines *Ambidextrous Mindset* bei vielen Führungskräften und Mitarbeitern zu fördern. Dabei kommen der Entwicklung von Fachkarrieren mit hochwertigen Expertenpositionen und einem neuen Laufbahnverständnis, das Karriere nicht mehr zwangsläufig mit hierarchischem Aufstieg in Verbindung bringt (Gasteiger), wesentliche Bedeutung zu. Nur so kann es gelingen, dass beispielsweise Mitarbeiter in der F&E ihre Karriere beginnen, über mehrere Stationen bis zum Leiter einer ausländischen Produktionsstätte aufsteigen und anschließend eine Aufgabe in einem der Produktentwicklungsbereiche übernehmen, in denen aber in der Regel deutlich weniger hochrangige Führungspositionen zu Verfügung stehen, als in Exploitation Bereichen wie der Produktion.

In Potenzialanalysen kann auf der Grundlage des entwickelten Kompetenzmodells gezielt überprüft werden, welche Mitarbeiter die für kontextuelle Ambidextrie notwendige Vielseitigkeit langfristig entwickeln können. Aufgrund der Konstitution des Konstruktes Ambidextrie durch die Verknüpfung der Lernmodi Exploitation und Exploration und der Bedeutung der lernbezogenen Metakompetenzen auf individueller Ebene dürfte das Instrument des Lernpotenzial Assessment Centers (AC) dafür geeignet sein. Bei diesem eignungsdiagnostischen Instrument ist eine Lernphase eingebettet in eine Vorher-Nachher-Messung, aus deren Unterschied sich die Lernfähigkeit eines Mitarbeiters ergibt (Sarges/Stracke 2005). Mitarbeiter sollten dahingehend überprüft werden, ob sie die für Exploitation und Exploration notwendigen Kompetenzausprägungen jeweils schnell erwerben können. Mit Bezugnahme auf die Übungen, die Sarges und Stracke (2005) für ein Lernpotenzial AC vorschlagen, könnten beispielsweise Schnittstellenbereiche zwischen Explorations- und Exploitationsbereichen im Rahmen von Fallstudien bearbeitet oder innovative Ideen für beide Bereich entwickelt und Probleme diskutiert werden. Zur Kompetenzentwicklung bei den Potenzialkandidaten, die den Anforderungen kontextueller Ambidextrie gerecht werden, tragen auch die angesprochenen Laufbahnmodelle (siehe dazu die „Verknüpfungen durch Human Resource Management" unter 3.2 Strukturfördernde Maßnahmen) mit funktionalen Bewegungen zwischen den Bereichen Exploitation und Exploration bei.

4. Resümee und Diskussion

Dieser Beitrag beschäftigte sich mit der Förderung von struktureller und kontextueller Ambidextrie im Zuge der Gestaltung der Wandlungsfähigkeit eines Automobilzulieferunternehmens. Dazu wurden Instrumente und Maßnahmen aus dem Bereich des Human Resource Managements und der Leadership-Forschung vorgestellt. Es wurde gezeigt, dass es im untersuchten Unternehmen notwendig war, neben der strukturellen auch die kontextuelle Ambidextrie zu fördern, um die hohe Komplexität zu bewältigen. Das Nebeneinander von struktureller und kontextueller Ambidextrie stellt jedoch hohe Anforderungen an die beteiligten Mitarbeiter und Führungskräfte. Die folgenden drei Aspekte wurden im Rahmen der Fallstudie erarbeitet:

Erstens wird in der Literatur für die Entwicklung organisationaler Ambidextrie sowohl unter der Perspektive der strukturellen als auch der kontextuellen Ambidextrie der Blick stark auf die Bedeutung des TMTs (O'Reilly/Tushman 2007; Raisch/Birkinshaw 2008; Hobus/Busch 2011) gerichtet. Deren hohe Bedeutung für die Generierung und Aktivierung von Werten und Leitbildern sowie für eine generelle Steuerung des Prozesses lässt sich auch im Rahmen unserer Fallstudie wiederfinden. Allerdings scheint strukturelle Ambidextrie mit Fokus auf das TMT in Organisationen, die mehreren Wandlungsprozessen (hoher externer Wandlungsdruck auf Exploration und Exploitation, Unternehmenswachstum etc.) unterworfen sind, nicht zur Aufrechterhaltung einer Balance von Exploitation und Exploration auszureichen. Vielmehr bedarf es hier einer größeren Anzahl von dezentralen Organisationseinheiten, in denen – im Sinne der kontextuellen Ambidextrie – Exploration und Exploitation direkt nebeneinander gelebt werden. Die verschiedenen Mitarbeitergruppen müssen insbesondere unter der Perspektive der kontextuellen Ambidextrie mit häufig wechselnden Anforderungen zurechtkommen und eigenverantwortlich Entscheidungen treffen, d.h. verantwortungsbewusst im Sinne der Organisation Risiken eingehen, Regeln brechen und neu schreiben.

Zweitens kann den hohen Anforderungen an die Leistungen der Mitarbeiter und Führungskräfte zunächst durch die Gestaltung der Organisationsstruktur und eine gute Zusammenarbeit im Top Management begegnet werden (O'Reilly/Tushman 2007; Hobus/Busch 2011). Zusätzlich bedarf es weiterer unterstützender Maßnahmen im kontextuellen Bereich: die Weiterentwicklung der Organisationskultur (Entwicklung und Kommunikation von Visionen und gemeinsamen Werten, die Leistungsorientierung, Vertrauen und Lernfreude vermitteln) und die Fokussierung der Führungskräfte auf einen flexiblen Führungsstil, der sowohl Exploration (transformationale Führung) als auch Exploitation (Zielsetzung und transaktionale Führung) fördert. Im Bereich der Führungsforschung konnte theoriekonform beobachtet werden, dass transaktionale Führung der angemessene Führungsstil in Bereichen mit Fokus auf Exploitation und transformationale Führung in solchen mit Fokus auf Exploration ist (Vera/Crossan 2004).

Drittens, selbst wenn Ambidextrie in Organisationen im Zusammenspiel vielfältiger Schnittstellen und Abteilungen in einer gesamten Organisation entsteht, wollen wir auf die hohen Kompetenzanforderungen an Individuen, Führungskräfte und Mitarbeiter, verweisen. Birkinshaw und Gibson (2004) führen an, dass Mitarbeiter, die unter den Bedingungen von struktureller Ambidextrie arbeiten, tendenziell eher Spezialisten sind, während solche unter kontextueller Ambidextrie eher Generalistenprofile haben sollten. In dieser Fallstudie werden derartige Überlegungen mit Kompetenzlisten (siehe dazu Heyse/Erpenbeck 2004; Heyse 2010) verbunden und es wird erläutert, welche Bedeutung einzelne individuelle Kompetenzen für die Unterstützung von Exploitations- und Explorationsprozessen haben. Dabei werden nicht nur die Kompetenzanforderungen des höheren Managements berücksichtigt, sondern die aller Mitarbeiter beziehungsweise des gesamten HR-Portfolios betrachtet. Für diese Analyse zeigt die Fallstudie auch die Verbindungslinien zwischen der Entwicklung der beiden psychologischen Konstrukte Metakompetenz (Briscoe/Hall 1999) und Eigenverantwortliches Handeln (Kaschube 2006) und der Ambidextrie auf. Darauf aufbauend wird der Bezug zwischen HR-Systemen und Ambidextrie dargestellt. Sie sollen in Anlehnung an Teece (2007) einen Beitrag zur Mikrofundierung einer speziellen Dynamic Capability, Ambidextrie, leisten. Zwar wird der Bezug von Kompetenzmodellen zur Unternehmensstrategie in der Literatur herausgestellt (Briscoe/Hall 1999; Green 1999), die Anbindung an Dynamic Capabilities und Ambidextrie ist aber bisher ungeklärt. Um die notwendigen Kompetenzen entwickeln zu können, muss das Human Resource Management allerdings nicht nur entsprechende Kompetenzen diagnostizieren, sondern beispielsweise Potenzialanalyseverfahren an die Anforderungen kontextueller Ambidextrie anpassen. Eine Möglichkeit dafür scheint ein entsprechendes Lernpotenzial Assessment Center (Sarges/Stracke 2005) zu sein. Zudem muss sich ein Human Resource Management, das Ambidextrie unterstützen will, mit neueren Laufbahnmodellen beschäftigen. Die vorliegende Fallstudie kann die genannten Aspekte sicherlich nicht abschließend erklären, sondern vielmehr den Weg für eine vertiefte Betrachtung der einzelnen Elemente aufzeigen.

Zusammenfassend sollte nochmals erwähnt werden, dass im vorliegenden Fall strukturelle Ambidextrie nicht ausreichte, um den Wandel zu gestalten und zusätzlich kontextuelle Ambidextrie nötig ist, um die Wettbewerbsfähigkeit aufrecht zu erhalten. Es sind einzelne Abteilungen notwendig, die sich fast ausschließlich der Exploration oder der Exploitation widmen, und zusätzlich eine Vielzahl von Einheiten in allen

Unternehmensbereichen, die beide Prozesse bedienen und zusammenführen. Zu ähnlichen Ergebnisse kommen auch Güttel et al. (2011), die eine Kombination von struktureller und kontextueller Ambidextrie in einer „hybriden" Prozessphase vorschlagen: Nach der Gründung eines Unternehmens arbeiten Unternehmen zunächst in kontextueller Ambidextrie. Mit zunehmender Größe ergeben sich ausdifferenzierte Strukturen und es kommt zu struktureller Ambidextrie. Um die Innovationsfähigkeit zu erhalten, werden schließlich beide Formen kombiniert (Güttel et al. 2011).

Weiterer Forschungsbedarf besteht auch darin, wie diese Einheiten optimalerweise miteinander interagieren, um die Wettbewerbsfähigkeit der Organisation zu fördern. Zusätzlich ist zu untersuchen, wie viele Mitarbeiter mit ausgeprägten Meta-Kompetenzen und hoher Eigenverantwortung eine Organisation für die Balance von Exploration und Exploitation benötigt und ob nicht eine zu große Anzahl mitdenkender Mitarbeiter eine Gefahr für relativ stabile Prozesse der Exploitation bedeutet.

Literatur

Abernathy, W.J. (1978): The Productivity Dilemma: Roadblock to Innovation in the Automobile Industry, Johns Hopkins University Press: Baltimore.

Adler, P.S./Goldoftas, B./Levine, D.I. (1999): Flexibility versus Efficiency? A Case Study of Model Changeovers in the Toyota Production System. In: Organization Science, 10, 1: 43-68.

Ammon, U. (2009): Delphi-Befragung. In: Kühl, S. (Hrsg.), Handbuch Methoden der Organisationsforschung, VS, Verl. für Sozialwiss.: Wiesbaden: 458–476.

Bass, B.M./Avolio, B.J. (1994): Improving Organizational Effectiveness through Transformational Leadership, Sage: Thousand Oaks, CA.

Benner, M.J./Tushman, M.L. (2002): Process Management and Technological Innovation: A Longitudinal Study of the Photography and Paint Industry. In: Administrative Science Quarterly, 47: 676-706.

Birkinshaw, J./Gibson, C. (2004): Building Ambidexterity into an Organization. In: MIT Sloan Management Review, 45, 4: 47-55.

Bortz, J./Döring, N. (2002): Forschungsmethoden und Evaluation: Für Human- und Sozialwissenschaftler, Springer: Berlin u.a.

Briscoe, J.P./Hall, D.T. (1999): Grooming and Picking Leaders Using Competency Frameworks: Do They Work? - An Alternative Approach and New Guidelines for Practice. In: Organizational Dynamics, 28, 2: 37-51.

Brunner, D.J./Staats, B.R./Tushman, M.L./Upton, D.M. (2010): Wellsprings of Creation: How Perturbation Sustains Exploration in Mature Organizations. Harvard Business School, Working Paper No. 11-022.

Burgelman, R.A. (1983a): A Model of the Interaction of Strategic Behavior, Corporate Context and the Concept of Strategy. In: Academy of Management Review, 8, 1: 61-70.

Burgelman, R.A. (1983b): A Process Model of Internal Corporate Venturling in the Diversified Major Firm. In: Administrative Science Quarterly, 28, 2: 223-244.

Christensen, C.M. (1998): The Innovator's Dilemma, Harvard Business School Press: Cambridge, MA.

Denison, R.D. (1990): Corporate Culture and Organizational Effectiveness, Wiley: New York.

Dimitrova, D. (2009): Das Konzept der Metakompetenz - Theoretische und empirische Untersuchung am Beispiel der Automobilindustrie, Gabler: Wiesbaden.

Duncan, R.B. (1976): The Ambidextrous Organization: Designing Dual Structures for Innovation. iI: Kilmann, R.H./Pondy, L.R./Slevin, D. (Hrsg.), The Management of Organization Design: Strategies and Implementation, Elsevier: New York: 167-188.

Easterby-Smith, M./Lyles, M.A./Peteraf, M.A. (2009): Dynamic Capabilities: Current Debates and Future Directions. In: British Journal Of Management, 20: 1-8.

Eisenhardt, K.M. (1989): Building Theories from Case Study Research. In: Academy of Management Review, 14, 4: 532-550.

Feldman, M.S.P., B. T. (2003): Reconceptualizing Organizational Routines as a Source of Flexibility and Change. In: Administrative Science Quarterly, 48, 1: 94-118.

Gasteiger, R.M. (2007): Selbstverantwortliches Laufbahnmanagement: Das proteische Erfolgskonzept, Hogrefe: Göttingen u.a.

Gibson, C./Birkinshaw, J. (2004): The Antecedents, Consequences, and Mediating Role of Organizational Ambidexterity. In: Academy of Management Journal, 47, 2: 209-226.

Gilbert, C.G. (2006): Change in the Presence of Residual Fit: Can Competing Frames Coexist? In: Organization Science, 17, 1: 150-167.

Goshal, S./Bartlett, C. (1994): Linking Organizational Context and Managerial Action: The Dimensions of Quality of Management. In: Strategic Management Journal, 15, S2: 91-112.

Graen, G.B./Uhl-Bien, M. (1995): Relationship-based approach to leadership: Developments of leader-member exchange (LMX) theory of leadership over 25 years: Applying a multi-level multi-domain perspective. In: Leadership Quarterly, 6, 2: 219-247.

Green, P.C. (1999): Building Robust Competencies. Linking Human Resource Systems to Organizational Strategies, Jossey-Bass: San Francisco.

Güttel, W.H./Garaus, C./Konlechner, S./Lackner, H./Müller, B. (2011): Head in the Clouds... Feet on the Ground: A Process Perspective on Organizational Ambidexterity. Institut of Human Ressource und Change Management, Johannes Kepler University Linz, Working Paper 2011.1.

Güttel, W.H./Konlechner, S.W. (2009): Continuously Hanging by a Thread: Managing Contextually Ambidextrous Organizations. In: Schmalenbach Business Review, 61, 2: 150-172.

Heimerl, P. (2007): Fallstudien als forschungsstrategische Entscheidung. In: Buber, R./Holzmüller, H.H. (Hrsg.), Qualitative Marktforschung: Konzepte - Methoden - Analysen, Gabler: Wiesbaden: 381-400.

Heyse, V. (2010): Verfahren zur Kompetenzermittlung und Kompetenzentwicklung: KODE® im Praxistest. In: Heyse, V./ Erpenbeck, J./Orthmann, S. (Hrsg.), Grundstrukturen menschlicher Kompetenz, Praxiserprobte Konzepte und Instrumente (Kompetenzmanagement in der Praxis, Bd. 5), Waxmann: Münster, 55–174.

Heyse, V./Erpenbeck, J. (2004): Kompetenztraining. 64 Informations- und Trainingsprogramme, Schäffer-Poeschel: Stuttgart.

Hinterhuber, H.H./Stadler, C. (2006): Leadership und Strategie als intangible Assets. In: Matzler, K./Hinterhuber, H.H./Renzl, B./Rothenberger, S. (Hrsg.), Immaterielle Vermögenswerte: Handbuch der intangible Assets, Erich Schmidt: Berlin: 531-548.

Hobus, B./Busch, M.W. (2011): Organisationale Ambidextrie. In: Die Betriebswirtschaft, 70, 2: 189-193.

Kaschube, J. (2006): Eigenverantwortung: eine neue berufliche Leistung, Vandenhoeck & Ruprecht: Göttingen.

Kaschube, J./Gasteiger, R. (2005): Eigenverantwortung im Spannungsfeld von Organisation und Individuum. In: Gruppendynamik und Organisationsberatung, 36, 2: 191-206.

Kaschube, J./Koch, S. (2005): Eine neuer Weg zur Beschreibung beruflicher Leistung: Eigenverantwortung. In: Gruppendynamik und Organisationsberatung, 36, 2: 141-156.

Konlechner, S.W./Güttel, W.H. (2009): Kontinuierlicher Wandel mit Ambidexterity - Vorhandenes Wissen nutzen und gleichzeitig neues entwickeln. In: Zeitschrift für Führung und Organisation, 78, 1: 45-53.

Levinthal, D.A./March, J.G. (1993): The Myopia of Learning. In: Strategic Management Journal, 14, S2: 95-112.

Lubatkin, M.H./Simsek, Z./Ling, Y./Veiga, J.F. (2006): Ambidexterity and Performance in Small- to Medium-Sized Firms: The Pivotal Role of Top Management Team Behavioral Integration. In: Journal of Management, 32, 5: 646-672.

Mansfield, R.S. (1996): Building Competency Models: Approaches for HR professionals. In: Human Resource Management, 35, 1: 7-18.

March, J.G. (1991): Exploration and Exploitation in Organizational Learning. In: Organization Science, 2, 1: 71-87.

Mayring, P. (2000): Qualitative Inhaltsanalyse. Grundlagen und Techniken, Deutscher Studien Verlag: Weinheim.

Motowidlo, S.J./Van Scotter, J.R. (1994): Evidence that Task Performance Should be Distinguished from Contextual Performance. In: Journal of Applied Psychology, 79, 4: 475-480.

Müller, J./Renzl, B./Hinterhuber, H.H./Lakomski, G. (2007): Leadership im Wissenszeitalter. In: Raich, M./Pechlaner, H./Hinterhuber, H.H. (Hrsg.), Entrepreneurial Leadership: Profilierung in Theorie und Praxis, DUV: Wiesbaden.

Nelson, R.R./Winter, S.G. (1982): An Evolutionary Theory of Economic Change, Belknap Press of Harvard Univ. Press: Cambridge, Mass. u.a.

Neuberger, O. (2002): Führen und führen lassen, UTB: Stuttgart.

O'Reilly, C./Tushman, M. (2007): Ambidexterity as a Dynamic Capability: Resolving the Innovator's Dilemma. In: Stanford Graduate School of Business Research Paper No. 1963, verfügbar unter SSRN: http://ssrn.com/abstract=978493.

O'Reilly, C.A./Tushman, M.L. (2004): The Ambidextrous Organization. In: Harvard Business Review, 82, April: 74-82.

Preisendörfer, P. (1985): Verantwortung im Betrieb: eine theoretische und empirische Analyse des Verantwortungskonzeptes sowie von Problemen der Verantwortung in betrieblichen Kontexten, Westdeutscher Verlag: Opladen.

Raisch, S./Birkinshaw, J. (2008): Organizational Ambidexterity: Antecedents, Outcomes, and Moderators. In: Journal of Management, 34, 3: 375-409.

Raisch, S./Birkinshaw, J./Probst, G./Tushman, M.L. (2009): Organizational Ambidexterity: Balancing Exploitation and Exploration for Sustained Performance. In: Organization Science, 20, 4: 685-695.

Sarges, W./Stracke, F. (2005): Das Lernpotential-Assessment-Center (LP-AC): Feedback schon während des Assessment Centers. In: Jöns, I./Bungard, W. (Hrsg.), Feedbackinstrumente im Unternehmen – Grundlagen, Gestaltungshinweise, Erfahrungsberichte, Gabler: Wiesbaden

Siggelkow, N./Levinthal, D.A. (2003): Temporarily Divide to Conquer: Centralized, Decentralized, and Reintegrated Organizational Approaches to Exploration and Adaptation. In: Organization Science, 14, 6: 650-669.

Stephan, M./Kerber, W. (2010): "Ambidextrie": Der unternehmerische Drahtseilakt zwischen Ressourcenexploration und -exploitation, Rainer Hampp: Mering.

Teece, D.J. (2007): Explicating dynamic capabilities: the nature and microfoundations of (sustainable) enterprise performance. In: Strategic Management Journal, 28, 13: 1319–1350.

Teece, D.J./Pisano, G./Shuen, A. (1997): Dynamic Capabilities and Strategic Management. In: Strategic Management Journal, 18, 7: 509-533.

Tushman, M.L./O'Reilly, C.A. (1996): The Ambidextrous Organization: Managing Evolutionary and Revolutionary Change. In: California Management Review, 38, 4: 8-30.

Vera, D./Crossan, M. (2004): Strategic Leadership and Organizational Learning. In: Academy of Management Review, 29, 2: 222-240.

Wollersheim, J. (2011): Exploration und Exploitation als zwei Seiten derselben Medaille: Eine systematische Zusammenführung bestehender Konzepte zur Förderung von Ambidextrie in Unternehmen. In: Stephan, M./Kerber, W. (Hrsg.), Jahrbuch Strategisches Kompetenz-Management, Rainer HamppVerlag: Mering: 3-26.

Zahra, S., A./George, G. (2002): Absorptive Capacity: A Review Reconceptualization, and Extension. In: Academy of Management Review, 27, 2: 185-203.

Zollo, M.W., S. G. (2002): Deliberate Learning and the Evolution of Dynamic Capabilities. In: Organization Science, 13, 3: 339-351.

Strategien beim Ablauf von Patenten in der Pharmaindustrie – Eine explorative Studie aus Sicht des Resource-based View of the Firm

Wolfgang Burr und Antje Koch

Zusammenfassung

Der vorliegende Beitrag untersucht, welche Reaktionsmöglichkeiten Pharmaunternehmen offen stehen, um auf den Ablauf des Patents auf einen Wirkstoff zu reagieren. Grundsätzlich bieten sich alternative Reaktionsmöglichkeiten für ein forschendes Pharmaunternehmen an: Weitere Nutzung und Verteidigung des bestehenden Wirkstoffs gegen Imitation (Exploitation vorhandener Ressourcen) oder offensive Erforschung neuer Wirkstoffe (Exploration neuer Ressourcen), um sich Erträge aus neuen Pharmainnovationen anzueignen oder eine Kombination beider Strategien als Reaktion auf den Ablauf eines Wirkstoffpatentes? Diese Frage wird in diesem Beitrag beantwortet, einerseits theoretisch mit Hilfe des Resource-based View und andererseits empirisch anhand von zwei Fallstudien mit führenden deutschen Pharmaunternehmen. Im Ergebnis zeigt sich, dass Unternehmen mit komplexen, unternehmensspezifischen Bündeln von exploitativen und explorativen Maßnahmen auf den Ablauf wichtiger Patente reagieren, und dass das Verhältnis zwischen Exploration und Exploitation stark vom Vorhandensein komplementärer Ressourcen bestimmt wird. Es wird damit ein Beitrag zur Ambidexterity-Forschung und zur genaueren Untersuchung des Trade-off von Exploitation und Exploration vor dem Hintergrund von zwei Praxisfallstudien geleistet.

Schlüsselwörter: Pharmaindustrie, Patentablauf, Resource based View of the Firm, verteidigungsfähiger Wettbewerbsvorteil

Abstract

The current article investigates what options pharmaceutical companies have to react on the expiration of patents on pharmaceutical substances. On the whole, pharmaceutical companies engaged in research have different possibilities to respond to this situation: further use and defense of the existing substance against imitation (exploitation of existing resources) or aggressive research of new substances (exploration of new resources), or a combination of the two strategies as a response to the expiration of a substance patent. The article tackles this question theoretically with the aid of the Resource-based View and empirically with two case studies from leading German pharmaceutical companies. Results show that companies react to the expiry of important patents with complex and specific bundles of exploitative and explorative measures and that the relation between exploration and exploitation is strongly determined by the availability of complementary resources. It performs a contribution to the ambidexterity research and a more accurate investigation of the trade-off among exploitation and exploration, on the background of two practice case studies.

Keywords: Pharmaceutical Industry, Patent Expiration, Resource-based View of the Firm, Sustainable Competitive Advantage

1. Einleitung

Warum ist der Ablauf wichtiger Patente eine erforschungswürdige Fragestellung? Der Ablauf wichtiger Patente ist eine entscheidende Zäsur für forschende Pharmaunternehmen. Die Pharmaindustrie ist eine besonders technologieintensive Branche, in der Patente eine überragende Bedeutung als Imitationsschutz haben und ihr Ablauf eine entscheidende Zäsur für die forschenden Unternehmen darstellt. Der Patentablauf stellt das Unternehmen nicht nur vor die generelle Notwendigkeit, nach Zeitablauf wieder neue Innovationen hervorzubringen. Gerade weil Pharmazeutika oftmals sehr leicht und schnell durch Generikahersteller kopierbar sind, bewirkt der Patentablauf für den bisherigen Patentinhaber eine drastisch und schnell veränderte Markt- und Wettbewerbsumgebung. Botazzi et al. (2001) bezeichnen den Ablauf von Patenten als „market shock“[1] und würdigen damit die große Bedeutung dieses Themas für forschende Pharmaunternehmen. Nach dem Ablauf wichtiger Patente treten sehr rasch Generikahersteller in den Markt ein, was für den ursprünglichen Patentinhaber sehr starke Umsatz- und Gewinnrückgänge in sehr kurzer Zeit bedeutet. Das Patent ist somit nicht nur Manifestation von erzielten Forschungserfolgen, die auf anderen Unternehmensressourcen (Labore, Forscher) basieren, sondern eine Ressourcenimitationsbarriere und eine Markteintrittsbarriere, bei deren Wegfall das Pharmaunternehmen in eine strategische Extremsituation gerät und sehr rasch auf dieses veränderte Umfeld reagieren muss. Die Fragestellung, wie Pharmaunternehmen auf den Ablauf wichtiger Patente reagieren, ist nach Kenntnis der Autoren bisher in der wissenschaftlichen Literatur noch überhaupt nicht untersucht worden. Ein Großteil der Arbeiten zu Patenten, ihre Begründung und Durchsetzung enthält volkswirtschaftliche Studien, z.B. wie sich das Patentrecht eines Landes auf die technologische Leistungsfähigkeit des Landes und seiner forschenden Industrien (vgl. Glass 2000; Horii/Iwaisako 2007 und Kanwar 2007; Qian 2007; Lambertini/Tedeschi 2007), auf ausländische Direktinvestitionen in einem Land (Glass 2000; You/Katayama 2005) und auf die Handelsströme zwischen Ländern auswirkt (vgl. Zugic 1997 und Al-Mawali 2005). Andere volkswirtschaftliche Studien untersuchen, wie das Patentrecht Anreize zu Innovationen schafft bzw. wie das Patentrecht ausgestaltet sein muss, damit es solche Anreize schafft (vgl. Encaoua et al. 2006; Qian 2007 und die dort genannte Literatur). Im Mittelpunkt der betriebswirtschaftlichen Patentforschung steht bisher eindeutig die Begründung, Aufrechterhaltung und Verteidigung sowie der strategische Einsatz von bereits bestehenden Patenten (vgl. Burr et al. 2007 und Gassmann/Bader 2006), nicht aber die Auswirkungen des Ablaufs von Patenten auf das Unternehmen und strategische Reaktionsmöglichkeiten von Unternehmen auf den Ablauf wichtiger Patente.

---

1 Botazzi et al. (2001: 1164). Zu den dramatischen Auswirkungen des Eintritts von Generikaanbietern in nicht mehr patentgeschützte Pharmamarktsegmente auf die Preise und Marktanteile des Originalmedikaments vgl. Grabowski (2002: 853). Zu den Reaktionen der vom Patentablauf betroffenen Pharmafirmen vgl. Hofmann (2007) und (2007a).

Andere Autoren untersuchen die Schwächung bestehender Patente durch inventing around vor dem gesetzlichen Patentablauf (Mukherjee 2006), d.h. durch „non-infringing imitation“ (vgl. Mukherjee 2006: 196) oder die bewusste, illegale Verletzung von bestehenden Patenten (vgl. Zigic 1997; You/Katayama 2005 sowie Burr et al. 2006: 274 ff.), die sich auf Patentverletzungen in China konzentrieren. Nur sehr wenige Forschungsarbeiten wenden bisher den Resource-based View auf Pharmaunternehmen an, im Mittelpunkt dieser Arbeiten stehen aber Fragen rund um den Aufbau, den Schutz und die Messung von FuE-Kompetenzen in Pharmafirmen (vgl. Bottazi et al. 2001; De Carolis 2003; Gonzàlez-Àlvarez/Muñoz-Doyague 2006; Kale/Little 2007; Lee 2003; Thomke/Kuemmerle 2002 mit Hinweisen auf drei weitere Studien, Oshba/Figueiredo 2007 und Rothaermel/ Hess 2007). Die Reaktionen von Pharmaunternehmen auf Patentabläufe sind in diesen Arbeiten überhaupt nicht untersucht worden.

Der vorliegende Beitrag untersucht, wie Pharmaunternehmen auf den Ablauf eines Wirkstoffpatentes reagieren. Alternative Reaktionsmöglichkeiten bieten sich für ein forschendes Pharmaunternehmen an: Verteidigung des bestehenden Wirkstoffs gegen Imitation (Ressourcenexploitation) oder offensive Erforschung neuer Wirkstoffe (Ressourcenexploration), um sich Erträge aus neu eingeführten Pharmainnovationen anzueignen, oder eine Kombination beider Strategien als Reaktion auf den Ablauf eines Wirkstoffpatentes? Diese Frage wird in diesem Beitrag theoretisch mit Hilfe des Resource-based View und mit ersten empirischen Vorstudien (zwei Fallstudien mit forschenden deutschen Pharmaunternehmen) beantwortet. Als zentrales Ergebnis zeigt sich, dass der Resource-based View of the Firm gut geeignet ist, um Reaktionsmuster von Pharmaunternehmen beim Ablauf wichtiger Patente zu strukturieren und zu analysieren. Ebenfalls wird deutlich, dass die Mischung zwischen Ressourcenexploration und Ressourcenexploitation stark vom Vorhandensein komplementärer Ressourcen bestimmt wird. Gewähren komplementäre Ressourcen nur einen schwachen Schutz gegen Nachahmer, so werden exploitative Ressourcenstrategien erschwert und die Unternehmen müssen in stärkerem Maße Ressourcenexploration betreiben. Ebenfalls zeigt sich, dass die untersuchten Unternehmen Mischstrategien entwickeln und sich nicht allein auf Exploration oder Exploitation konzentrieren.

Zum Aufbau des vorliegenden Beitrags: Abschnitt 2 gibt einen Überblick zu den theoretischen Grundlagen des Beitrags. Referenzpunkte der theoretischen Analyse sind das Konzept des ressourcenbasierten, verteidigungsfähigen Wettbewerbsvorteils sowie die strategischen Optionen der Ressourcenexploitation und der Ressourcenexploration. In Abschnitt 3 werden die theoretischen Grundlagen auf die Fragestellung des Papers (Reaktionsmuster auf Patentabläufe in der Pharmaindustrie) angewandt. Es werden anhand dieses Bezugsrahmens grundsätzliche Reaktionsmöglichkeiten auf das Schwinden eines Sustainable Competitive Advantage (Exploitation bestehender Ressourcen oder Exploration neuer Ressourcen) aufgezeigt und der erste Bezug zur Pharmaindustrie hergestellt. In Abschnitt 4 werden dann die empirische Forschungsmethodik und die Vorgehensweise bei der Erstellung der empirischen Unternehmensfallstudien dargelegt. Abschnitt 5 stellt die Ergebnisse aus der Zusammenführung und

Konfrontation der theoretischen Grundlagen mit den beiden empirischen Fallstudien zu zwei deutschen forschenden Pharmaunternehmen dar. Abschnitt 6 diskutiert und reflektiert die Forschungsergebnisse. In diesem letzten Abschnitt wird zu der Frage Stellung genommen, ob der Resource-based View of the Firm ein nützlicher Erklärungsansatz ist, um Managemententscheidungen betreffend den Ablauf wichtiger Patente zu strukturieren.

2. Theoretischer Hintergrund: Resource-based View of the Firm

Theoretische Grundlage bildet der Resource-based View of the Firm (RBV). Die Autoren haben sich für diesen Ansatz aus 3 Gründen entschieden: Das Forschungsproblem „Reaktionen auf den Patentablauf" ist sehr komplex und vielschichtig, da Unternehmen mit sehr verschiedenartigen Maßnahmen auf Patentabläufe reagieren können (z.B. Fusionen mit Konkurrenten, Lizenznahmen von kleinen Firmen, verstärkte Kooperationen zwecks Beschleunigung der eigenen Forschung etc.). Daher war es wichtig, einen theoretischen Fokus auf Ressourcen und unternehmensinterne Kompetenzen des Unternehmens einzunehmen, um andere Aspekte des Forschungsproblems (z.B. marktbezogene Handlungen des Managements, institutionelle Rahmenbedingungen des Patentrechts) auszublenden und das Forschungsproblem fokussieren zu können. Zweitens bietet sich der Resource-based View als Theorie an, weil mit dieser Theorie gleichzeitig Aspekte des strategischen Managements (zu ressourcenökonomischen Arbeiten im Bereich des strategischen und operativen Managements vgl. beispielsweise Freiling/Reckenfelderbäumer 2007: 274 ff.) und des Innovationsmanagements (vgl. z.B. ressourcenökonomische Arbeiten zum Innovationsmanagement bei Burr 2004; Gerybadze 2004) behandelt werden können, die für ein vertieftes Verständnis von Patentabläufen erforderlich sind. Drittens haben sich die Autoren an einer bestehenden Forschungsrichtung mit einigen wenigen, eingangs genannten Publikationen orientiert, die Fragen des Innovationsmanagements (aber bisher noch nicht Fragen des Ablaufs von Patenten, die Innovations- und Strategiebezug aufweisen) in der Pharmaindustrie mit Hilfe des Resource-based View analysiert hat.

Nachfolgend werden ausgewählte Basiskonzepte des Resource-based View im Überblick dargestellt, um die Anwendung dieser theoretischen Grundlagen auf das Forschungsthema „Patentablauf in der Pharmaindustrie" im nächsten Kapitel vorzubereiten.

2.1 Das Konzept des ressourcenbasierten verteidigungsfähigen Wettbewerbsvorteils (Sustainable Competitive Advantage)

Zwischen den Vertretern des ressourcenbasierten Ansatzes gibt es keine Übereinstimmung, welche Merkmale eine Ressource aufweisen muss, damit sie einem Unternehmen einen verteidigungsfähigen Wettbewerbsvorteil (Sustainable Competitive

Advantage) verleiht . Ein verteidigungsfähiger Wettbewerbsvorteil liegt vor, wenn er trotz der Anstrengungen von Konkurrenten, diesen Wettbewerbsvorteil zu duplizieren weiter besteht, und daher die Anstrengungen der Konkurrenten mangels Erfolgsaussichten beendet worden sind (vgl. Barney 1991: 102).

Abbildung 1: Ressourcenmerkmale und verteidigungsfähiger Wettbewerbsvorteil, in Anlehnung an Barney (1991)

Die vorstehende Abbildung orientiert sich vor allem an der Arbeit von Barney (1991), ergänzt sie aber durch nachfolgende Argumente und Ressourcenmerkmale von anderen Autoren (z.B. Mahoney/Pandian 1992; Schoemaker/Amit 1994; Cool/Dierickx 1994). Sie verdeutlicht das Konzept des verteidigungsfähigen Wettbewerbsvorteils im Überblick. Das zentrale Axiom innerhalb des Resource Based View of the Firm ist, dass sich Unternehmen in ihrer Ressourcenausstattung unterscheiden und dass sich daraus Unterschiede in der Effizienz und der Profitabilität von Unternehmen erklären lassen. Ein verteidigungsfähiger Wettbewerbsvorteil (vgl. z.B. Barney 1991; Cool/Dierickx 1994; Schoemaker/Amit 1994) liegt vor, wenn eine Ressource die in der obigen Abbildung genannten Ressourcen- und Umweltmerkmale alle simultan erfüllt. Dann kann dieser verteidigungsfähige Wettbewerbsvorteil zu einem nachhaltigen Rentenstrom für das Unternehmen führen. Ressourcen, die alle o.g. Kriterien erfüllen, sind die „Kronjuwelen" des Unternehmens (vgl. Montgomery 1995), die seinen strategischen Wettbewerbsvorteil gegenüber den Wettbewerbern begründen. Einen verteidigungsfähigen Wettbewerbsvorteil kann ein Unternehmen erringen, indem es einzelne Ressourcen i.e.S. (z.B. Sachanlagevermögen, Humankapital, Reputation, Markennamen, Patente etc.) besitzt bzw. kontrolliert oder indem es Kernkompetenzen bzw. Kompetenzen entwickelt, die die o.g. Merkmale erfüllen[2].

2 Der (Kern-)Kompetenzbegriff ist in der Literatur nicht eindeutig definiert. Eine Reihe von Autoren versteht eine Kompetenz als die Fähigkeit eines Unternehmens, seine Ressourcen

In der Pharmaindustrie können Patente auf Wirkstoffe als isolierte Ressourcen i.e.S. die Basis verteidigungsfähiger Wettbewerbsvorteile sein, wenn sie im Einzelfall die in der obigen Abbildung skizzierten Anforderungen für das Vorliegen eines verteidigungsfähigen Wettbewerbsvorteils erfüllen[3].

Die große Bedeutung von Patenten in der Pharmaindustrie wurde auch durch die klassische und sehr bekannt gewordene empirische Untersuchung von Levin et al. (1987) bestätigt: Nur in einer einzigen von über 100 untersuchten Branchen, nämlich jener der Pharma-Hersteller, wurden Patente von der Mehrheit der Befragten eindeutig als effektivstes Instrument zur Appropriierung von Innovationserträgen angesehen[4]. In der Untersuchung von Levin et al. (1987) stellte sich heraus, dass Patente die Imitationskosten bei neuen Medikamenten um 40% erhöhen (vgl. Levin et al. 1987: 811). Die wahrscheinlichste Erklärung für das signifikante Ergebnis, dass Patente besonders in der pharmazeutisch-chemischen Industrie effektiv sind, ist die Existenz vergleichsweise klarer Standards, um die Gültigkeit eines Patents in diesem Wirtschaftszweig zu belegen und um das Patent gegen Verletzung zu verteidigen[5]. Neuere Untersuchungen bestätigen die große Bedeutung von Patenten in der Pharmaindustrie (vgl. den Überblick bei Encacoua et al. 2006: 1427 sowie Grabowski 2002: 849-851, 853 und Qian 2007: 436).

Neben Patenten bilden auch spezifische Unternehmenskompetenzen die Basis für verteidigungsfähige Wettbewerbsvorteile in der Pharmaindustrie. Aus der bisherigen empirischen Forschung (vgl. Kale/Little 2007; Henderson/Cockburn 1994 und De Carolis 2003) ist bekannt, dass forschende Pharmaunternehmen für ihren Markterfolg besondere Kompetenzen in folgenden Bereichen benötigen: Forschungskompetenz in einem bestimmten Krankheitsfeld bzw. Indikationsgebiet (z.B. Krebserkrankungen, Herz-Kreislauf-Krankheiten, Nervenleiden etc.) und in einzelnen Pharmatechnologien (z.B. gentechnische Entwicklung und Herstellung von Pharmazeutika), zusätzliche Kompetenzen in den Bereichen Marketing, Umgang mit der Regulierungsinstanz (z.B. Management des Zulassungsprozesses) und Management intellektueller Eigentumsrechte.

---

zielorientiert einzusetzen. Vgl. z.B. Sanchez/Heene/Thomas (1996: 8) oder Mahoney/Pandian (1992: 365). Kernkompetenz wird von Prahalad/Hamel (1990: 82) definiert als „the collective learning in the organization, especially how to coordinate diverse production skills and integrate multiple streams of technology".

3 Hill/Deeds (1996: 435) betonen die Patentfunktion, dass Patente in einigen Fällen Imitationsbarrieren darstellen.

4 Vgl. Levin et al. (1987: 796 f., 816) sowie die Aufzählung von Appropriierungsmechanismen bei Gonzàlez-Àlvarez/Muñoz-Doyague (2006: 842).

5 Die Einzigartigkeit eines bestimmten Moleküls kann wesentlich einfacher demonstriert werden als z. B. die Neuheit einer Komponente eines komplexen technischen oder mechanischen Produktsystems, vgl. Levin et al. (1987: 798).

2.2 *Ressourcenexploitation und Ressourcenexploration als strategische Optionen eines Unternehmens*

Der Resource-based View of the Firm eignet sich sowohl für die Anwendung auf Fragen des strategischen und operativen Managements als auch auf Fragen des Innovationsmanagements; er wird auch in breitem Umfang und in vielfältiger Weise auf diese beiden Teilgebiete der Managementlehre angewandt. Darin spiegelt sich sowohl der eher statisch-gleichgewichtsorientierte Charakter einer Forschungsrichtung im Resource-based View (z.B. Konzept des verteidigungsfähigen Wettbewerbsvorteils) als auch der dynamisch-prozessorientierte Charakter einer anderen Forschungsrichtung im Resource-based View (Aufbau neuer Kompetenzen im Unternehmen, Dynamic Capabilities-Ansatz, vgl. Schreyögg und Klisch-Eberl 2007) wider (vgl. zu diesen beiden Forschungsrichtungen im Resource-based View auch Burr 2002). Dieser duale Charakter des Resource-based View zeigt sich auch in zwei zentralen Erklärungskonzepten, die zueinander in einer ergänzenden, aber auch in einer konfliktären Beziehung stehen: dem Konzept der Ressourcenexploitation und dem Konzept der Ressourcenexploration[6].

Für den Fall, dass es einem Unternehmen aufgrund Nichterfüllung einiger oder aller der oben genannten Bedingungen (vgl. Abb. 1) nicht mehr möglich ist, einen ressourcenbasierten, verteidigungsfähigen Wettbewerbsvorteil zu erzielen oder sich die Renten aus seinen Ressourcen anzueignen, gibt der ressourcenorientierte Ansatz der Unternehmensführung Gestaltungsempfehlungen für das Management. Interessant ist in diesem Zusammenhang, dass nach Kenntnis der Verfasser kein Vertreter des Exploitationsansatzes der ressourcenorientierten Unternehmensführung explizite Aussagen dazu macht, wie relevant (d.h. wie häufig und mit welcher Bedeutung für den Unternehmenserfolg) jeweils der Fall des verteidigungsfähigen bzw. des nicht-verteidigungsfähigen Wettbewerbsvorteils in der Praxis ist. Falls ein Unternehmen einen Wettbewerbsvorteil besitzt, der nicht verteidigungsfähig ist und damit z.B. durch Imitation oder Substitution erodiert werden kann, so ergibt sich als grundsätzliche Handlungsoption eine Strategie der Exploitation des schwindenden Wettbewerbsvorteils oder eine Strategie der Exploration neuer Wettbewerbsvorteile oder eine Mischstrategie, die Exploration und Exploitation kombiniert[7]. Sowohl die Exploi-

---

6 Vgl. hierzu auch *Rotharmel/Deeds* (2004) und (2001), die Ressourcenexploitation und Ressourcenexploration auf Allianzen in der Biotechnologie-Industrie anwenden.

7 Fragen des Einsatzes bestehender Ressourcen (Exploitation) und des Aufbaus neuer Ressourcenpotentiale (Exploration) werden in der Literatur unter vielfältigen alternativen Begriffsverwendungen erörtert. Wertvoll ist in diesem Zusammenhang der bei Christensen (1996: 129), Anmerk. 5 aufgeführte Überblick über die Begriffsverwendung in der Literatur. Es finden sich in der Literatur die korrespondierenden Begriffspaare „static routines" versus „dynamic capabilities" (Teece et al., 1994), „competence maintaining and leveraging" versus „competence building" (Sanchez/Heene/Thomas 1995). Zum Trade-off zwischen Exploitation und Exploration vgl. March (1991).

tation vorhandener als auch die Exploration neuer Ressourcenpotentiale trägt zur kurz- bzw. langfristigen Gewinnerzielung eines Unternehmens bei (so auch die Ansicht von Teece et al. 1997: 515). Die initiierenden Forschungsimpulse im Themenbereich Exploitation versus Exploration von Ressourcen kamen durch den klassischen Beitrag von March (1991) zustande.

Exploitation zielt auf die Nutzung bestehender Ressourcenpotenziale und Kompetenzen (vgl. Konlechner/Güttel 2009: 45, Hobus/Busch 2011: 189, Danneels 2002: 1095, grundlegend March 1991). Im Pharmabereich bedeutet dies den fortgesetzten Einsatz der vorhandenen Wirkstoffe trotz Patentablauf und ihre Verteidigung gegen Imitation und Imitatoren z.B. durch Erzielung von Kostensenkungen.

Exploration bedeutet hingegen das Erforschen und Entwickeln neuer Ressourcen, Ressourcenkombinationen und Kompetenzen (vgl. Konlechner/Güttel 2009: 45, Hobus/Busch 2011: 189, Danneels 2002: 1095, grundlegend March 1991). Exploration bedeutet in der Pharmaindustrie z.B. die Entwicklung neuer pharmazeutischer Wirkstoffe, also die Realisierung pharmazeutischer Innovationen.

Das Verhältnis zwischen Ressourcenexploitation und Ressourcenexploration ist in mehrfacher Hinsicht problematisch. Zum einen gibt es in der Literatur keine eindeutige Grenzziehung zwischen den beiden Konzepten. So rechnen beispielsweise Benner und Tushman (2003: 238) inkrementelle Innovationen der Exploitation zu. Inkrementelle Innovationen sind zwischen Exploitation und Exploration angesiedelt, da sie vorhandene Lösungen maßvoll weiterentwickeln und verbessern. In diesem Paper wird hingegen inkrementelle Innovation der Exploration zugerechnet, da neues Wissen erarbeitet werden muss. Exploration und Exploitation werden im vorliegenden Beitrag somit stärker polarisiert dargestellt. Zum anderen stellt sich neben dem definitorischen Abgrenzungsproblem auch ein inhaltliches Dilemma: Zwischen (kurzfristiger) Ressourcenexploitation und (langfristig angelegter) Ressourcenexploration (in der Literatur finden sich hierfür auch die Begriffe statische Effizienz und dynamische Effizienz (so die Begriffsverwendung bei Ghemawat/Costa 1993; Sanchez/Heene 1997 und Marengo 1994) existiert in vielen Fällen ein Spannungsverhältnis (so auch die Ansicht von Ghemawat/Costa 1993: 59 sowie Marengo (1994: 554, 561, 569). Abernathy (1978) hat darauf hingewiesen, dass ein Unternehmen nicht hocheffizient (im statischen Sinne) sein und gleichzeitig eine hohe Innovationsrate aufweisen kann. Heskett (1987) unterscheidet zwischen einer Organisation vom Typ A, der auf Regelmäßigkeit und (statische) Effizienz von Abläufen ausgelegt ist und einer Organisation vom Typ B, der auf Innovation und Flexibilität hin optimiert ist. Ghemawat/Costa (1993) kommen zu der vorsichtigen Schlussfolgerung: „... organizational arrangements that promote static efficiency may be inconsistent with arrangements that promote dynamic efficiency." (Ghemawat/Costa 1993: 63). Sie zeigen im Einzelnen auf, dass die beiden Effizienzorientierungen sehr unterschiedliche Anforderungen an die Organisationsstrukturen, die sie unterstützen und die Mitarbeiter, die sie umsetzen sollen, stellen (vgl. hierzu Ghemawat/Costa 1993: 65, 68). Sanchez/Heene (1997) weisen darauf hin, dass die Ressourcenexploitation (in ihrer Terminologie: competence leveraging) den kurzfristigen Wettbewerbserfolg des Unternehmens bestimmt und daher einen Großteil der Aufmerksamkeit des Managements und der Ressourcenallokation innerhalb von Unternehmen bindet, der für die Ressourcenexploration (competence building) zur Sicherung der langfristigen Unternehmenszukunft nicht mehr zur Verfügung steht (vgl. hierzu Sanchez/Heene 1997a: 307). Exploitation zielt auf die Verfeinerung und Ausdehnung bestehender Kompetenzen und Technologien. Die Erfolge von Exploitationsbemühungen sind im Regelfall positiv, schnell realisierbar und vorhersagbar. Exploration bedeutet Experimentieren mit neuen Alternativen und Problemlösungsmethoden. Explorationsbemühungen sind demgegenüber unter Erfolgsgesichtspunkten oftmals unsicher, nur langfristig realisierbar und mit der Gefahr der Fehlinvestition verbunden. Aus diesen Gründen herrscht in vielen Organisationen eine Tendenz vor, die Exploitation bekannter Alternativen der Exploration unbekannter Alternativen vorzuziehen, was jedoch langfristig für die Entwicklungsfähigkeit des Unternehmens nachteilig ist.

Die Entscheidung eines Unternehmens, welcher Anteil seiner knappen Ressourcen in Exploitation und welcher Anteil in Exploration investiert wird, d.h. die Verwirklichung einer angemessenen Balance zwischen Exploration und Exploitation, ist für die langfristige Überlebensfähigkeit und den Erfolg von Unternehmen von entscheidender Bedeutung (so auch die Ansicht von De Carolis 2003: 46 unter direkter Bezugnahme auf die Pharmaindustrie. Ähnliche Aussagen finden sich bei Konlechner und Güttel 2009: 45, Marengo 1994: 554). Die weitere Unternehmensentwicklung wird hingegen behindert durch eine einseitige und übermäßige Betonung von statischer Effizienz und Exploitation ebenso wie durch eine einseitige und übermäßige Betonung von dynamischer Effizienz und Explorierung (vgl. Scheurer 1997: 233).

Marengo bringt dieses kritische Entscheidungsproblem auf den Punkt:

> „*Organizations always face the dilemma between concentrating their resources on the exploitation of the knowledge which is already available to them and the exploration of new possibilities. Both exploitation and exploration are necessary for the survival of an organization*" (Marengo 1994: 554).

Eine Balance zwischen Exploration und Exploitation kann über die Implementierung ambidextrer Strukturen erfolgen. Die grundlegenden Forschungsarbeiten auf dem Gebiet ambidextrer Strukturen stammen von Duncan (1976), Birkinshaw und Gibson (2004), Tushman und O´Reilly (1996). Hobus und Busch definieren Ambidextrie als die „... Fähigkeit einer Organisation ..., exploitative und explorative Aktivitäten in einem ausbalancierten Verhältnis parallel zu betreiben." (Hobus und Busch 2011: 189, sehr ähnlich ist auch die Definition eines ambidextren Organisationsdesigns bei Konlechner und Güttel 2009: 47). Solche ambidextren Strukturen können entweder durch strukturelle Ambidextrie (vgl. Konlechner und Güttel 2009: 48 sowie Hobus und Busch 2011: 190 f.) oder durch kontextuelle Ambidextrie (vgl. Konlechner und Güttel 2009: 49 f. sowie Hobus und Busch 2011: 190 f.) realisiert werden. Die empirischen Forschungsbelege, ob und inwiefern ambidextre Strukturen zum Erfolg der

Unternehmung beitragen, sind bisher allerdings nicht eindeutig (vgl. Hobus und Busch 2011: 190 f., einen positiven Zusammenhang stellen He und Wong 2004 fest). Im Vordergrund des vorliegenden Beitrags steht allerdings nicht die Frage, mit welchen strukturellen Lösungen Unternehmen Ambidextrie erreichen, sondern die strategische Frage, ob Pharmaunternehmen angesichts des strategischen Ausnahmecharakters infolge Ablauf wichtiger Patente überhaupt eine Mischung von Exploitation und Exploration realisieren oder einseitig auf eine der beiden Strategien der Ressourcennutzung setzen. Im Vordergrund steht somit die strategische, von der Unternehmensführung zu beantwortende (vgl. Konlechner und Güttel 2009: 48) Frage nach dem Mischungsverhältnis von Exploitation und Exploration, nicht die Frage, wie die Balance zwischen beiden Modi der Ressourcennutzung durch geeignete organisatorische Lösungen erreicht und gehalten wird. Im Vordergrund dieses Beitrags stehen also Fragen nach der ambidextren Strategie, nicht nach der ambidextren Organisation von Pharmaunternehmen angesichts einer tiefgreifenden strategischen Zäsur, wie sie der Ablauf wichtiger Patente in dieser Branche darstellt.

3. Ressourcenexploitation und/oder Ressourcenexploration als Reaktion auf Patentabläufe in der Pharmaindustrie

Nachfolgend werden Maßnahmen der Exploitation und Exploration von Ressourcen erst theoretisch aus dem Resource-based View abgeleitet. Anschließend erfolgt gleich eine Bezugnahme und Anwendung auf die Pharmaindustrie.

3.1 Exploitation von Ressourcenpotentialen

Grundsätzliche Handlungsoptionen beim Schwinden eines verteidigungsfähigen Wettbewerbsvorteils sind aus Sicht des Resource-based View of the Firm der Aufbau und die Nutzung von Ressourcenimitationsbarrieren (isolating mechanisms).

Ein zentraler Forschungsgegenstand des Resource-based View of the Firm sind Ressourcenmerkmale, die die Imitation einer Ressource durch Wettbewerber erschweren. Unter den Begriffen „Imitationsbarrieren" (vgl. Teece et al. 1997: 526) und „Isolationsmechanismen" (isolating mechanisms) (vgl. Conner 1991: 138 unter Berufung auf Rumelt 1984: 567, der unter isolating mechanisms „phenomena that limit the *ex post* equilibration of rents among individual firms" versteht) werden in der ressourcenbasierten Forschungsliteratur Barrieren beschrieben und systematisiert, die die Nivellierung bestehender Rentenunterschiede zwischen den Firmen einer Branche durch imitierendes Verhalten von Konkurrenten erschweren oder verhindern können.[8] Es gibt

8 Zu einem Überblick über verschiedene isolating mechanisms, die insbesondere imitierendes Verhalten von Wettbewerbern erschweren oder unterbinden, vgl. Mahoney/Pandian (1992: 372 f.), Barney (1994: 119) sowie Levinthal (1995: 35).

eine Vielzahl von Faktoren, die Einfluss darauf haben, zu welchen Kosten, innerhalb welcher Zeitspanne und mit welcher Erfolgswahrscheinlichkeit Wettbewerber die Ressourcen eines anderen Unternehmens imitieren können. Folgende Faktoren tragen dazu bei, die Imitation eines Ressourcenbestandes durch Wettbewerber zu erschweren:

3.1.1 Merkmale der Technologie und kausale Ambiguität als Imitationsbarriere in der Pharmaindustrie

Eine Imitationsbarriere ist die der Innovation zugrunde liegende Technologie. Der Anteil an implizitem Wissen innerhalb des technologischen Ressourcenbestands (vgl. zum impliziten Wissen Polanyi 1962; Franck 1991 sowie Teece et al. 1997: 526. Zu implizitem Wissen innerhalb einer Technologie vgl. De Carolis 2003: 36) oder andere Merkmale der Technologie (z.B. ihre Komplexität) bestimmen die Imitierbarkeit der technologischen Ressource per se[9]. In der ressourcenökonomischen Theorie wird diese Thematik unter dem Stichwort kausale Ambiguität behandelt: Wenn Wettbewerber die Ursachen des Wettbewerbserfolges nicht erkennen oder nicht verstehen können, so schützt dies das eigene Unternehmen gegen Nachahmung seiner Wettbewerbsvorteile. Kausale Ambiguität um technologische Kompetenzen des eigenen Unternehmens herum erschwert aber nicht nur, wie die neuere empirische Forschung belegt hat, die Imitation durch Wettbewerber, sondern auch das unternehmensinterne Management von technologischen Ressourcenpotenzialen und Erfolgsquellen bzw. Erfolgspositionen, da das Management den Beitrag dieser Ressourcen und Kompetenzen zum Wettbewerbserfolg des Unternehmens nur unzureichend versteht (vgl. hierzu Gonzàlez-Àlvarez/Nieto-Antolin 2005 sowie Gonzàlez-Àlvarez/Muñoz-Doyague 2006).

In der Technologie, die dem zu imitierenden Wirkstoff zugrunde liegt, kann die erste Imitationsbarriere bestehen, um das vom Patentablauf bedrohte Pharmazeutikum zu schützen. Neben der chemischen Synthese, auf der die meisten pharmazeutischen Wirkstoffe basieren, ist die Gentechnologie zu nennen (vgl. VFA 2003: 8ff.). Der Einsatz der Gentechnologie in der Wirkstoffproduktion ermöglicht es, noch komplexere Wirkstoffkombinationen herzustellen als durch chemische Synthese vgl. VFA 1998: 10. Beispiele für gentechnisch hergestellte Wirkstoffe sind körpereigene Antikörper, Enzyme und Proteine). Wenn gentechnisch erzeugte Wirkstoffe für Nachahmer schwerer imitierbar sind als die auf den Grundlagen der klassischen Pharmazie (chemisch) hergestellten Wirkstoffe, dann sind gentechnisch hergestellte Pharmazeutika auch nach Ablauf der Patente besser gegen Imitation geschützt. Für den Pharmahersteller kann daraus ein Anreiz resultieren, den Anteil gentechnisch basierter, in hochkomplexen Produktionsprozessen hergestellter Wirkstoffe zukünftig zu erhöhen

9 *Teece* (1986) nennt die Art der zugrunde liegenden Technologie als eine wesentliche Voraussetzung, die erfüllt sein muss, damit sich ein Innovator die Erträge aus seiner Innovation aneignen kann.

(dieses klassische Argument der imitationsorientierten Technologieentwicklung findet sich bereits bei Magee 1977)[10].

3.1.2 Komplementäre Ressourcen als Imitationsbarriere in der Pharmaindustrie

Auch die Kontrolle über komplementäre Ressourcen kann eine Imitationsbarriere darstellen. Komplementäre Ressourcen sind nach Teece (1992: 8 f.) erforderlich zur Markteinführung und Kommerzialisierung einer Innovation[11]. Die Verteilung der komplementären Ressourcen zwischen dem Innovator, den potentiellen Imitatoren und den Zulieferern bzw. Subdienstleistern ist nach Teece (1992) entscheidend für den Wettbewerbserfolg des Innovators sowie die Verteilung des Innovationsgewinns zwischen Innovator, Imitatoren und Zulieferern bzw. Subdienstleistern. Die Verteilung komplementärer Ressourcen entscheidet auch über die Möglichkeiten des Innovators, durch Kontrolle komplementärer Ressourcen Imitatoren abzuwehren. In der Pharmaindustrie können Produktionsanlagen für pharmazeutische Wirkstoffe, Zugang/Zusammenarbeit/Vernetzung mit Zulieferern (Wirkstofflieferanten) und Vertriebskanälen (Ärzte/Apotheker/Großhandel) als bedeutende komplementäre Ressourcen bezeichnet werden.

In der Pharmaindustrie bedeutet ein Patentablauf nicht automatisch, dass sich Generikahersteller, die den frei gewordenen Wirkstoff kopieren, die Renten aus den FuE-Anstrengungen des Originalherstellers aneignen können. Der Markterfolg eines Pharmaunternehmens hängt von den zum Wirkstoff/Medikament komplementären Ressourcen/Kompetenzen (z.B. Kontrolle über Produktionsanlagen, Vertriebsnetze und Vertriebskompetenzen, enge Vernetzung und gefestigte Beziehungen mit anderen Marktteilnehmern, wie z.B. Ärzten und Apothekern) ab. Entscheidend sind hier die Möglichkeiten des innovativen Pharmaunternehmens zur Kontrolle über diese komplementären Ressourcen und die Fähigkeit zum effizienten und effektiven Einsatz komplementärer Ressourcen. Generikahersteller, die keinen Zugang zu den erforderlichen komplementären Ressourcen besitzen, oder diese nicht zu nutzen verstehen, werden die Wirkstoffimitation entweder gar nicht realisieren können (z.B. beim Fehlen von spezialisierten Produktionsanlagen) oder einen imitierten Wirkstoff nicht gewinnbringend vermarkten können (z.B. bei mangelhaften Vertriebskompetenzen oder bei schwacher Vernetzung mit verschreibenden Ärzten).

---

[10] Von den im Januar 2003 auf den deutschen Arzneimittelmarkt befindlichen Medikamenten basieren 2,9 Prozent auf gentechnischen Wirkstoffen. Die zu diesem Zeitpunkt in den frühen Phasen der klinischen Untersuchung befindlichen Wirkstoffe basierten zu 25,9 Prozent auf gentechnischer Herstellung (vgl. *VFA* (2003: 9).

[11] Teece (1992: 8 f.) nennt als Beispiele für komplementäre Ressourcen die Fähigkeit eines Unternehmens zur qualitativ hochwertigen Herstellung von Gütern, After Sales-Dienstleistungen und Marketingdiensten oder die Beherrschung komplementärer Technologien. Vgl. zu komplementären Ressourcen auch Encacoua et al. (2006: 1428).

3.1.3 Andere intellektuelle Eigentumsrechte als Imitationsbarriere in der Pharmaindustrie

Die Wirksamkeit der vom System intellektueller Eigentumsrechte eröffneten Schutzmöglichkeiten ist eine weitere wesentliche Bestimmungsgröße der Imitierbarkeit von Ressourcenbeständen[12]. Zum System intellektueller Eigentumsrechte zählen im wesentlichen Patente, Gebrauchs- und Geschmacksmuster, Urheberrechte und Marken sowie Geschäftsgeheimnisse. Stehen Patente nicht (mehr) als Schutzmechanismus zur Verfügung, kann ein Schutz gegen Nachahmung oftmals mit den anderen genannten intellektuellen Eigentumsrechten erreicht werden (vgl. Levin et al. 1987). Dabei ist oftmals nicht nur das intellektuelle Eigentumsrecht per se ein Schutzmechanismus, sondern manchmal auch die Möglichkeit, mit der Behauptung der Verletzung von intellektuellen Eigentumsrechten Gerichtsprozesse zu führen und auf diese Weise den Markteintritt von Imitatoren zu behindern bzw. zu verzögern.

Für Arzneimittel ist es möglich, nach Ablauf des Patentschutzes ein sogenanntes ergänzendes Schutzzertifikat zu erhalten und damit den Patentschutz für zugelassene Arzneimittel um bis zu fünf Jahre zu verlängern (vgl. Fischer/Breitenbach 2003: 178).

Gebrauchs- und Geschmacksmuster haben in der Pharmaindustrie nur eine geringe Bedeutung (vgl. ebd.: 169). Neben dem Patent gilt in der Pharmaindustrie vor allem die Marke als wichtiges Instrument zum Schutz geistigen Eigentums (vgl. ebd.: 167). Ein Nachahmer kann nach Ablauf des Patentschutzes zwar den Wirkstoff des Originalherstellers kopieren, die Marke des Medikaments genießt jedoch separaten Schutz, d.h., die Verwendung des Markennamens ist auch nach Ablauf des Patentschutzes nur für den Originalhersteller möglich (vgl. Guminski/Rauland 2002: 237 f.). Kompetenz im Markenmanagement kann deshalb einen bedeutenden Wettbewerbsvorteil gegenüber Imitatoren darstellen. Gut eingeführte Premiummarken mit einem ausgezeichneten Image (z.B. Aspirin®) sind in der Lage, sich gegen preiswertere Generika zu behaupten (vgl. Fischer/Breitenbach 2003: 152, 170), auch wenn das Patent bereits lange abgelaufen ist.

Geheimhaltung und die Begründung von Geschäftsgeheimnissen können ebenfalls Imitationsversuche verhindern: Das Pharmazeutikum selbst lässt sich nicht geheim halten, da im Markt verkaufte Arzneimittel von Konkurrenten einer chemischen Analyse unterzogen werden können. Das Unternehmen kann aber Anstrengungen unternehmen, um die Beobachtbarkeit der Organisation, ihrer Ressourcen und der Lei-

[12] Vgl. Teece (1986) sowie Eriksen/Mikkelsen (1996: 63), die als Barrieren gegen Imitation zum einen die Merkmale der Ressource an sich und zum anderen rechtliche Schutzmechanismen ansprechen. Teece et al. (1997: 526) schätzen die Wirksamkeit von intellektuellen Eigentumsrechten als Schutz gegen Imitation differenziert ein: „One should not, however, overestimate the overall importance of intellectual property protection; yet it presents a formidable imitation barrier in certain particular contexts.“

stungserstellungsprozesse zu vermindern und Unbefugten den Zugang zur Organisation zu verweigern[13].

Ein speziell in der Pharmaindustrie verbreitetes Instrument zur Abwehr von Imitatoren ist der Gerichtsprozess. Dabei geht es nicht immer um die Abwehr einer tatsächlichen Patentverletzung, sondern Behauptungen von Patentverletzungen und Patentklagen sind zu einem strategischen Instrument geworden, um den Marktzutritt von Konkurrenten zu verhindern oder zumindest zu verzögern. Wie das Beispiel von Astra-Zeneca zeigt, kann man durch eine Klage bei Gericht die Zulassung eines Konkurrenzprodukts für 30 Monate blockieren (vgl. Seidlitz 2003: 13).

Die bisher genannten Ressourcenimitationsbarrieren dienen primär der Exploitation vorhandener Ressourcen und ihrer Verteidigung gegen Imitatoren. Die Alternative hierzu ist die Exploration neuer Ressourcenkombinationen als Vorwärtsstrategie, um sich gegen nachrückende Imitatoren zu behaupten.

3.2 Exploration von Ressourcenpotentialen

Grant (1991) empfiehlt dem Management eine Strategie, die nicht auf die Verteidigung bestehender, sondern auf die Schaffung neuer Wettbewerbsvorteile in kurzer Zeit abzielt und zwar schneller als Konkurrenten die bestehenden Wettbewerbsvorteile durch Imitation oder Substitution erodieren können (vgl. Grant 1991: 130 f.) . So verstandene Exploration kann grundsätzlich auf drei Wegen stattfinden: Das Unternehmen kann erstens die bestehenden Ressourcen so verändern (z.B. durch Erhöhung ihres Spezifitätsgrades und ihrer Nichtimitierbarkeit oder durch Reorganisation des Ressourceneinsatzes), dass sie zu Ressourcen transformiert werden, auf denen das Unternehmen einen erneuten verteidigungsfähigen Wettbewerbsvorteil aufbauen kann. Dies ist meistens gleichbedeutend mit inkrementalen Innovationen. Die Alternative hierzu wäre die Hervorbringung gänzlich neuer Ressourcenkombinationen, d.h. von Wirkstoffen und Pharmaprodukten mit radikal innovativem Charakter. Inkrementelle und radikale Innovationen liegen im Kern einer Fast Pace-Strategie zugrunde. Der zweite Weg der Exploration für das Unternehmen neuer Ressourcenkombinationen ist die Diversifikation des Unternehmens in ganz neue Geschäftsfelder, die mit dem bisherigen Geschäft verwandt oder unverwandt sind.

Als Möglichkeiten der Ressourcenexploration in der Pharmaindustrie sollen die folgenden drei Optionen unterschieden werden:

---

[13] Vgl. Grant (1991), der im Falle eines nicht (mehr) verteidigungsfähigen Wettbewerbsvorteils unter anderem die möglichst lange Geheimhaltung des Wettbewerbsvorteils empfiehlt.

Inkrementale Pharmainnovationen	*Radikale Pharmainnovationen*	*Diversifikation*
durch Modifikationen bestehender Wirkstoffe und Pharmaprodukte	durch völlig neu entwickelte Wirkstoffe und Pharmaprodukte	neue Geschäftsfelder jenseits des angestammten forschungsintensiven Pharmageschäftes

Tabelle 1: Möglichkeiten der Ressourcenexploration in der Pharmaindustrie

3.2.1 Fast Pace Strategien: Eigenerstellung von Pharmainnovationen im Innovations- und Zeitwettbewerb

Neben der Verteidigung bestehender Wirkstoffe gegen Imitation kann sich ein Unternehmen alternativ auf die Erforschung neuer Wirkstoffe konzentrieren, um auf diese Weise mit Hilfe inkrementaler oder radikaler Pharmainnnovationen die Imitatoren auf Abstand zu halten (Fast Pace-Strategie, d.h. Erzielung immer neuer Vorsprünge im Innovationswettbewerb).

Eigenerstellung inkrementaler Pharmainnovation durch Wirkstoff- und Produktmodifikation

Explorative Ressourcenveränderung wird in der Pharmaindustrie als Wirkstoffmodifikation verstanden, die zur Neupatentierung und zu neuen Medikamenten führt und auf folgenden Prinzipien beruht (vgl. Guminski/Rauland 2002: 236f.):

- Wirkstoffveränderungen: (geringfügige) Molekülvariationen des bekannten Wirkstoffs führen zu so genannten Me-too-Präparaten, die als inkrementale Innovationen (Schrittinnovation) einen eigenen Patentschutz erlangen können.
- Verwendung des Wirkstoffs in einem neu entwickelten Kombinationspräparat mit anderen Wirkstoffen.
- Veränderungen der Wirkstoffstärke (Dosierung) in dem Medikament, das den Wirkstoff enthält.
- Entdeckung neuer Indikationsgebiete für den bekannten Wirkstoff, für die dann ein Verwendungspatent beantragt werden kann.
- Neue Anwendergruppen für den bekannten Wirkstoff: z.B. Modifikation des bisher für Erwachsene verwendeten Wirkstoffs, so dass er bei Säuglingen und Kindern eingesetzt werden kann.
- Neue Darreichungsformen (Galenik) für den bewährten Wirkstoff: z.B. Aerosole, Pflaster, Cremes oder so genannte Drug Delivery Systems, die eine ver-

zögerte Wirkstofffreisetzung ermöglichen und dem Patienten die häufige Tabletteneinnahme ersparen (vgl. Fischer/Breitenbach 2003: 22 f.).

In all den oben genannten Fällen entstehen inkrementale Innovationen, die zu einem neuen Patent und damit einem neuen patentbasierten Sustainable Competitive Advantage führen können. Die zielgerichtete Suche nach solchen geplanten Wirkstoffveränderungen zur Generierung inkrementeller Pharmainnovationen wurde bei den im Rahmen des Forschungsprojektes in den beiden Fallstudien interviewten Pharmafirmen als Lifecycle Management bezeichnet[14].

Erforschung von radikal innovativen Wirkstoffen und Pharmaprodukten

Grant (1991: 130 f.) empfiehlt dem Management eine Strategie, die nicht auf die Verteidigung bestehender, sondern auf die Schaffung neuer Wettbewerbsvorteile in kurzer Zeit abzielt und zwar schneller als Konkurrenten die bestehenden Wettbewerbsvorteile durch Imitation oder Substitution erodieren können. Bei einer Fast Pace-Strategie ist das Ziel des Pharmaunternehmens die Erforschung ganz neuer Pharmazeutika, schneller als die alten Wirkstoffpatente auslaufen und Generikaanbieter die alten Pharmazeutika imitieren können. Eine solche Strategie erfordert hohe FuE-Ausgaben und talentierte Forscher (Input), eine hohe Erfolgsquote bei FuE-Projekten (Output, gemessen z.B. an der Zahl der patentierten Wirkstoffe als Anteil an allen geprüften potenziellen Wirkstoffkandidaten), sowie schnelle und effiziente Abläufe in FuE, um Zeitvorsprünge zu erzielen und zu verteidigen (FuE-Prozesse). Ziel dieser Strategie ist letztlich der Aufbau einer FuE-Pipeline, um radikal innovative Pharmazeutika auf den Markt bringen zu können und die Vorteile aus der Vermarktung patentgeschützter Arzneimittel weiterhin zu sichern.

Der Prozess der Arzneimittelentwicklung kann als extrem risikobehaftet, kostenintensiv und zeitaufwendig bezeichnet werden. Die Neuentwicklung von Wirkstoffen, evtuell sogar unter großem Zeitdruck (Fast Pace Strategien) birgt im Pharmabereich ein hohes Risiko des Scheitern der entsprechenden FuE-Projekte. Von ca. 10.000 erforschten Substanzen erreicht letztlich nur eine einzige die Zulassung und damit die Marktreife (vgl. Breyer et al. 2003: 428). Die Entwicklungszeit von der Synthese von Wirkstoffkandidaten bis zur Zulassung des neuen Medikamentes erhöhte sich von zwei Jahren in den 1950er Jahren auf heute durchschnittlich zehn bis zwölf Jahre. Die Verlängerung der Entwicklungsphase und eine im Vergleich zu früheren Jahren aufgrund strengerer Zulassungsprüfungen abnehmende Erfolgswahrscheinlichkeit haben die FuE-Kosten für ein zugelassenes Arzneimittel von 7,5 Mio. US-Dollar in den 1950er Jahren auf rund 400 Mio. US-Dollar im Jahr 2000 (vgl. ebd.: 429 f. sowie DiMasi et al. 2003: 116) steigen lassen. Jüngste Schätzungen nennen sogar Kosten von bis zu 1200 Mio. US-Dollar für ein neu entwickeltes Medikament der Schweizerischen Pharmaindustrie heute (vgl. Scienceindustries 2011: 23). In diesen Kosten

14 Der Lifecycle von pharmazeutischen Produkten wird auch bei Botazzi et al. (2001: 1161) erwähnt, aber nicht vertieft untersucht.

sind die Kosten für die zahlreichen gescheiterten Innovationsprojekte anteilig zugerechnet, was die sehr hohen Gesamtkosten erklärt. Gerade weil die Entwicklung radikal innovativer Medikamente so kosten- und zeitintensiv und mit hohen Risiken befrachtet ist, erscheint in manchen Unternehmen die Durchführung inkrementaler Innovationsprojekte mit geringeren Kosten-, Zeit- und Risikoproblemen als attraktive Handlungsoption.

3.2.2 Fast Pace Strategien: Eigenerstellung von Pharmainnovationen im Innovations- und Zeitwettbewerb

Basierend auf bestehenden Kompetenzen in FuE könnte das Pharmaunternehmen beispielsweise selbst in das Generikageschäft einsteigen (eigenes Angebot von Generika bzw. Akquisition eines Generikaherstellers), wie es z.B. das forschende Pharmaunternehmen Novartis getan hat. Denkbar ist auch die Verstärkung weniger FuE-intensiver Pharmafelder, wie z.B. nicht verschreibungspflichtige OTC-Präparate. Denkbar ist auch, dass das Unternehmen ganz neue Geschäftsfelder sucht und sich neben dem Pharmageschäft ein zweites Standbein aufbaut (z.B. Merck AG mit Flüssigkristallen für TFT-Bildschirme oder Johnson&Johnson, die das Geschäft mit Medizintechnik zusätzlich zum Pharmageschäft aufgebaut haben).

4. Empirische Forschungsmethodik: Fallstudienforschung

Nachfolgend werden die Kernergebnisse von zwei empirischen Unternehmensfallstudien mit forschenden Pharmaunternehmen in Deutschland präsentiert. Die beiden Fallstudien dienen der weiteren Exploration des empirischen Feldes, insbesondere einer Untersuchung, wie das Thema Patentablauf in der Unternehmenspraxis gehandhabt wird.

Die theoretische Analyse wird ergänzt und überprüft durch die Kernergebnisse von zwei vergleichenden, empirischen Fallstudien mit zwei forschenden Pharmaunternehmen in Deutschland, die ein besseres Verständnis des empirischen Feldes und eine erste kritische Reflexion der theoretisch abgeleiteten Aussagen ermöglichten.

Die zwei empirischen Studien dienen primär der weiteren Explorierung des praktischen Feldes und ergänzen die theoretische Analyse. Der Hauptfokus des vorliegenden Beitrags ist nicht der empirische Test von Hypothesen, sondern die explorative Erschließung eines bis heute unbehandelten Forschungsthemas und die Gewinnung von Erkenntnissen, ob und inwieweit der Resource-based View eine prinzipiell geeignete Theorie ist, um den Ablauf von Patenten beschreiben und erklären zu können. Die theoretisch abgeleiteten Aussagen werden daher mit den Ergebnissen von zwei empirischen Fallstudien konfrontiert, um ein besseres Verständnis der komplexen Thematik „Reaktionsmöglichkeiten auf Patentabläufe“, auf die mit den grundlegenden Alternativen der Ressourcenexploitation oder der Ressourcenexploration reagiert werden kann, zu erreichen. Der vorliegende explorative Beitrag bezweckt somit die Eruierung der grundsätzlichen Zusammenhänge und die Identifikation der unternehmerischen Handlungsmöglichkeiten von Unternehmen beim Ablauf wichtiger Patente auf der Basis theoretischer und erster empirischer Ergebnisse. Hierfür wird eine theoretische Analyse mit ersten empirischen Vorstudien kombiniert, um dieses bisher noch weitgehend unerforschte Thema für nachfolgende Studien vorzubereiten.

Die methodische Durchführung der Fallstudien orientierte sich an den klassischen Beiträgen und methodischen Empfehlungen zur Durchführung von Case Study Research, wie sie von Eisenhardt (1989), Yin (2003) sowie Eisenhardt und Graebner (2007) gegeben wurden. Die Auswahl der Unternehmen war motiviert davon, dass gerade in der Pharmaindustrie Patente als Imitationsschutz eine viel größere Bedeutung als in anderen Branchen haben (vgl. Levin et al. 1987). Es erschien den Autoren lohnenswert, gerade in dieser Branche Reaktionsmuster auf Patentabläufe zu untersuchen. Innerhalb der Branchen haben wir forschungsintensive Pharmafirmen (keine Generikahersteller, keine Firmen, deren Fokus auf wenig forschungsintensiven, nicht rezeptpflichtigen, frei verkäuflichen Over the Counter-Pharmazeutika liegt) ausgewählt. Denn forschende Pharmaunternehmen sind von Patentabläufen stark negativ betroffen, während Generikahersteller von Patentabläufen profitieren. Es wurden gezielt deutsche forschende Pharmahersteller angesprochen. Nach Gewinnung von zwei kooperierenden Firmen wurde auf die Akquisition weiterer Firmen bewusst verzichtet. Das Ziel der Studie (Explorierung eines empirischen Feldes, erste Konfrontation vorhandener Theorien und ihrer Empfehlungen mit der unternehmerischen Praxis) ist mit zwei Fallstudien erreichbar. In jedem Unternehmen wurde 1 Interview durchgeführt. Es wurde dabei darauf geachtet, dass die Interviewpartner thematisch einschlägig waren, d.h. mit dem Ablauf wichtiger Patente konfrontiert waren und in ihrer Position auch die Reaktion des Unternehmens auf den Patentablauf mitgestalten konnten.

Zum Pharmageschäft des Unternehmens 1: Der Geschäftsbereich Pharma ist eines der größten Pharmaunternehmen Deutschlands; er erzielt einen Umsatz von mehr als 1 Mrd. EUR (ohne das OTC-Geschäft) im Geschäftsjahr 2007. Weltweit gehört das Unternehmen zu den 30 größten Pharmaherstellern. Interviewpartner war der stellvertretende Leiter des Unternehmensbereich Pharmaceuticals, Finanzen/Kooperationen. Das Interview wurde am 5.8.2004 durchgeführt; es dauerte von 14.00 bis 15.50 Uhr.

Zum Unternehmensbereich Pharma des Unternehmens 2: Unternehmen B ist eines der ältesten pharmazeutisch-chemischen Unternehmen der Welt. Es handelt sich hierbei um einen breit diversifizierten Mischkonzern mit zwei Hauptgeschäftsfeldern. Der Unternehmensbereich Pharma erzielte im Geschäftsjahr 2007 einen Umsatz von mehr als 1 Mrd. Euro. Der Geschäftsbereich Pharma gehört damit zu den 100 größten Pharmaunternehmen weltweit. Der Interviewpartner war der Leiter von Patents Pharmaceuticals, Corporate Legal & Intellectual Property. Das Interview wurde am 8.10.2004 durchgeführt; es dauerte von 13:00 bis 14:50 Uhr.

Die Interviews basierten auf einem semistrukturierten Fragebogen mit 20 Fragen, der vorab den Interviewpartnern übermittelt wurde. Die Fragen wurden aus dem theoretischen Fundament des Forschungsprojektes (Resource-based View) und dem von beiden Autoren vorab erarbeiteten (Literaturstudium) Verständnis über die ökonomischen Grundlagen, Innovationsprozesse und Marktstrukturen der Pharmaindustrie entwickelt. Während der Interviews wurden die Antworten der Interviewpartner dokumentiert, auf Tonbandaufnahmen wurde verzichtet. Die Interviews fanden in beiden Fällen am Stammsitz des Unternehmens in Deutschland statt, wo auch Teile der Pharmaforschung und zentrale Unternehmensfunktionen bei beiden Unternehmen angesiedelt sind. Die Interviews wurden bei Unternehmen A allein von einem Autor, bei Unternehmen B von beiden Autoren gemeinsam durchgeführt. Die Interviewprotokolle wurden anhand von weiteren Dokumenten und Unterlagen, anhand von Geschäftsberichten und Berichten in der Wirtschaftspresse über diese beiden Unternehmen überprüft und vervollständigt. Die Verschriftlichung der Interviewergebnisse orientierte sich an den Fragen des Fragebogens, so dass sich zwei strukturell sehr ähnliche Fallstudien ergaben, was die Vergleichbarkeit der beiden Fallstudien erleichterte. Es erfolgte eine kritische Durchsicht und Freigabe der Interviewprotokolle durch die Interviewpartner, die in beiden Fällen auf der strikten Anonymisierung der Interviewergebnisse bestanden. Ergebnis waren zwei Unternehmensfallstudien mit einem Umfang von 12 Seiten (Unternehmen A) bzw. 6 Seiten (Unternehmen B). Die Interpretation der Fallstudien erfolgte durch vergleichende Gegenüberstellung der beiden Firmen und unter Bezugnahme auf den Resource-based View of the Firm.

5. Wesentliche Ergebnisse der Fallstudien und Unterschiede zwischen den untersuchten Unternehmen

Wesentliche Ergebnisse der beiden Fallstudien sind in Tabelle 2 zusammengefasst.

Es werden deutliche Unterschiede, aber auch Gemeinsamkeiten zwischen den beiden Unternehmen erkennbar, wie sie auf den Ablauf wichtiger Patente reagieren. Unternehmen A setzt neben der Forschung sehr stark auf den Schutz der nicht mehr patentgeschützten Medikamente durch Vertriebsnetze und Aufbau von Markennamen als komplementäre Ressourcen. Für Unternehmen B haben komplementäre Ressourcen eine deutlich geringere Bedeutung. Beide Unternehmen stimmen aber darin überein, dass sie die Schutzmöglichkeiten gegen Nachahmer insgesamt als unzureichend einschätzen.

Die Durchführung inkrementeller und radikaler Pharmainnovationen besitzt in beiden Unternehmen, was typisch für die forschungsintensive Pharmaindustrie ist, hohe Priorität. Deutliche Unterschiede sind aber beim Aufbau neuer Geschäftsfelder erkennbar. Unternehmen A setzt hier auf OTC-Medikamente (keine Forschungsarbeit erforderlich, dafür Markenführung für Medikamente, die wie Konsumgüter vermarktet werden), bei denen es seine Marketingkompetenz als Wettbewerbsvorteil einbringen kann. Unternehmen B setzt hier auf den Aufbau eines eigenen Generikageschäftes, das sehr preis- und kostensensitiv ist, bei denen das Unternehmen seine Forschungskompetenz aber nicht als Wettbewerbsvorteil einbringen kann. Gesamtbeurteilung: Unternehmen A setzt relativ gleichmäßig auf Nutzung und Verteidigung bestehender Medikamente und gleichzeitig auf die Erforschung neuer Medikamente. Unternehmen B setzt insgesamt stärker auf eine forschungsorientierte Strategie, die das Erzielen neuer Innovationsvorsprünge bezweckt, vernachlässigt die Verteidigung bestehender Medikamente aber nicht. Gemeinsam ist beiden Unternehmen, dass sie sowohl Exploitation als auch Exploration nach Ablauf wichtiger Patente betreiben (aber mit unterschiedlichen Gewichtungen und Schwerpunktsetzungen).

Unternehmen A	Merkmale und Charakteristika im Pharmabereich	Unternehmen B
	1) Ressourcenexploitation	
gering	Bedeutung komplexer Technologie als Schutzmechanismus (Ausnahme: Gentechnik)?	gering
hoch	Bedeutung komplementärer Ressourcen als Schutzmechanismus?	mittel
hoch	Bedeutung einer Patentverlängerung ergänzendes Schutzzertifikat)?	hoch
hoch	Bedeutung des Markenaufbaus?	mittel
hoch	Bedeutung von Geschäftsgeheimnissen?	hoch
hoch	Bedeutung von Gerichtsprozessen?	gering
schlecht	Gesamtbeurteilung der Schutzmöglichkeiten nach Ablauf eines Wirkstoffpatentes?	schlecht
	2) Ressourcenexploration	
hoch	Bedeutung inkrementaler Pharmainnovationen (Lifecycle Management)	hoch
hoch	Bedeutung radikaler Pharmainnovationen?	hoch
Rezeptfreie Arzneimittel (Marketingkompetenz)	Diversifikation: Neue Geschäftsfelder?	Generika (Kosten/Preis)
	3) Gesamtbeurteilung	
Mischstrategie (Exploitation und Exploration relativ gleichmäßig)	Strategie (Exploitation und/oder Exploration)?	Mischstrategie (Fokus auf Exploration)
Pharmavertrieb, Marken, Marketing	Primäre Orientierung der Schutzstrategie?	Forschung, neue Medikamente

Tabelle 2: Zusammengefasste Ergebnisse der beiden empirischen Fallstudien im Überblick

Nachfolgend werden noch einige ergänzende Erläuterungen zum besseren Verständnis der empirischen Ergebnisse aus den beiden Fallstudien gegeben.

5.1 Ressourcenexploitation nach Ablauf von Patenten in der Pharmaindustrie

5.1.1 Imitationsschutz durch Merkmale der Technologie

Auf die Frage, ob eine komplexe Technologie, die der Wirkstoffentwicklung und -herstellung zugrunde liegt, einen wirksamen Schutz gegen Imitation darstellt, antworteten beide befragten Unternehmen, dass eine komplexe Technologie kaum wirksam vor Imitationen schützt. Beide Unternehmen haben aber als Ausnahme hierzu genannt, dass der Einsatz von Gentechnik in der Arzneimittelentwicklung und –

herstellung ein wirksames oder sogar sehr wirksames Instrument zum Schutz vor Imitation ist. Insofern lässt sich vermuten, dass die kausale Ambiguität um bestimmte (aber nicht um alle) technologische Kompetenzen herum zur Verteidigungsfähigkeit der nicht mehr patentbasierten Wettbewerbsvorteile in der Pharmaindustrie einen Beitrag leisten kann.

5.1.2 Imitationsschutz durch Kontrolle komplementärer Ressourcen und Kompetenzen

Die Bedeutung komplementärer Ressourcen zum Schutz vor Imitation wurde von den beiden befragen Unternehmen unterschiedlich eingestuft. Während Unternehmen A komplementären Ressourcen bei der Abwehr von Imitatoren eine große Bedeutung zuspricht, haben für Unternehmen B komplementäre Ressourcen nur eine mittlere Bedeutung.

Gerade bei der Bedeutung komplementärer Ressourcen lassen sich deutliche Unterschiede zwischen den befragten Unternehmen feststellen. Dies zeigen die nachfolgend wiedergegebenen Ergebnisse aus den Interviewprotokollen:

Bedeutung komplementärer Ressourcen bei Unternehmen A:

Unternehmen A beurteilt die Bedeutung der komplementären Ressourcen, um sich nach dem Ablauf des Patentschutzes Marktanteile erhalten zu können und sich vor Imitationen zu schützen, in einer sehr differenzierten Weise. Insgesamt hält Unternehmen A komplementäre Ressourcen beim Schutz gegen Imitation für wichtig.

Die Kontrolle über knappe Produktionskapazitäten bietet nach Ansicht von Unternehmen A keinen Schutz gegen Imitation. Die chemische Zusammensetzung der Medikamente und die Herstellverfahren sind in der Branche bekannt. Unternehmen A hält eine Verengung der Produktionskapazitäten, um den Markt zu schützen, für nicht machbar.

Auch die enge und exklusive Zusammenarbeit mit Wirkstofflieferanten gibt Unternehmen A keinen Schutz gegen Imitation, da die Inhaltsstoffe und Herstellverfahren für Medikamente in der Branche bekannt sind.

Ein sehr wichtiger Schutzhebel gegen Imitatoren ist die hohe Qualität und Dichte des Vertriebsnetzes von Unternehmen A. Konkurrenten ohne ein gut ausgebautes Vertriebsnetz sind bei der Imitation behindert. Ein gut ausgebautes Vertriebsnetz ist nach Ablauf des Wirkstoffpatentes sehr wichtig, um Marktanteile zu halten. Denn der Arzt ist der Point of Sale, der durch sein Verschreibungsverhalten für Unternehmen A die Nachfrage generiert (im Gegensatz dazu das OTC-Geschäft, das auf Werbung basiert und von freien Kaufentscheidungen der Endverbraucher lebt). Aufgabe des Vertriebsnetzes ist es dabei, den Arzt an die Medikamente von Unternehmen A zu binden. Dies geschieht über Symposia, Kongresse, Events, sowie eine in langen Jahren aufgebaute Vertrauensbeziehung zwischen Arzt und Pharmavertreter. Auf diese Bindung des Arztes arbeitet Unternehmen A während der Patentlaufzeit 20 Jahre lang hin. Nach Ablauf des Patentes auf den Wirkstoff wird die erzeugte Bindung des Arztes sehr wichtig, um Imitation zu erschweren. Die bestehende Beziehung zum Arzt und die Beratung des Arztes durch den Außendienst haben für Unternehmen A dementsprechend eine sehr hohe Bedeutung.

Bestehende Kontakte zu Pharmagroßhändlern und Apotheken (der Vertriebsschiene für Pharmazeutika) haben für Unternehmen A keine Bedeutung als Schutzmechanismus gegen Imitation bzw. Imitatoren.

Die Zusammenarbeit mit und Kontakte zu forschenden Krankenhäusern sind für Unternehmen A beim Schutz gegen Imitation sehr wichtig. Zum einen sind die Krankenhäuser Teil der Vertriebsschiene für Pharmazeutika, die direkt für oder gegen den Einsatz von Medikamenten entscheiden, und bei den klinischen Studien für neue Medikamente arbeitet Unternehmen A mit den forschenden Krankenhäusern eng zusammen.

Bedeutung komplementärer Ressourcen bei Unternehmen B:

Unternehmen B beurteilt die Bedeutung der komplementären Ressourcen, um sich nach dem Ablauf des Patentschutzes Marktanteile erhalten zu können und sich vor Imitationen zu schützen, in einer sehr differenzierten Weise und teilweise deutlich geringer als Unternehmen A.

Die Kontrolle über knappe Produktionskapazitäten (die eigenen und die von Auftragnehmern) bietet im Moment einen hohen Schutz gegen Imitation.

Die enge und exklusive Zusammenarbeit mit Wirkstofflieferanten gibt Unternehmen B keinen Schutz gegen Imitation. Wirkstofflieferanten streben nach der maximalen Auslastung ihrer Kapazitäten und wollen daher keine exklusive Verträge mit einem bestimmten Hersteller.

Der Qualität und Dichte des Vertriebsnetzes als Schutzinstrument gegen Imitation misst Unternehmen B eine mittlere Bedeutung zu.

Die Bedeutung bestehender Kontakte zu Ärzten wird, im Gegensatz zu früher, als gering eingeschätzt. Die Ärzte sind heute vor allem durch gesetzliche Regelungen, Budgetrestriktionen u. ä. in ihrem Verschreibungsverhalten stärkeren Restriktionen ausgesetzt als früher, so dass bei den Ärzten Generikahersteller heute ebenso akzeptiert sind wie die Hersteller von Originalpräparaten.

Als Schutzmechanismus gegen Imitation bzw. Imitatoren haben bestehende Kontakte zu Pharmagroßhändlern und Apotheken (der Vertriebsschiene für Pharmazeutika) für Unternehmen B eine mittlere Bedeutung. Besonders wichtig sei es, die Präsenz des Medikaments beim Großhändler zu sichern und in der Listung weit vorn zu stehen. Ein oberer Listenplatz ist deshalb von Bedeutung, weil die Apotheken meist via Internet bestellen und oben gelistete Medikamente die besseren Absatzchancen haben.

Die Zusammenarbeit mit und Kontakte zu forschenden Krankenhäusern sind für Unternehmen B von geringer Bedeutung, wenn es darum geht, Wirkstoffe gegen Imitatoren zu verteidigen.

5.1.3 Imitationsschutz durch sonstige abwehrende Maßnahmen, vor allem aus dem System intellektueller Eigentumsrechte

Bei den beiden befragten Unternehmen ergaben sich folgende Ergebnisse bezüglich der Bedeutung sonstiger, vor allem aus dem System intellektueller Eigentumsrechte resultierender Abwehrmöglichkeiten gegenüber Imitationen:

Für beide Unternehmen hat es große Bedeutung, ein ergänzendes Schutzzertifikat für das auslaufende Patent zu beantragen, um so die Patentlaufzeit für den Wirkstoff zu verlängern.

Der frühzeitige Aufbau einer Marke bietet für Unternehmen A einen hohen, für Unternehmen B nur einen durchschnittlichen Schutz gegen Imitationen.

Beide Unternehmen halten Geschäftsgeheimnisse, die die Entwicklung und den Herstellungsprozess eines Wirkstoffs/Arzneimittels betreffen, für insgesamt gut geeignet, um sich gegen Imitationen zu schützen.

Unternehmen A spricht Gerichtsprozessen, die das Patent verteidigen bzw. den Markteintritt von Generikaherstellern verzögern, eine hohe, Unternehmen B hingegen nur eine mittlere Bedeutung zu.

Insgesamt kommen beide Unternehmen durchaus zu differierenden Einschätzungen. Die Vorhersage der Ressourcenökonomik, dass auch sonstige Maßnahmen zum Imitationsschutz geeignet sind, kann der empirische Befund aus den zwei Fallstudien aber insgesamt nicht widerlegen.

5.2 Ressourcenexploration nach Ablauf von Patenten in der Pharmaindustrie

5.1.2 Inkrementale Innovation in der Pharmaindustrie (Lifecycle Management)

Beide Unternehmen messen dem Lifecycle Management eine sehr hohe Bedeutung bei. Die verschiedenen Möglichkeiten und Ansatzpunkte zu inkrementaler Produktinnovation[15] im Rahmen des Lifecycle Managements werden von den befragten Unternehmen differenziert beurteilt.

5.2.2 Radikale Innovationen in der Pharmaindustrie

Neben inkrementalen Innovationen streben beide befragten Unternehmen auch nach radikal innovativen Pharmazeutika. Dies äußert sich in den sehr hohen FuE-Ausgaben beider Firmen und dem Bestreben, Blockbuster mit großem Weltmarktpotenzial und grundlegend neue Pharmazeutika mit hohem Therapienutzen zu entwickeln.

---

15 Wirkstoffe, deren Patent abgelaufen ist, werden systematisch variiert und einer weiteren Nutzung zugeführt, um einen neuen Patentschutz zu erlangen.

5.2.3 Aufbau neuer Geschäftsfelder unter Nutzung vorhandener Ressourcen und Kompetenzen

Dem Aufbau neuer Geschäftsfelder als Reaktion auf den Patentablauf messen die beiden befragten Unternehmen eine mittlere Bedeutung bei. Auffällig sind hier die Unterschiede in der Unternehmensstrategie, während Unternehmen A sich auf den weiteren Ausbau seines Geschäfts mit verschreibungsfreien OTC-Markenpräparaten konzentrieren möchte (wobei es seine Marketingkompetenzen als Wettbewerbsvorteil einbringen kann), konzentriert sich Unternehmen B auf den Ausbau des kosten- und preissensitiven Generikageschäftes, das es aber 2 Jahre später an einen Wettbewerber veräußert hat. Hierin zeigt sich die auch in der Pharmaindustrie in den letzten Jahren deutlich erkennbare Tendenz zur Konzentration auf das Kerngeschäft und die Kernkompetenzen des Unternehmens.

6. Eignung des Resource-based View of the Firm für die Erklärung von Managementherausforderungen beim Ablauf von Patenten

In der Praxis werden Exploitation und Exploration im Regelfall kombiniert eingesetzt. Dies deckt sich auch mit den Ergebnissen der empirischen Untersuchung von Levin et al. (1987), die sowohl Maßnahmen mit Exploitations- als auch Explorationscharakter als Schutzstrategien gegen Imitation herausgearbeitet hat. Wie der Beitrag aus einer ressourcentheoretischen Perspektive zeigt, realisieren Pharmaunternehmen komplexe Bündel aus exploitativen und explorativen Maßnahmen. Als Reaktionsmuster auf den Ablauf wichtiger Patente wurde offenbar, dass die beiden interviewten Firmen auf eine firmenindividuelle Kombination von Exploitationsmaßnahmen (Abwehr von Imitatoren) und Explorationsmaßnahmen (Erzielung neuer Wettbewerbsvorsprünge durch inkrementelle und/oder radikale Pharmainnovationen oder durch Aufbau neuer Geschäftsfelder jenseits des forschungsintensiven Pharmageschäftes) setzten. Dabei überwiegt bei den beiden befragten Unternehmen deutlich die Exploration neuer Ressourcenkombinationen als Antwort auf den Ablauf wichtiger Patente. Beide untersuchten Unternehmen haben aber eine einseitige Orientierung nur in Richtung Exploitation (Gefahr der Kompetenzfalle) oder nur in Richtung Exploration (Gefahr der Innovationsfalle, d.h. Generierung vieler Ideen, die nur unzureichend umgesetzt und verwertet werden) vermieden (vgl. hierzu auch Hobus und Busch 2011: 189). Bei der strategischen Bestimmung des Mischungsverhältnisses zwischen Exploration und Exploitation spielen bei beiden Unternehmen insbesondere die komplementären Ressourcen eine wichtige Rolle. Denn komplementäre Ressourcen können jenseits des auslaufenden Patentes verteidigungsfähige Wettbewerbsvorteile generieren. Fehlen dem Unternehmen hingegen solche komplementären Ressourcen oder geben sie, wie bei den beiden untersuchten Pharmaunternehmen, nur einen schwachen Schutz gegen Nachahmer, dann wird die strategische Option der fortgesetzten Ressourcenexploitation schwer realisierbar und es bleibt den Unternehmen nur eine explorationsorientierte Vorwärtsstrategie als hauptsächliche Handlungsoption. Die Rolle komplementärer Ressourcen bei der Bestimmung des Verhältnisses von

Exploration und Exploitation ist bisher nach Kenntnis der Verfasser nur wenig untersucht worden. Hierin bietet sich eine Möglichkeit für zukünftige Forschungsanstrengungen im strategischen Ressourcenmanagement.

Insgesamt haben beide Fallstudienunternehmen in den Interviews die Ansicht geäußert, dass es insgesamt betrachtet nur schlechte Möglichkeiten gibt, um einen Wirkstoff nach Patentablauf wirksam vor Imitationen zu schützen. Dieses Ergebnis ist insgesamt überraschend: Es widerspricht zum einen einzelnen Schutzmöglichkeiten, die von den Interviewpartnern bei den vorigen Fragen mehrfach als verfügbar und durchaus wirksam beurteilt wurden. Es widerspricht zum anderen den theoretischen Vorhersagen des Resource-based View, die durchaus Ansatzpunkte zur Verteidigung gegen Nachahmer erkennen lassen. Diese Widersprüche können aus Sicht der Verfasser wie folgt erklärt werden: Die Interviewpartner konzedierten, dass sie Gewinnrückgänge von bis zu 80 % nach dem Patentablauf hinnehmen mussten. Angesichts der Tatsache, dass besonders erfolgreiche Pharmafirmen Umsatzrenditen von 15 bis 25% erzielen, würde ein Gewinnrückgang um die von Unternehmen A genannten 80 % bedeuten, dass Pharmaunternehmen nach Ablauf von Patenten immer noch eine Rendite erzielen, die in etwa dem gesamtwirtschaftlichen Durchschnitt von Industrie- und Dienstleistungsunternehmen entspricht. Ohne verbliebene Schutzmöglichkeiten wären solche Gewinne, angesichts der sehr leichten Kopierbarkeit von nicht auf Gentechnik basierenden Pharmazeutika, vermutlich nicht erzielbar. Die theoretischen Aussagen des Resource-based View sind somit nach Ansicht der Autoren durch die festgestellten empirischen Fakten der beiden Fallstudien nicht widerlegbar.

Auch die deutlich unterschiedlichen Antworten der befragten Unternehmen zur Bedeutung komplementärer Ressourcen als Schutz gegen Imitationen sind erklärungsbedürftig. Sie reflektierten zum einen Unterschiede in der Unternehmensstrategie (primär forschungsorientierte Strategie versus forschungs- und marketingorientierte Strategie), zum anderen Unterschiede in den Einschätzungen der Interviewpartner zur künftigen Entwicklung des Pharmamarktes (z.B. zur Wirksamkeit und zu den Auswirkungen von Gesundheitsreformen). Dies verweist auf die Notwendigkeit, Aussagen zu Ressourcen und Ressourcenbündeln immer auch vor dem Hintergrund der verfolgten Unternehmensstrategie und der Entwicklungen in den relevanten Absatzmärkten zu interpretieren.

Die durchgeführten zwei empirischen Fallstudien haben die grundlegenden, aus dem Resource-based View abgeleiteten Handlungsmöglichkeiten von Unternehmen beim Ablauf wichtiger Patente im Kern nicht widerlegen können. Die wichtigsten theoretisch basierten Aussagen konnten einer ersten Spiegelung an der unternehmerischen Realität unterzogen werden. Es zeigte sich, dass eine Analyse mit dem Resource-based View zu einem besseren Verständnis der Managementprobleme beim Ablauf wichtiger Patente beitragen und einige dieser Probleme gut aufzeigen und strukturieren kann. Die Alternativen der Exploitation und Exploration sind als gedanklicher Bezugsrahmen für Managemententscheidungen rund um das Thema Patentablauf sinnvoll und hilfreich. Insbesondere ermöglicht eine Analyse mit dem Resource-based View ein besseres Verständnis der Managementprobleme beim Ablauf wichtiger Patente, gerade indem sie bei einem sehr bedeutenden Managementproblem der Unternehmenspraxis einen relevanten Teilausschnitt (Ressourcen- und Kompetenzfragen) isoliert und systematisch analysiert. Das Managementproblem „Patentablauf" ist extrem vielschichtig; seine Komplexität besteht vor allem in der Vielzahl weiterer Handlungsalternativen (z.B. Fusionen zwischen Pharmaunternehmen, die durch den Ablauf wichtiger Patente motiviert werden, Intensivierung von Kostensenkungsbestrebungen, Lizenznahme von anderen Pharmaherstellern), die für das Management besteht. Eine ressourcenökonomische Betrachtung kann und muss viele der markt- und marktstrukturbezogenen Aspekte des Entscheidungsproblems ausblenden und kann gerade deshalb den Blick für Ressourcen- und Kompetenzfragen (Ressourcenexploitation und Ressourcenexploration) nach dem Ablauf von Patenten schärfen. Auch Aspekte des Lobbying gegenüber dem Gesetzgeber (Gesundheitspolitik) und der Einflussnahme eines Pharmaunternehmens auf Regulierungs- und Zulassungsinstanzen werden bei einer streng ressourcenökonomischen Betrachtung ausgeschlossen, obwohl sie in der Praxis der Pharmaindustrie sicherlich Bedeutung haben.

Limitationen der Untersuchungsergebnisse sind in folgenden Punkten begründet: Unsere Ergebnisse basieren auf zwei Fallstudien. Mit einer so geringen Zahl an Fallstudien könnten Phänomene der betrieblichen Praxis (Patentabläufe) besser verstanden, auch Theorien weiterentwickelt werden, aber keine empirischen Tests und Überprüfungen durchgeführt werden. Zudem ist die Pharmaindustrie hinsichtlich zentraler Charakteristika ihrer Innovationsprozesse (sehr lange Dauer, hohe Kosten, extreme Risiken bei der Entwicklung bahnbrechend neuer Pharmazeutika) eine extreme Industrie. Die Innovationsprozesse in anderen Industrien (z.B. Maschinenbau, Chemieindustrie) weisen deutlich andere Charakteristika auf. Auch die komplementären Ressourcen und die Bedeutung von Patenten als Schutzmechanismus haben in anderen Industrien einen anderen Stellenwert. Die Forschungsergebnisse sind somit nicht direkt übertragbar auf andere Branchen und Unternehmen in diesen Branchen.

Es stellt sich in künftigen Forschungsarbeiten die großzahlig-quantitativ zu untersuchende Frage, welche Strategie bzw. Strategiekombination (Exploration, Exploitation, kombinierte Strategie) unter welchen externen Umwelt- und internen Unternehmensgegebenheiten die erfolgreichere (z.B. unter den Aspekten Umsatzwachstum, Gewinn, Börsenwert des Unternehmens) ist. Langfristig muss sowohl Exploration als auch Exploitation erfolgen, weil mit Hilfe des Abschöpfens von Gewinnen (Exploitation) aus bereits eingeführten Arzneimitteln die Entwicklung neuer Arzneimittel (Exploration) finanziert wird. Fraglich ist aber, welches genaue Mischungsverhältnis von Exploitation und Exploration für das einzelne Pharmaunternehmen (und andere Unternehmen aus anderen Industrien, die mit Patentabläufen konfrontiert werden) zu beobachten ist bzw. welche markt- und unternehmensbezogenen Einflussfaktoren den Mix bestimmen.

Literatur

Abernathy, W.J. (1978): The Productivity Dilemma, 1. Aufl., Baltimore, MD.

Al-Mawali, N. (2005): Bilateral intra-industry trade flows and intellectual property rights protection: first empirical evidence. In: Applied Economics Letters, 12: 823-828.

Barney, J. (1991): Firm Resources and Sustained Competitive Advantage. In: Journal of Management, 17: 99-120.

Barney, J. (1994): Commentary: Brumagim, A.L.: Hierarchy of Corporate Resources. In: Shrivastava, P./Huff, A.S./Dutton, J.E. (Hrsg.): Advances in Strategic Management. Greenwich, Connecticut/London, England, 10a: 113-125.

Benner, M.J. /Tushman, M.L. (2003): Exploitation, Exploration and Process Management: The Productivity Dilemma Revisited. In: Academy of Management Review, 28: 238-256.

Birkinshaw, J./Gibson, C. (2004): Building Ambidexterity into an Organization. In: MIT Sloan Management Review, 45: 47-55.

Botazzi, G./Dosi, G./Lippi, M./Pamolli, F./Riccarboni, M. (2001): Innovation and corporate growth in the evolution of the drug industry. In: International Journal of Industrial Organization, 19: 1161-1187.

Breyer, F./Zweifel, P.S./Kifmann, M. (2003), Gesundheitsökonomie, Springer: Berlin.

Burr, W. (2002): Service Engineering bei technischen Dienstleistungen, 1. Aufl., Deutscher-Universitäts-Verlag: Wiesbaden.

Burr, W. (2004): Innovationen in Organisationen, 1. Aufl., Kohlhammer: Stuttgart.

Burr, W./Musil, A./Stephan, M./Werkmeister, C. (2004): Unternehmensführung, 1. Aufl., Vahlen: München.

Burr, W./Stephan, M./Soppe, B./Weisheit, S. (2007): Patentmanagement, 1. Aufl., Schäffer-Poeschel: Stuttgart.

Christensen, C.M. (1996): The Drivers of Vertical Disintegration. In: Division of Research: Working Papers, http://www.hbs.edu/dor/abstracts/9596/96-008htm.

Conner, K.R. (1991): A Historical Comparison of Resource-Based Theory and Five Schools of Thought within Industrial Organization Economics: Do We Have a New Theory of the Firm? In: Journal of Management, 17: 121-154.

Cool, K./Dierickx, I. (1994), Comentary: Schoemaker, P.J.H./Amit, R.: Investments in Strategic Assets. In: Shrivastava, P./Huff, A.S./Dutton, J.E. (Hrsg.): Advances in Strategic Management. Greenwich, Connecticut/London, England, 10a: 35-44.

De Carolis, D. M. (2003): Competencies and Imitability in the Pharmaceutical Industry: An Analysis of Their Relationship with Firm Performance. In: Journal of Management, 29: 27-50.

Danneels, E. (2002): The Dynamics of Product Innovation and Firm Competences. In: Strategic Management Journal, 23: 1095–1121.

DiMasi, J.A./Hansen, R.W./Grabowski, H.G. (2003): The Price of Innovation: New Estimates of Drug Development costs. In: Journal of Health Economics, 22: 151-185.

Duncan, R.B. (1976): The ambidextrous organization: designing dual structures for innovation". In: Kilmann, R.H./Pondy, L.R./Slevin, D.P. (Hrsg.): The Management of Organization Design: Strategies and Implementation, 1: 167–188.

Eisenhardt, K.M. (1989): Building theories from case study research. In: Academy of Management Review, 14, 4: 532–550.

Eisenhardt, K.M. /Graebner, M.E. (2007): Theory building from cases: Opportunities and challenges. In: Academy of Management Journal, 50, 1: 25-32.

Encaoua, D./Guellec, D./Martinez, C. (2006): Patent systems for encouraging innovation: Lessons from economic analysis. In: Research Policy, 35: 1423-1440.

Eriksen, B./Mikkelsen, J. (1996): Competitive advantage and the concept of core competence. In: Foss, N. und Knudsen, C. (Hrsg.): Towards a competence theory of the firm, 1. Aufl., London: 54-74.

Fischer, D./Breitenbach, J. (2003): Die Pharmaindustrie. Einblick-Durchblick-Perspektiven. Spektrum Akademischer Verlag: Heidelberg/Berlin.

Franck, E. (1991): Künstliche Intelligenz: Eine grundlegende Diskussion der Einsatzmöglichkeiten und –grenzen, Mohr: Tübingen.

Freiling, J./Reckenfelderbäumer, M. (2007): Markt und Unternehmung, 2. Aufl., Gabler: Wiesbaden.

Gassmann, O./Bader, M.A. (2006): Patentmanagement, 1. Aufl., Springer: Berlin.

Gerybadze, A. (2004): Technologie- und Innovationsmanagement, 1. Aufl., Vahlen: München.

Ghemawat, P./Costa, J. (1993): The Organizational Tension Between Static and Dynamic Efficiency. In: Strategic Management Journal, 14: 59-73.

Glass, A.J. (2000): Costly R&D and intellectual property rights protection. In: Technology Management, 19: 179-193.

Gonzalez-Alvarez, N./Munoz-Doyague, M.F. (2006): Causal ambiguity of technological competencies, human resource practices and competitive advantage. In: International Journal Technology Management, 35: 308-328.

Gonzalez-Alvarez, N./Nieto-Antolin, M. (2005): Protection and internal transfer of technological competencies: The role of causal ambiguity. In: Industrial Management & Data Systems, 105: 841-856.

Grabowski, H. (2002): Patents, Innovation and Access To New Pharmaceuticals. In: Journal of International Economic Law, 849-860.

Grant, R.M. (1991): The Resource-Based Theory of Competitive Advantage: Implications for Strategy Formulation. In: California Management Review, 33, 3: 114-135.

Guminski, W./Rauland, M. (2002): Produktlebenszyklus und die Möglichkeiten seiner Gestaltung. In: Schöffski, O./Fricke, F./Guminski, W./Hartmann, W. (Hrsg.): Pharmabetriebslehre, Berlin u. a.: 229-242.

He, Z.L./Wong, P.K. (2004): Exploration vs. Exploitation: An Empirical Test of the Ambidexterity Hypothesis. In: Organization Science, 15, 4: 481-494.

Henderson, R./Cockburn, I. (1994): Measuring competence? Exploring Firm Effects in Pharmaceutical R&D. In: Strategic Management Journal, 15: 63-84.

Heskett, J.L. (1987): Establishing strategic direction: Aligning elements of strategy. In: Harvard Business School Note # 9-388-033.

Hill, C.W.L./Deeds, D.L. (1996): The importance of industry structure for the determination of firm profitability: A neo-Austrian perspective. In: Journal of Management Studies, 33, 4: 429-451.

Hobus, B./Busch, M.W. (2011): Organisationale Ambidextrie – Organizational Ambidexterity. In: DBW, 70, 2: 189-193.

Hofmann, S. (2007): Konzerne ringen um Pharmamarkt: Hersteller von Originalmedikamenten greifen Generikabranche mit Rabattverträgen an. In: Handelsblatt, 248: 1.

Hofmann, S. (2007a): Pharma-Riesen specken ab: Nachahmer-Produkte setzen Branche unter Druck: Weltweit 50 000 Arbeitsplätze in Gefahr. In: Handelsblatt, 236: 1.

Horii R./Iwaisako, T. (2007): Economic Growth with Imperfect Protection of Intelleual Property Rights. In: Journal of Economics, 90: 45-85.

Kale, D./Little, S. (2007): From Imitation to Innovation: The Evolution of R&D Capabilities and Learning Processes in the Indian Pharmaceutical Industry. In: Technology Analysis & Strategic Management, 19: 589-609.

Kanwar, S. (2007): Business enterprise R&D, technological change, and intellectual property protection. In: Economic Letters, 96: 120-126.

Konlechner, S.W./Güttel, W.H. (2009): Kontinuierlicher Wandel mit Ambidexterity. Vorhandenes Wissen nutzen und gleichzeitig neues entwickeln. In: zfo, 78, 1: 45-53.

Lambertini, L./Tedeschi, P. (2007): On the Social Desirability of Patents for Sequential Innovations in a Vertically Differentiated Market. In: Journal of Economics, 90, 2: 193-214.

Lee, J. (2003): Innovation and Strategic Divergence: An Empirical Study of the U.S. Pharmaceutical Industry from 1920 to 1960. In: Management Science, 49: 143-159.

Levin, R.C./Klevorick, A.K./Nelson, R.R./Winter, S.G. (1987): Appropriating the Returns from Industrial Research and Development. In: Brookings Papers on Economic Activity, 3: 783-831.

Levinthal, D. (1995): Strategic Management and the Exploration of Diversity. In: Montgomery,

C.A. (Hrsg.): Resource-based and Evolutionary Theories of the Firm, Boston u. a.: 19-42.

Magee, S. (1977): Multinational Corporations, the Industry Technology Cycle and Development. In: Journal of World Trade Law, 11: 297-321.

Mahoney, J.T./Pandian, J.R. (1992): The Resource-based View within the Conversation of Strategic Management. In: Strategic Management Journal, 13: 363-380.

March, J.G. (1991): Exploration and Exploitation in Organizational Learning. In: Organization Science, 2, 1: 71-87.

Marengo, L. (1994): Knowledge Distribution and Coordination on Organizations: On some Social Aspect of the Exploration-Exploitation Trade-Off. In: Revue Internationale de Systemique, 7: 533-571.

Montgomery, C.A. (1995): Of Diamonds and Rust: A New Look at Resources. In: Montgomery, C.A. (Hrsg.): Resource-bases and Evolutionary Theories of the Firm. Boston u. a.: 251-268.

Mukherjee, A. (2006): Patents and R&D with imitation and licensing. In: Economic Letters, 93: 196-201.

Oshba, M. /Figueiredo, P.N. (2007): Collaborating to compete: A search into capabilities and strategic alliances in the pharmaceutical industry. In: Journal of Technology Management & Innovation, 2, 2: 18-30.

Polanyi, M. (1962): Personal Knowledge. The University of Chicago Press: Chicago.

Peteraf, M.E./Bergen, M.E. (2003): Scanning dynamic competitive landscapes: A market-based and resource-based framework. In: Strategic Management Journal, 24: 1027-1041.

Qian, Y. (2007): Do National Patent Laws Stimulate Domestic Innovation in a Global Patenting Environment: A Cross-Country Analysis of Pharmaceutical Patent Protection, 1978-2002. In: The Review of Economics and Statistics, 89: 436-453.

Rothaermel, F.T/Deeds, D.L. (2001): More good things are not necessary better: An empirical study of strategic alliances, experience effects, and innovative output in high-technology start-ups. In: Academy of Management Proceedings, TIM: F 1.

Rothaermel, F.T/Deeds, D.L. (2004): Exploration and exploitation alliances in biotechnology: a system of new product development. In: Strategic Management Journal, 25: 201-221.

Rothaermel, F.T./Hess, A.M. (2007): Building Dynamic Capabilities: Innovation driven by individual-, firm-, and network-level effects. In: Organization Science, 18, 6: 898-921.

Rumelt, R.P. (1984): Towards a Strategic Theory of the Firm. In: Lamb, R.B. (Hrsg.): Competitive Strategic Management, New York: 556-570.

Sanchez, R./Heene, A./Thomas, H. (1996): Introduction. Towards the Theory and Practice of Competence-based Competition. In: Sanchez, R./Heene, A./Thomas, H. (Hrsg.): Dynamics of Competence-based Competition: Theory and Practice in the New Strategic Management, Oxford: 1-35.

Sanchez, R./Heene, A. (1997): Reinventing strategic management. New theory and practice for competence based competition. In: European Management Journal, 15, 3: 303-317.

Schreyögg, G./Kliesch-Eberl, M. (2007): How dynamic can organizational capabilities be? Towards a dual-process model of capability dynamization. In: Stategic Management Journal, 28, 9: 913-933.

Scienceindustries (2011): Schweizerische chemische und pharmazeutische Industrie, Zürich, Download am 10.10.2011 unter: http://www.sgci.ch/plugin/article/sgci/10134

Scheurer, S. (1997): Strategische Steuerung zwischen Planung und Selbstorganisation. In: Die Unternehmung, 3: 215-236.

Schoemaker, P.J.H./Amit, R. (1994): Investments in Strategic Assets. In: Shrivastava, P./Huff, A.S./Dutton, J.E. (Hrsg.): Advances in Strategic Management. Greenwich, Connecticut/London, England, 10a: 3-33.

Seidlitz, F. (2003): Die Pharma-Fehde. In: Die Welt vom 3.9.2003, S. 16.

Teece, D.J.(1992): Competition, Cooperation, and Innovation. In: Journal of Economic Behavior and Organization, 18: 1-25.

Teece, D.J./Rumelt, R.P./Dosi, G./Winter, S. (1994): Understanding Corporate Coherence: Theory and Evidence. In: Journal of Economic Behavior and Organization, 23: 1-30.

Teece, D.J. (1986): Profiting from technological innovation, in: Research Policy, 15, 6: 285-305.

Teece, D.J./Pisano, G./Shuen, A. (1997): Dynamic Capabilities and Strategic Management. In: Strategic Management Journal, 18: 509-533.

Thomke, S./Kuemmerle, W. (2002): Asset Accumulation, Interdependence and Technological Change: Evidence From Pharmaceutical Drug Discovery. In: Strategic Management Journal, 23: 619-635.

Tushman, M.L./O'Reilly, C.A. (1996): Ambidextrous Organizations: Managing Evolutionary and Revolutionary Change. In: California Management Review, 38, 4: 8-30.

VFA (Verband Forschender Arzneimittelhersteller e.V.) (1998): Innovation – Schlüssel zum Erfolg. Bonn.

VFA (Verband Forschender Arzneimittelhersteller e.V.) (2003): Forschung für das Leben. Entwicklungsprojekte für innovative Arzneimittel. Berlin.

Yin, R.K. (2003) Case study research: Design and methods, 3. Aufl., Thousand Oaks.

You, K./Katayama, S. (2005): Intellectual Property Rights Protection and Imitation: An Empirical Examination of Japanese F.D.I in China. In: Pacific Economic Review, 10: 591-604.

Zigic, K. (1997): Strategic trade policy, intellectual property rights protection and North-South trade. In: Journal of Development Economics, 61: 27-60.

Expertenwissen: Entstehungsbedingungen – Identifikation – Weitergabe und Bewahrung

Michael W. Busch und Dietrich von der Oelsnitz

Zusammenfassung

Bei der Kombination unternehmensspezifischer Inputfaktoren spielen Mitarbeiterfähigkeiten eine herausragende Rolle. Der Resource-based View hat bislang allerdings zu wenig die Genese individuellen Expertentums analysiert, obwohl die Expertise- und Hochbegabungsforschung hierzu bereits wertvolle Einsichten geliefert hat. Ziel des Beitrags ist es, anhand einer umfassenden Literaturanalyse aufzuzeigen, wie sich Expertenwissen im Zeitverlauf entwickelt, wie das für Unternehmen relevante Expertenwissen identifiziert werden kann und welche Möglichkeiten es schließlich gibt, um das Wissen und die Erfahrungen speziell altersbedingt ausscheidender Experten zu sichern bzw. zu transferieren. Hierbei werden folgende Entstehungsbedingungen von Expertise herausgearbeitet: Frühzeitige Fokussierung auf ein Spezialgebiet; bewusste Übung; Unterstützung durch Mentoren; Disziplin und Durchhaltevermögen; Selbststeuerungskompetenz; Leistungswille und Rastlosigkeit; Begeisterung, Neugierde und Offenheit für ein Thema.

Schlüsselwörter: Expertenwissen; Deliberate Practice; Identifikation von Experten; Wissens- und Erfahrungstransfer.

Abstract

The evolution of expertise has long been studied in the cognitive science of expertise and giftedness. Yet the resource-based view largely did not take notice of these findings, although the importance of knowledge, skills, and abilities of human resources as a scource of competitive advantage is widely recognized within this approach. By analyzing the conditions underlying the development of expertise we want to deepen our understanding about individual knowledge in organizations. We identify seven conditions of expertise: early beginning of training; deliberate practice; coaching and mentoring; discipline and the will power to defer gratifications; self-regulation; achievement motive; enthusiasm and curiosity. Finally, we show how expertise is identified in organizations, and also how knowledge is transferred as experts leave the organization.

Keywords: Expertise; Deliberate Practice; Identifying and Transferring Expert Knowledge

1. Einleitung

Gemäß der Sichtweise des Resource-based View (RBV) gründen Wettbewerbsvorteile letztlich in der Kombination unternehmensspezifischer Inputfaktoren, deren Ergebnisse – Sachgüter oder Dienstleistungen – sich marktseitig bewähren und von Konkurrenten nur schwer zu durchschauen bzw. zu imitieren sind (vgl. Freiling 2001: 20 ff.). Neben Strukturen, Verfahren und Technologien zählen zu diesen Ressourcen vor allem Mitarbeiter, deren eminente Bedeutung für den Erfolg von Unternehmen immer wieder herausgestellt wird (vgl. Scholz 2011: 461). Insbesondere in wissensintensiven Branchen ist die Abhängigkeit von hochqualifizierten Fachkräften sehr hoch, doch auch in der Erbringung komplexer Dienstleistungen spielt die Erfahrung von Mitarbeitern im Umgang mit Kunden eine tragende Rolle (vgl. Nissen: 2007: 6 ff.).

Ohne Zweifel anerkennt der RBV die hohe Bedeutung individueller Kompetenzen für den Unternehmenserfolg, speziell im Hinblick auf die erforderliche Anpassungs- und Lernfähigkeit (vgl. Wollersheim 2010: 13 f.). Die genaue Klärung der Entstehungsbedingungen individueller Kompetenz als Basis der unternehmerischen Kompetenz bleibt hingegen unterbelichtet: „Zum einen werden Kompetenzen (...) letztlich als situationsdeterminiert begriffen und (...) mittels Konstrukte höherer Ordnung („dynamic capabilities“ oder auch „high-level routines“) zu erklären versucht. Zum anderen führt die starke Betonung des implizit-kollektiven Charakters von (...) Kompetenz zu einer Vernachlässigung von Aspekten wie etwa Expertenwissen, Kognition, Reflexivität (...) oder auch der Motivation einzelner Akteure“ (Martin/Hansen 2010: 59). *Diese offenkundige Lücke, nämlich das Übersehen oder Übergehen individueller Kompetenz im Rahmen des Strategischen Kompetenzmanagements, gilt es zu schließen.*

Hierzu sollte der RBV verstärkt Anleihen bei der traditionsreichen Expertise- und Hochbegabungsforschung nehmen, von deren grundlegenden Erkenntnissen er profitieren kann. Expertentum (synonym: Expertenwissen, Expertise) beruht gemäß dieser Sichtweise „auf Voraussetzungen, die nicht zufällig sind, sondern das letzte Glied einer langen Entwicklungskette persönlicher Eigenschaften und Handlungsweisen bilden“ (Busch 2011: 22; vgl. auch Sternberg 2002: 62 f.). Verlässt nun ein Experte altersbedingt oder – was ebenso verstärkt zu beobachten ist – durch Abwerbung von Headhuntern das Unternehmen, so gehen mit ihm nicht nur sein Fachwissen, sondern auch sein Beziehungswissen, sein Organisations- und Branchenwissen, vor allem aber seine ihn als Experten auszeichnenden Persönlichkeitsmerkmale verloren, also sein Zusammenhänge erfassender und vernetzender »Kennerblick«.

Wir betrachten nachfolgend die Aufbereitung und Weitergabe des Wissens ausscheidender Experten als eine komplexe, letztlich nie restlos zufriedenstellend lösbare Herausforderung. Dazu werden zunächst die Hintergründe und Grundmerkmale von Expertentum beschrieben. Wir wollen diese Frage an einigen Stellen »lebensnah« beantworten und ziehen daher bewusst Beispiele und wörtliche Zitate bekannter Persönlichkeiten heran. Hierauf wird die Frage geklärt, wie strategisch bedeutsame Experten im Unternehmen identifiziert werden können. Fehlt die Kenntnis, wer im eigenen Unternehmen über einen Expertenstatus verfügt und welchen Stellenwert er für das Unternehmen besitzt, so besteht die Gefahr, dass fluktuationsbedingte Kompetenzverluste unbemerkt bleiben und nachher auch niemand darüber Aufschluss zu geben vermag, wo das notwendige Fachwissen verlorengegangen ist bzw. wie es erneut entwickelt oder beschafft werden kann. Die Identifikationsphase hat also zu analysieren, wessen Wissen überhaupt von »strategischem Wert« für ein Unternehmen ist. Leicht ersetzbare oder hinfällig gewordene Kompetenzen brauchen nicht transferiert zu werden. Schließlich werden Maßnahmen zur Bewahrung und Externalisierung von Expertenwissen sowie in diesem Zusammenhang auftretende Hindernisse aufgezeigt.

Wir konzentrieren uns dabei auf das altersbedingte Ausscheiden eines Mitarbeiters, stellt diese Art der Fluktuation doch eine im Vergleich zu sonstigen Fluktuationen besser zu bewältigende Managementaufgabe dar, da Unternehmen hierüber frühzeitig Kenntnis besitzen und die Wissensteilungsbereitschaft bei diesen Mitarbeitern in der Regel ausgeprägter ist als etwa bei solchen, die noch Karriereabsichten hegen oder die unfreiwillig gehen müssen, weil ihnen gekündigt wurde. Die altersbedingte Fluktuationsbewältigung liefert durch ihre systematische Durchführung zugleich die *gestalterische Vorlage* für andere Fluktuationsfälle. Der Hauptunterschied zu anderen Fällen (vor allem Versetzungen oder Kündigungen) besteht darin, dass der Grund für das Verlassen des Unternehmens evident ist – eben altersbedingt – und daher nicht in gesonderten »Exit Interviews[1]« aufgedeckt werden muss.

Zusammenfassend soll in unserem Beitrag geklärt werden

- *was Expertenwissen ist und wie es entsteht (Kapitel 2)*
- *wie Expertenwissen im Unternehmen identifiziert werden kann (Kapitel 3) und*
- *wie Unternehmen den altersbedingten Verlust dieses Wissens durch rechtzeitig geplante und gezielt eingesetzte Transfer- und Bewahrungsmaßnahmen wenn nicht vermeiden, so doch spürbar reduzieren können (Kapitel 4).*

---

1 Die Erforschung von Exit Interviews reicht bis in die 1950er Jahre zurück (vgl. Smith/Kerr 1953). Letzten Endes ist deren Stoßrichtung aber eine andere als die von Maßnahmen zur Wissens- und Erfahrungssicherung. Exit Interviews sollen Gründe aufdecken, die Mitarbeiter dazu bewogen haben, das Unternehmen zu verlassen (z. B. fehlende Herausforderungen, keine Weiterqualifizierungsangebote, mangelnde Unterstützung, schlechtes Betriebsklima, unzureichende Bezahlung, vgl. Neal 1989: 37 f.). Daraus lassen sich dann Hinweise für organisationale bzw. bindungsbezogene Verbesserungen ableiten. Hierin ähneln Exit Interviews Ansätzen zur Messung der Kunden(un)zufriedenheit (z. B. Critical Incident Technique, Lob- und Beschwerdeanalyse).

2. Expertenwissen

2.1 Hintergrund

Die Analyse der Hintergründe überragender Leistung reicht bis zu den olympischen Wettkämpfen bei den alten Griechen zurück. Menschen haben sich seit jeher dafür interessiert, wie außergewöhnliche Taten – sei es im sportlichen, sei es im künstlerisch-handwerklichen, sei es im wissenschaftlichen Bereich – letztlich erklärt werden können. Diese »individuelle Erfolgsfaktorenforschung« hat sich dabei stets zwischen den beiden Erklärungspolen genetische Prädisposition versus gesellschaftliche Sozialisation bzw. Anlagen versus Umwelt (englisch: born or made / nature or nurture) bewegt (vgl. Tannenbaum 2000: 49 f.). Der erste Strang, d.h. die Erforschung der intellektuellen bzw. kognitiven Merkmale von Experten, wird traditionell von der *Psychologie* verfolgt; dem zweiten Strang, d.h. der Analyse der gesellschaftlichen Voraussetzungen für die Entstehung von Expertise und der Analyse der Rolle, die Experten in Gesellschaften spielen, widmet sich schwerpunktmäßig die *Soziologie* (vgl Huber 1999: 6 ff.).

Die Frage, ob Talent angeboren oder Ergebnis zahlreicher, außerhalb der Person liegender Voraussetzungen ist, konnte bis heute nicht wirklich befriedigend beantwortet werden.[2] Die aktuelle Neurowissenschaft geht von einer Verschränkung beider Bereiche aus, so dass heute weniger von einer sich ausschließenden Entweder-Oder-Logik als vielmehr von einer sich ergänzenden Sowohl-als-auch-Beziehung ausgegangen wird: „Es erfolgt zunächst eine allein durch genetische Abläufe geprägte Entwicklung. Diese wird anschließend durch Einflüsse aus der Umwelt moduliert und so weit umgestaltet, dass sie auf bestimmte Gegebenheiten passt. Die Anlage liefert das Material, an welchem die Umwelt ansetzt. Diese verändert im Feinen, was das grobe genetische Programm bereitgestellt hat" (Siefer 2009: 189 f.).

Die Entwicklung von Talent und von Expertentum lässt sich somit durch Rahmenbedingungen, Trainingsmaßnahmen und eigenes Bemühen beeinflussen, zwar nicht vorherbestimmen, aber doch indirekt steuern. Fehlt ein solcher Einfluss, so ist das Auftreten von Höchstleistung wesentlich unwahrscheinlicher. Die amerikanische Soziologin Annette Lareau spricht in diesem Zusammenhang von »konzertierter Kultivierung«. Eltern lassen ihre Kinder dabei nicht »natürlich« aufwachsen, sondern fördern sie aktiv und gezielt, machen sie mit vielfältigen Angeboten vertraut, um ihre Begabungen zu entdecken, geben ihnen Feedback und stärken ihr Selbstbewusstsein

---

2 Ein populärer Verfechter der »Talent ist kein Zufall«-These ist der amerikanische Bestsellerautor Malcolm Gladwell: Talentierte Menschen kamen „alle in den Genuss verborgener Vorteile, außergewöhnlicher Chancen und eines kulturellen Umfeldes, die es ihnen ermöglichten, anders zu lernen und zu arbeiten als andere Menschen (...) Die größte Eiche in einem Wald ist nicht nur deshalb die größte, weil sie aus der kräftigsten Eichel stammt, sondern sie ist es auch deshalb, weil ihr kein anderer Baum die Sonne genommen hat, weil die Erde tief und nährstoffreich ist, weil kein Hase den Schößling gemümmelt und kein Forstarbeiter den jungen Baum vorzeitig gefällt hat" (Gladwell 2009: 23).

(vgl. Gladwell 2009: 93 ff.; Bauer 2011: 37 f.). Sie sind zunächst der formende »Töpfer« und werden erst später zum »Gärtner«, der wachsen lässt und auf die Selbststeuerung des Kindes vertraut (vgl. Bueb 2007: 15 f.).

2.2 Begriffsbestimmung

Die Bestimmung von Experten erfolgt in der Forschung häufig im kontrastiven Vergleich zu Neulingen (Novizen) (vgl. Farrington-Darby/Wilson 2006: 25 f.). Experten nähern sich Problemen mehr aus der Vogelperspektive, sie sehen das Ganze und verstricken sich nicht wie Neulinge in Details. Dies wurde zuerst bei fortgeschrittenen Schachspielern beobachtet. „Der frappierendste Befund der Expertiseforschung ist zweifellos der Nachweis der überragenden Fähigkeit von Experten, sich an Gegenstände bzw. Konstellationen ihrer Domäne zu erinnern: Präsentiert man z.B. einem Schachmeister eine ihm unbekannte Schachposition für wenige Sekunden, so ist er in der Lage, diese perfekt oder nahezu perfekt aus dem Gedächtnis zu rekonstruieren. Ein Novize kann allenfalls fünf oder sechs Figuren erinnern" (Gruber/Mandl 1996: 20).

Eine wissenschaftlich eindeutige Definition von Expertise lässt sich bisher nur sehr schwer finden, denn die untersuchten Experten entstammen ganz unterschiedlichen Bereichen (Sport, Musik, Medizin, Mathematik), was eine Vergleichbarkeit der Ergebnisse erschwert. Ein gemeinsamer Bezugspunkt aller Definitionen ist jedoch die *komplexe Domäne*, d.h. ein abgrenzbares Aufgabengebiet, dessen Aneignung in etwa zehn Jahre in Anspruch nimmt (vgl. Kap. 2.3.2). Diese lange Anlernzeit erlaubt es, Parallelen zwischen verschiedenen Domänen aufzuzeigen. Außerdem können „triviale" Alltagskompetenzen, die prinzipiell jeder beherrscht bzw. rasch erlernen kann (z.B. Schuhe schnüren, ein Faxgerät bedienen), ausgeschlossen werden. Ein weiterer gemeinsamer Bezugspunkt betrifft die *beobachtbare Leistung* von Experten, sobald diese auf der höchsten Entwicklungsstufe angekommen sind. Experten auf der höchsten Entwicklungsstufe sind in der Lage, dauerhaft, d.h. weder zufällig noch singulär, überdurchschnittliche Leistungen innerhalb ihrer Domäne zu erbringen (vgl. Salas/Rosen 2010: 105). Expertise ist daher allgemein als *individuelle Kompetenz* zu begreifen, in der sich die Anforderungen eines komplexen Aufgabenfeldes mit dem Wissen einer Person – verstanden als ein Set an Kenntnissen und Fähigkeiten – weitgehend decken und in Form von konkreten, in der Regel fehlerfreien Arbeitsergebnissen beobachten lassen (vgl. von Krogh/Roos 1995: 62; Probst/Raub/Romhardt 2010: 23).

Diese *ergebnisbezogene* Sicht auf Expertise ist abzugrenzen von der prozessualen Betrachtung, die die Entwicklung von Expertise untersucht. Hierbei ist nochmals zu unterscheiden in die Analyse der Abfolge einzelner Entwicklungsstufen (z.B. Anfänger – Fortgeschrittener Schüler – Kompetenter Schüler – Experte – Koryphäe, vgl. etwa Dreyfus/Dreyfus 2005: 782 ff.) und den allgemeinen Entstehungsvoraussetzungen, d.h. den vielen ineinanderwirkenden Bausteinen, welche zur Evolution von Expertise beitragen. Eingrenzend sollen nachfolgend nur diese betrachtet werden.

2.3 Entstehungsvoraussetzungen von Expertise

In der Literatur werden zahlreiche Entstehungsvoraussetzungen von Expertise analysiert (vgl. Gruber/Ziegler 1996; Heller et al. 2002; Ericsson et al. 2006; Ziegler 2008). Tabelle 1 fasst die am häufigsten diskutierten Aspekte zusammen. Die Intensität der einzelnen Aspekte und ihr jeweiliges Zusammenspiel kann durchaus variieren. Ihre generelle Auftrittswahrscheinlichkeit jedoch ist sehr hoch. Sicherlich ist jede Biographie eines Experten einmalig (z.B. was die Umstände seiner Ausbildung, seinen persönlichen Hintergrund, seinen Kontakt zu bestimmten Personen oder die geschichtlichen Rahmenbedingungen seiner Entwicklung betrifft); dennoch lassen sich – ähnlich wie bei der Analyse der Handschrift in der Graphologie – wiederkehrende Muster erkennen, die es erlauben, von der individuellen Lebenssituation und Persönlichkeit zu abstrahieren. Beispielsweise wird es keinen Experten auf seinem Gebiet geben, der nicht unermüdlichen Ehrgeiz bei der Erkundung und praktischen Erschließung seines Themengebiets an den Tag gelegt hat. Auch wird es schwerlich möglich sein, einen Meister seines Fachs anzutreffen, der nicht durch Vorbilder – ob reale oder imaginierte – angeleitet, unterstützt und motiviert wurde.

Entstehungsbedingungen von Expertise
1. Frühzeitige Fokussierung auf ein Spezialgebiet 2. Bewusste Übung (Deliberate Practice) 3. Unterstützung durch Mentoren 4. Disziplin und Durchhaltevermögen 5. Selbststeuerungskompetenz 6. Leistungswille und Rastlosigkeit 7. Begeisterung, Neugierde und Offenheit für ein Thema

Tabelle 1: Entstehungsbedingungen von Expertise

2.3.1 Frühzeitige Fokussierung auf ein Spezialgebiet

Als erste Entstehungsbedingung von Expertise ist die *frühzeitige Fokussierung auf ein Spezialgebiet* zu nennen. In bestimmten Gebieten, die vor allem körperliches Geschick erfordern (Erlernen einer Sportart oder eines Musikinstruments) muss diese Fokussierung bereits im Kindesalter erfolgen, um später überhaupt Virtuosentum zu erlangen. In anderen Gebieten (wie dem schriftstellerischen Schaffen) zeigen Beispiele wie Theodor Mommsen, Theodor Fontane oder Ernst Jünger, dass ebenso in hohem Alter noch Spitzenleistung erbracht werden kann. Aber auch die späte Ernte setzt in der Regel eine frühe Aussaat, d.h. die langjährige Beschäftigung mit einem bestimmten Thema voraus. Schließlich ist selbst bei Wunderkindern als häufig angeführten Beispielen für (vermeintlich) angeborenes Talent eine zumeist extrem früh vorgenommene thematische Beschränkung beobachtbar, die in der Regel durch Eltern(teile) vorbereitet und gelenkt wird – von Mozart über Steffi Graf, Michael Jackson bis hin zu den berühmten Polgár-Töchtern, die durch ihren Vater von Kindesbeinen an systematisch und intensiv im Schachspiel unterwiesen wurden. In all diesen Fällen wirkte die thematische Einflussnahme der Eltern auf das Kind schicksalsbestimmend (vgl. ausführlicher Freeman 2002: 574 ff.).

Zusammen genommen ist diese frühe Heranführung oder Entdeckung einer eng umgrenzten Leidenschaft geradezu der Schlüssel zum späteren Erfolg: „Fast alle Menschen, die in irgendeiner Weise durch ihre Leistungen bekannt oder gar berühmt geworden sind, haben sich auf eine Sache, auf eine Aufgabe, auf ein Problem konzentriert. Das ging und geht oft bis zur Besessenheit und manchmal an die Grenze des Krankhaften" (Malik 2006: 111).

2.3.2 Bewusste Übung (Deliberate Practice)

Die Konzentration auf ein Themenbereich geht einher mit *fordauerndem Üben* und Experimentieren in diesem Gebiet. Das Sprichwort »Übung macht den Meister« (englisch: Practice makes perfect) zeigt, dass diese Einsicht auch im kollektiven Gedächtnis gespeichert ist. Übung ist allerdings nicht gleich Übung. Wer Fortschritte in seinem Fachgebiet machen will, darf nicht das üben, was er bereits beherrscht (auch wenn dies einfacher und lustvoller ist), sondern hat sich dem zuzuwenden, was er noch nicht vollauf beherrscht (und was daher Überwindung kostet). Diese Form der bewussten, einen bestimmten Teilaspekt einer Gesamtaufgabe betreffenden, strukturierten und hochkonzentriert ausgeführten Übung wird als *Deliberate Practice* bezeichnet: „practice that focuses on tasks beyond your current level of competence and comfort (...) It entails considerable, specific, and sustained efforts to do something you can't do well – or even at all" (Ericsson/Prietula/Cokely 2007: 116, 118). Da diese Art des Trainings extrem anstrengend (und auch eintönig) ist, kann es nur an wenigen Stunden pro Tag ausgeführt werden (vgl. Schneider 2002: 169).

Eine Tätigkeit immer wieder durchzugehen ist unentbehrlich, um in sich die Fähigkeit zur Selbstkritik zu entwickeln. Allerdings: „In der modernen Erziehung gilt repetitives Lernen als geisttötend. Aus Angst, die Kinder zu langweilen, und in dem Bemühen, ihnen ständig neue Anreize zu bieten, mögen aufgeklärte Lehrer Routine vermeiden – doch damit nehmen sie den Kindern die Erfahrung, eine eingeschliffene Praxis zu überprüfen und von innen heraus zu verändern" (Sennett 2008: 56).

Beispiele für Deliberate Practice sind bestimmte Wurftechniken im Basketball, die Trainierung der Stimm-Modulation in der Rhetorik, die Aneignung unregelmäßiger Verben im Fremdsprachenerwerb oder das Rückwärtseinparken beim Autofahrenlernen. Intelligentes Üben versucht demnach

- die Lernaktivität auf konkrete Lernzuwächse hin auszurichten,
- den Schwierigkeitsgrad dem individuellen Leistungsstand anzupassen, d.h. genau einen Schritt darüber anzusetzen,
- aussagekräftiges Feedback über Erfolge und Misserfolge zu vermitteln und
- ausreichend Übungsgelegenheiten zur Fehlerkorrektur zu bieten (vgl. Ziegler 2008: 42).

Ziel ist die fehlerfreie Beherrschung einer Domäne. Um diesen Exzellenzstatus zu erlangen, geht die Forschung von etwa 10.000 Stunden oder 10 Jahren Übung aus (vgl. Ericsson/Krampe/Tesch-Römer 1993: 368; Horn/Masunaga 2006: 601 f.; Gladwell 2009: 36 ff.). Noch einmal anders: „*Repetitio est mater studiorum.* Die kleinen menschlichen Kräfte können Unmögliches bewirken, wenn sie mit dem längeren Weg der Übung multipliziert werden (...) Dass die Meister nicht vom Himmel fallen, weiß jeder, der sich an das Curriculum der älteren Handwerksberufe erinnert“ (Sloterdijk 2009: 312, 459).

2.3.3 Unterstützung durch Mentoren

Unmittelbares Feedback spielt eine zentrale Rolle, damit die erwünschten Übungseffekte erzielt werden. Ohne eine konkrete inhaltliche Rückmeldung über das eigene Verhalten bleiben leistungssteigernde Verbesserungen unerkannt, Fehler können sich dauerhaft »einnisten« und die für ein höheres Kompetenzniveau erforderlichen *Ent*lernprozesse bleiben aus. Zudem kann übersehen werden, wann der rechte Zeitpunkt gekommen ist, um eine Öffnung des Verhaltensrepertoires bzw. eine Schwierigkeitssteigerung vorzunehmen.

Hierzu bedarf es der professionellen *Unterstützung durch einen Mentor*: „Das beste bekannte Lernsetting zur Förderung von Leistungsexzellenz ist individueller Unterricht durch einen Mentor (...) [das Aufwachsen] in individuell zugeschnittenen Lernumgebungen“ (Ziegler 2008: 91). Es dürfte sich schwerlich ein Beispiel von Höchstleistung finden lassen, wo es nicht einen solchen Mentor (oder gleich mehrere davon) gegeben hat (vgl. Olsson 2011: 73 f.). Der Fall Michael Jackson, dessen Vater für ihn Segen und Fluch zugleich war – Segen, weil er die Grundlage seiner Karriere legte, Fluch, weil er ihm die Kindheit raubte –, zeigt allerdings auch die Ambivalenz des »frühen Drills« (vgl. hierzu auch das aktuell sehr kontrovers diskutierte Buch der »Tigermutter« Amy Chua 2011). Mentoren dienen als Vorbilder, Rollenmodelle und/oder »Antreiber« (vgl. Feldhusen 2005: 70 f.). Neben dem inhaltlichen Aspekt der Förderung der beruflichen Entwicklung sind Mentor-Mentee-Beziehungen oft auch durch eine persönliche und emotionale Komponente geprägt (vgl. Reichelt 2008: 393). Eine solche Vertrauensbasis ist notwendig, denn ehrliches Feedback kann verletzend sein und vor den Kopf stoßen. Nur wenn der Lernende bereit ist, sich in regelmäßigen Abständen in Frage zu stellen und wenn er in der Lage ist, die damit verbundenen negativen Gefühle auszuhalten, kommt es zu persönlichem Wachstum (vgl. Martens/Kuhl 2009: 77). Der Mentor übernimmt hier die Rolle eines »Sparringspartners«, der den Leistungswillen und den Ehrgeiz seines Schützlings anstachelt, der unerschrocken Defizite benennt, der aber auch Auswege aufzeigt. Offenheit für konstruktive Kritik ist allerdings nur möglich, wenn der Kritisierte trotz aller Schärfe letztlich das tieferliegende Wohlwollen des Kritikers spürt (vgl. Busch 2009: 78).

2.3.4 Disziplin und Durchhaltevermögen

Ein guter Mentor bzw. Coach gibt Hilfe zur Selbsthilfe. Er schafft es nicht nur, dass sein Protegé ihm vertraut, sondern auch, dass er sich mit der Zeit immer mehr selbst vertraut und sich eigenständig neue Herausforderungen steckt. So wandelt sich die Pflicht allmählich zur Neigung und aus Disziplin entwickelt sich Selbstdisziplin (vgl. Bueb 2007: 42). *Disziplin und Durchhaltevermögen* sind weitere Grundvoraussetzungen zur Entstehung von Expertenwissen. Ein angehender Experte arbeitet hart an sich und wirft bei Rückschlägen nicht gleich die »Flinte ins Korn«. Zum Erfolg eines Experten führt nicht der Fahrstuhl, sondern die Treppe, wie sich der Schweizer Verleger Emil Oesch einmal bildlich ausdrückte. Beispielhaft sei hier eine Äußerung des Drei-Sterne-Kochs Eckart Witzigmann aufgeführt. Danach gefragt, ob Kochen ein Fleiß- oder ein Talentberuf sei, antwortete er: „Beides. Ich habe im Jahr 1957 angefangen zu lernen. Da wusste ich noch nichts von einem Michelin oder Paul Bocuse. Manche meiner Karrierestationen empfand ich wie Quarantänestationen. Man kam gar nicht raus. Aber da habe ich auch jeden Tag geackert und Bücher gelesen und Rezepte gelernt. Das war das Trampolin in die Weltspitze" (o.V. 2011: 129).

Während *Disziplin* die Bereitschaft zum gegenwärtigen Triebverzicht bzw. -aufschub bedeutet, um ein in der Zukunft liegendes Ziel zu erreichen, beinhaltet *Durchhaltevermögen* vor allem die Fähigkeit, mit Misserfolgen umzugehen, diese schnell abzuhaken und den Blick wieder konsequent nach vorne zu richten. Die Eigenschaft, sich selbst zu disziplinieren und Verzicht zu üben, gilt als einer der wenigen empirisch robusten Persönlichkeitsmerkmale, die den anschließenden Erfolg junger Menschen vorhersagen (z.B. höhere Durchschnittsnoten in der Schule, berufliche Karriere). Als Teil der emotionalen Intelligenz wird sie als mindestens genauso wichtig wie der Intelligenzquotient betrachtet (vgl. Duckworth/Seligman 2005: 939). „To be able to delay immediate satisfaction for the sake of future consequences has long been considered an essential achievement of human development" (Shoda/Mischel/Peake 1990: 978; Mischel/Ayduk 2011). Eine Person, die über Impuls- und Selbstkontrolle, d.h. über die Willenskraft verfügt, Belohnungen aufzuschieben (deferred/delayed gratification) kann beispielsweise die Unannehmlichkeiten, die mit Deliberate Practice einhergehen, in Kauf nehmen, weil ein höheres Ziel lockt, nämlich die Erlangung von Leistungsexzellenz, die Aussicht, einmal zu den Besten auf seinem Gebiet zu gehören.

Zuerst konnte dies in den berühmten Marshmallow-Experimenten des Stanforder Psychologen Walter Mischel gezeigt werden. Sich unbeobachtet wähnende Kinder sollten es dabei schaffen, für eine Zeitlang auf den Verzehr einer Süßigkeit zu verzichten. Sie sollten also die ‚instant gratification' aufschieben. Dafür wurde ihnen versprochen, anschließend zwei von den Süßigkeiten zu bekommen. Diejenigen von ihnen, denen dies gelang, waren später auch erfolgreicher in der Schule, wiesen eine höhere Sozialkompetenz auf und neigten weniger zum Drogenkonsum. Kurzfristige Askese zahlt sich daher langfristig aus, ist nicht lebensfeindlich, sondern lebenssteigernd (vgl. Bueb 2007: 43). Ähnlich funktioniert jede Form der temporären Entsagung (z.B. Essenseinschränkung), die durch die Hoffnung auf die Erreichung fernerer Ziele genährt wird (z.B. Gewichtsabnahme, gesteigerte Fitness, höheres Wohlbefinden).

In diese Logik ist auch der Umgang mit Misserfolgen einzuordnen. Nur wer an einem Thema »dranbleibt« und nicht vorzeitig aufgibt, kann auf lange Sicht die Früchte seiner Arbeit einfahren. Erfolgreiche Menschen schaffen es bei Rückschlägen, rasch wieder in den Modus »Handlungsorientierung« umzuschalten. Lageorientierte Menschen dagegen kreisen frustriert und jammernd um die missliche Lage, in der sie sich verfangen haben, katapultieren sich in die Opferrolle, fühlen sich überfordert. Ihre Selbstberuhigung und Selbstmotivierung ist derart beeinträchtigt, dass es ihnen nicht oder nur unzureichend gelingt, ihre Energie in zukünftiges Handeln zu lenken (vgl. Martens/Kuhl 2009: 67).

2.3.5 Selbststeuerungskompetenz

Um eine solche Form der Paralyse zu vermeiden, entwickeln angehende Experten eine geschärfte Selbst- und Umweltwahrnehmung. Sie wissen, wie sie auf bestimmte Rahmenbedingungen und Ereignisse reagieren und sind ihnen damit nicht hilflos ausgesetzt. Sie haben ein Bewusstsein über das eigene Denken und Lernen, das eigene Fühlen und Empfinden, das eigene Wollen und über das eigene Handeln (vgl. Busch 2008: 82). Daniel Goleman sieht in der Selbstwahrnehmung, besonders im Erkennen eigener Gefühle zum Zeitpunkt ihres Auftretens, die Grundlage emotionaler Intelligenz: „Wer die eigenen Gefühle nicht zu erkennen vermag, ist ihnen ausgeliefert" (Goleman 1997: 65). Zorn ist hierfür ein gutes Beispiel.

Die allgemeine Fähigkeit, mit Frustrationen konstruktiv umzugehen und das Schicksal im Vertrauen auf die eigenen Kompetenzen bewusst und aktiv zu bewältigen, soll hier zusammenfassend mit *Selbststeuerungskompetenz* bezeichnet werden. Begriffe wie Metakognition, Achtsamkeit (mindfulness) und Selbstregulation weisen in eine ähnliche Richtung. Stets geht es um eine Sensibilisierung von Bewusstseins- und Handlungskräften des Übenden:

- Metakognition bezieht sich auf übergeordnete mentale Prozesse im Zusammenhang mit Lernen, d.h. auf die Lernplanung, die Überwachung der Lernentwicklung und die Vorhersage der Lernleistung (vgl. Coutinho et al. 2005: 322).
- Achtsame *Beobachtung* ist die bewusste Wahrnehmung innerer und äußerer Phänomene (z.B. Gedanken, Gefühle, Geräusche, Gerüche, körperliche Reaktionen). Achtsames *Handeln* bedeutet, sich einer Aufgabe vollkommen, d.h. mit ungeteilter Aufmerksamkeit zuzuwenden. Dazu gehört auch die urteilsfreie *Akzeptanz* eigener Erfahrungen in der Gegenwart. Achtsame *Beschreibung* schließlich bezieht sich auf die Fähigkeit, gewonnene Beobach-

tungen und Erfahrungen unmittelbar und ohne Wertungen zu benennen (vgl. Dekeyser et al. 2008: 1236).
- Selbstregulation kennzeichnet selbstgesteuerte Gedanken, Gefühle und Handlungen, die planvoll auf die Erreichung persönlicher Ziele abgestimmt sind und regelmäßig angepasst werden (vgl. Zimmerman 2005: 14).

Jeder Experte entwickelt diese feinen »Antennen« gegenüber sich selbst und seiner Umwelt. Simon Ammann, der vierfache Olympiasieger im Einzelspringen auf der Normal- und Großschanze, hat eine solche Sensibilität in Bezug auf den motorischen Bewegungsablauf des Skisprungs aufgebaut. Gefragt danach, wie er sich seine Erfolge selber erklären könne, antwortete er: „Ich habe nie aufgehört, diesen Sport zu erkunden (...) Ich habe einen Weg gefunden, den vertikalen Druck beim Absprung zu verbessern (...) Ich habe die technischen Grenzen ausgelotet und *meinen Körper den Anforderungen angepasst*" (Brinkbäumer/Pfeil 2010: 147, Hervorhebungen durch die Verf.). Die Antwort Ammanns zeigt, wie akribisch er sich selbst beobachtet hat bzw. von seinem Trainer beobachten hat lassen, um seine Leistung zu steigern. Gleichzeitig kommen darin auch die beiden letzten für die Entwicklung von Expertise notwendigen Entstehungsbedingungen zum Ausdruck, nämlich einerseits Leistungswille und Rastlosigkeit, und andererseits Begeisterung, Neugierde und Offenheit für die jeweils gehegte »Passion«.

2.3.6 Leistungswille und Rastlosigkeit

Die Entstehung des *Leistungsmotivs* ist bis heute rätselhaft. Mit Sicherheit spielen Bezugs- bzw. Vergleichspersonen in der Kindheit wie Eltern, Geschwister und Spielkameraden eine Rolle. Besonders leistungsmotivierte Personen wollen sich mit anderen messen und suchen neue Herausforderungen. „Es erfüllt sie mit Befriedigung, wenn sie etwas Neues geschaffen oder etwas besonders gut gemacht haben. Als Perfektionisten, die sie sind, geben sie sich nicht damit zufrieden, dass eine Aufgabe einfach nur erledigt wurde: Sie arbeiten dafür, alles, was ihnen wichtig erscheint, so gut wie möglich zu machen" (Schmalt/Sokolowski/Langens 2000: 31 f.). Etwas besser zu machen, um dem Lehrer zu gefallen, Kritik zu vermeiden oder die Anerkennung einer geschätzten Person zu erlangen, hat allerdings noch nicht unbedingt etwas mit einem hohen Leistungsmotiv zu tun: „What should be involved in the achievement motive is doing something better for its own sake, for the intrinsic satisfaction of doing something better" (McClelland 1987: 228). Bezeichnend ist hier die Antwort der Geigerin Anne-Sopie Mutter auf die Frage, ob sie als Kind jemand habe antreiben müssen: „Ich treibe mich selber, ich bin mein eigenes Perpetuum mobile. Auch heute noch" (o.V. 2005: VIII). Dieser innere Antrieb (drive to excel) erzeugt in besonders leistungsmotivierten Menschen eine gewisse *Rastlosigkeit* und Unruhe. Leistungsmotivierte geben sich nicht mit dem einmal Erreichten zufrieden, sondern suchen sich fortwährend neue Ziele: „Es braucht diesen gierigen Willen, der die Besten dazu bringt, 15 Prozent mehr zu üben als alle Schwächeren" (Thomas Niendorf, zitiert in Brinkbäumer/Pfeil 2010: 146). Eben dieser Drang führt dazu, dass sie mehr als gewillt sind, zusätzliche Belastungen und persönliche Opfer auch im Privatleben in Kauf zu nehmen, um vorwärtszukommen (vgl. Ready/Conger/Hill 2010: 82).

2.3.7 Begeisterung, Neugierde und Offenheit für ein Thema

Dies kann nur gehen, wenn die Betreffenden mit *Begeisterung* bei der Sache sind und sich mit dem, was sie tun, vollkommen identifizieren. Franz Beckenbauer hat dies so beschrieben: „Bei mir war es die Freude am Ball. Am Ball war ich glücklich. Dein Glück ist, wenn deine Passion zum Beruf wird“ (zitiert in Olsson 2011: 48). Und eine Freundin der Koloratursopranistin Edita Gruberová sagte über sie: „Sie *liebt* das Singen. Wenn sie nicht singen würde, wäre sie unglücklich“[3]. Experten werden aufgrund dieser positiven Grundeinstellung nie müde, die Breiten und Tiefen ihres Fachgebiets auszuloten. Die Freude an ihrer Arbeit erweckt in ihnen den ausgeprägten Wunsch, immer weiter zu lernen und Neues zu erschließen. Sie bemühen sich anhaltend um eine Erweiterung und Aktualisierung ihres Wissens, bleiben sozusagen auf »Entdeckungskurs«, hören nie auf, Fragen zu stellen (vgl. Shanteau 1992: 16).

2.4 Leistungen von Experten

Ein Experte erbringt auf der Höhe seines Könnens dauerhaft, also nicht nur zufällig und singulär auf einem bestimmten Gebiet herausragende Leistung (vgl. Gruber/Lehmann 2007: 6; Ready/Conger/Hill 2010: 80). Sein Handeln ist mit konkreten Ergebnissen verknüpft (z.B. reicht es nicht, dass ein Chirurg mit dem Skalpell umgehen kann, er muss damit auch erfolgreich Operationen durchführen) und lässt sich idealerweise unter Laborbedingungen messen und replizieren (vgl. Ericsson/Prietula/Cokely 2007: 117). Gruber/Mandl (1996: 19) fassen Expertise in folgendem *Leistungsprofil* zusammen: große Wissensbasis; reichhaltige Erfahrung im Umgang mit domänenspezifischen Anforderungen; überdurchschnittlicher Erfolg beim Erkennen und Bearbeiten von Problemen; metakognitive Kontrolle über Handlungen (diese ist sowohl Entstehungsbedingung als auch Ergebnis von Expertise); Effizienz, Fehlerfreiheit und große Genauigkeit der Handlungen; hohe Flexibilität gegenüber neuen Problemsituationen.[4]

---

3 Edita Gruberová: Die Kunst des Belcanto, Dokumentation von Claus Wischmann und Stefan Pannen, Deutschland 2008, ZDF.

4 Zu einer ähnlichen Auflistung der Merkmale von Expertise gelangen Sternberg (2002: 57), Klein (1992: 171 ff.) sowie Glaser/Chi (1988: XVII ff.): Experts excel mainly in their own domains; experts perceive large meaningful patterns in their domain; experts are fast; they are faster than novices at performing the skills of their domain, and they quickly solve problems with little error; experts have superior short-term and long-term memory; experts see and represent a problem in their domain at a deeper (more principled) level than novices; novices tend to represent a problem at a superficial level; experts spend a great deal of time analyzing a problem qualitatively; experts have strong self-monitoring skills.

Die Forschung hat also durchaus fundierte Kenntnisse über die Leistungsmerkmale von Expertise herausgearbeitet, was jedoch noch nicht heißt, dass auch die dahinterliegenden Mechanismen verstanden wurden. „In general, we seem to know quite a bit about characteristics of expertise, but unfortunately, we know very little about the cognitive structures and processes underlying these characteristics“ (Cooke 1992: 33). Kognitive »Alleinstellungsmerkmale« von Experten sind

- gesteigerte Gedächtnisleistung,
- Mustererkennung,
- Erfassung schwacher Signale und
- Handlungsautomatismen.

Hierbei muss deutlich betont werden, dass es sich stets um Leistungen von Experten innerhalb ihres Gebietes bzw. ihrer Domäne handelt. Außerhalb ihrer fachlichen Grenzen gilt dies nicht. Mehrfachexzellenz ist höchst selten anzutreffen (z.B. Schachgroßmeister und Geigenvirtuose).

Zunächst führt die im Zeitverlauf aufgebaute Erfahrung dazu, dass sich Experten in ihrer Wahrnehmung und in ihrer Art, Informationen zu verarbeiten und sich Problemen zu nähern, von Laien bzw. Anfängern unterscheiden. Auf die *gesteigerte Gedächtnisleistung* (skilled memory) wurde bereits verwiesen. Diese lässt Experten rascher *Muster erkennen* (pattern recognition) und Verbindungen zwischen Teilaspekten ihrer Domäne erfassen (vgl. Cooke 1992: 34).[5] Wer über ausdifferenzierte Gedächtnisstrukturen verfügt, kann eingehende Informationen schlicht besser verarbeiten und zuordnen (vgl. Salas/Rosen 2010: 107 ff.). Erklärt wird dies mit der Chunking-Theorie (vgl. Gobet 1996: 59 ff.). Chunks sind Einheiten der Informationsverarbeitung. Es wird angenommen, dass Informationen in Chunks gebündelt, abgespeichert und verarbeitet werden: „chunks are closely knit units of knowledge structure“ (Chi/Glaser/Rees 1982: 9). Während der Anfänger etwa bis zu sieben Informationseinheiten im Kurzzeitgedächtnis abspeichern kann (heute geht man eher von drei bis vier aus), merkt sich der Experte sieben Gruppierungen (Miller 1956). Er greift auf verästeltere Wissensstrukturen im Langzeitgedächtnis zurück. Dies ermöglicht es ihm, sich an Spielstellungen und nicht bloß an einzelne Figuren eines Schachbretts zu erinnern. Ein solches Denken in großen Chunks steigert seine Gedächtnisleistung um ein Vielfaches (vgl. Kahnemann 2011: 23 f.). Der Unterschied zwischen einem Leseanfänger und einem Leseexperten kann dies noch besser veranschaulichen. Grundschüler müssen beim Erlernen der Lesefähigkeit zunächst jeden einzelnen Buchsta-

5 Für den medizinischen Bereich konnte nachgewiesen werden, dass Ärzte im Praktikum (Novizen) „ihr Wissen in Form von Kausalnetzwerken auf der Basis physiologischen und pathophysiologischen Faktenwissens, das gut durch Lehrbücher angeeignet werden kann, strukturieren. Bei Experten hingegen entwickelt sich eine „Enkapsulierung“ des Wissens, die einer effektiveren Organisation und Zusammenfassung des Faktenwissens unter Schlüsselkonzepten entspricht (...) Als Voraussetzung (...) wird die Bearbeitung möglichst vieler Fälle angegeben, d.h. eine Arbeitsumgebung, die vielfältige Anforderungen stellt und zum Kennenlernen vieler Beispiele führt“ (Bergmann 2008: 66 f.).

ben betrachten, um die Bedeutung und Aussprache eines Wortes korrekt zu erfassen, während Leseexperten ganze Wörter oder gar Wortgruppen auf einen Blick erkennen, selbst dann, wenn Buchstaben innerhalb von Wörtern in falscher Reihenfolge stehen (vgl. Posner 1988: XXXI).

Das Wahrnehmungsvermögen eines Experten ist jedoch nicht nur in quantitativer Hinsicht entwickelter als das eines Laien, sondern auch in qualitativer Hinsicht. Der Experte verfügt über den sog. Kennerblick, *erfasst Nuancen und schwache Signale in seiner Domäne*, was sich besonders in kritischen Situationen unter Zeitdruck positiv bemerkbar macht. „[He] has learned to be sensitive to spatial, causal, and temporal relationships“ (Klein 1992: 171). Mistele (2007: 166) nennt hierfür ein konkretes Beispiel: „So wurde von einem befragten Feuerwehrmann berichtet, dass Spraydosen in einem brennenden Bad ein großes Gefahrenpotenzial darstellen (...) Allerdings kündigt ein Zischen von entweichender Luft eine bevorstehende Explosion an. Dieses Geräusch nimmt ein unerfahrener Feuerwehrmann tendenziell weniger wahr, während ein erfahrener Feuerwehrmann vor Betreten des Bads ganz bewusst auf dieses schwache Signal achtet und sein Handeln entsprechend ausrichtet“ (zu weiteren Beispielen vgl. Neuweg 2004: 176 f.). Die Erfahrung sorgt nicht nur für ein feineres Sensorium, sondern auch für eine größere Gelassenheit angesichts widriger Umstände. Der Experte hat größeres Vertrauen in die eigene Kompetenz (self-efficacy).

Die rasche Aufdeckung von Mustern, aber auch die geschärfte Situationswahrnehmung (situation awareness) sind Eigenschaften, die – ähnlich wie das Erkennen von Gesichtern – weitgehend unbewusst ablaufen. Durch die Entwicklung von *Handlungsautomatismen* wird der Experte entlastet und kann sich uneingeschränkt den wesentlichen Aspekten einer Situation oder eines Problems zuwenden.[6] Ein guter Leser etwa kann sich vollauf dem inhaltlichen Verständnis eines Textes widmen, weil er sich nicht auf das Lesen als solches konzentrieren muss; dieses läuft automatisch und weitgehend unbewusst ab. Lesen ist zu implizitem bzw. prozeduralem Wissen (knowing how) geworden (vgl. Rothe/Schindler 1996: 39), wirkt also wie eine stillschweigend funktionierende »Hintergrundkompetenz«.[7] Ein Ausspruch von Alfred North Whitehead, den dieser auf die Zivilisation bezog, lässt sich uneingeschränkt auch auf Experten münzen: „Die Behauptung, dass wir die Gewohnheit annehmen sollen, gründlich zu bedenken, was wir tun, ist ein völlig abwegiger Gemeinplatz (...) Es verhält sich genau umgekehrt. Die Zivilisation erzielt ihren Fortschritt, indem sie die Zahl der wichtigen Vorgänge vermehrt, die wir ohne Nachdenken ausführen können“ (zitiert in Gigerenzer 2008: 49).

6 Natürlich baut auch jeder »Laie« Handlungsautomatismen auf (etwa ein angelernter Arbeiter in der tayloristischen Fertigungsstruktur). Der Unterschied zum Experten besteht darin, dass sich diese Automatismen sehr viel schneller einstellen und übertragen lassen als dies bei der Aneignung eines komplexen Themengebiets möglich erscheint.

7 Eine umfassende Analyse über den komplexen Zusammenhang zwischen Könnerschaft und implizitem Wissen liefert Neuweg 2004: 12 ff.; vgl. auch Gueldenberg/Helting 2007: 118.

3. Identifikation von Expertenwissen

Die bisherigen Ausführungen zeigen, dass die Entwicklung von Expertise in der Regel schon lange vor dem Eintritt eines Mitarbeiters in ein Unternehmen eingesetzt hat. In Unternehmen wird diese dann in einen konkreten Arbeitskontext gerückt, der die Gelegenheit zur Vertiefung fachlicher und unternehmensspezifischer Erfahrungen liefert.

3.1 Identifikation strategisch relevanter Experten in Unternehmen

Experten in Unternehmen gibt es in sämtlichen funktionalen Bereichen (Controlling, Marketing, Entwicklung, Beschaffung, Vertrieb, Fertigung, Qualitätsprüfung), auf allen Ebenen (oberes, mittleres, unteres Management), in operativen (Schweißen, Feilen, Anlagenelektronik) oder in dispositiven Aufgabenfeldern (Projektmanagement, Budgetierung, Verhandlungsführung, strategische Planung). Allerdings sind nicht alle Experten für das Unternehmen von strategischem Wert, sondern nur die, „die einen Großteil des wettbewerbsrelevanten Wissens auf sich vereinen" (Knaese/Probst 2001: 37). „Therefore, we can replace the question, 'Who is an expert?' with the question, 'Where is the expertise in a given organization?'" (Klein 1992: 175). Bevor Experten identifiziert werden, ist also zu prüfen, wo die erfolgskritischen Geschäftsprozesse eines Unternehmens verortet sind: Was sind die primären, d.h. unmittelbar wertschöpfenden bzw. kundennutzenstiftenden Aktivitäten? Über welche Kernkompetenz(en) verfügt das Unternehmen? In welchem Bereich liegt sein komparativer Konkurrenzvorteil: im Bereich Logistik&Vertrieb (Versandhandel), in der Technologieentwicklung (Maschinenbau), in besonders effizienten Fertigungsverfahren oder in professionellen Dienstleistungen (Unternehmensberatung, Instandhaltung)? Welche Verbindung besteht zwischen diesen Bereichen und anderen Unternehmensbereichen?

Hierbei ist nämlich zu berücksichtigen, dass sich Expertise innerbetrieblich oft erst im prozess- bzw. bereichsübergreifenden Verbund voll entfaltet, beispielsweise im Rahmen von Teamarbeit. Die Identifikation von Experten hat sich demnach an drei Grundfragen zu orientieren:

1. Wo liegen die erfolgskritischen organisationalen Kompetenzen? Welchen Bereichen kommt dabei besondere strategische Relevanz zu?
2. Gibt es innerhalb dieser Bereiche Experten (Wissensträger), die in absehbarer Zeit das Unternehmen verlassen werden?
3. Welches Kompetenzlevel besitzen diese Experten?

Von der Beantwortung dieser Fragen hängen die Dauer und die Intensität anzusetzender Transfermaßnahmen ab. Die Bestimmung organisationaler Kompetenzen ist aufgrund kausaler Ambiguität, sozialer Komplexität und Implizität (vgl. Güttel 2006: 423 ff., auch zu entsprechenden Identifikationsansätzen) vermutlich schwieriger vorzunehmen, als die Bestimmung individueller Kompetenzen. Je nach *Strukturiertheit einer Domäne* stellt jedoch auch die Identifizierung von Experten ein keineswegs leichtes Unterfangen dar.

3.2 Beurteilung und Messung der Expertenleistung

In Domänen, in denen eindeutige Ratingskalen existieren oder gute Vergleichsmöglichkeiten gegeben sind (z.B. im Einzelsport), ist das Erkennen von Expertise noch verhältnismäßig einfach. Experten liegen hier in ihrer Leistung mindestens zwei Standardabweichungen über dem Mittelwert erfasster Leistungswerte (vgl. Ericsson/Charness 1994: 731). Wie aber kann Könnerschaft in *schlecht definierten Domänen* identifiziert werden? Nicht immer sind objektiv messbare Leistungskriterien bzw. Produktivitätskennzahlen wie Patentanmeldungen, Verkaufsabschlüsse oder die Anzahl gefertigter Einheiten verfügbar (vgl. Weiss/Shanteau 2003: 105). In schlecht definierten Domänen erschöpft sich Expertise nicht in der Produktion eindeutiger Outputs oder in der Fähigkeit, auf bestimmte Fragen korrekte Antworten geben zu können. „The difficulty is that experts are needed precisely in domains where correct answers seldom exist (...) Indeed, if we could compute (or look up) correct answers, why would we need an expert at all?“ (Shanteau et al. 2002: 253). Was macht einen guten Verkäufer, Manager oder Erfinder aus?[8] An Erklärungen hierüber mangelt es in Büchern wahrlich nicht, allein die exakte Bestimmung des Könners anhand eines »Goldstandards« oder »Urmeters« ist nicht möglich, sonst hätte es die Personalauswahl leicht. Die Identifikation muss also Umwege gehen und nach indirekten Messgrößen Ausschau halten.

Einfache, jedoch nicht zwingend aussagekräftige Kriterien zur Identifikation von Expertise sind die *Erfahrung* eines Mitarbeiters (gemessen nach der Anzahl seiner Berufsjahre oder den bisher bearbeiteten Aufgaben), seine hierarchische *Position* bzw. sein Fachlaufbahn-Status, seine akademischen oder anderweitig erworbenen *Qualifikationen und Titel* sowie verliehene Auszeichnungen auf Basis bedeutender Leistungen (vgl. Farrington-Darby/Wilson 2006: 26 f.; Simonton 2006: 323 f.). Differenziertere Urteile lassen *Selbsteinschätzungen* erwarten, wobei diese mit der Wahrnehmung Dritter abzugleichen sind. Die Ermittlung des Ansehens von Mitarbeitern unter Kollegen und anderen Kontaktpersonen (peer selection), etwa im Rahmen soziometrischer Erhebungen[9], ist ein deutlicher Hinweis für Expertise: „In most domains it is easier to identify individuals who are socially recognized as experts than it is to specify observable performance at which these individuals excel“ (Ericsson/Charness

---

8 Auch in der Wissenschaft wird aktuell sehr kontrovers darüber diskutiert, ob es sinnvoll ist, Forschungsleistungen allein auf Publikationsleistungen zu reduzieren (vgl. hierzu handelsblattranking.wordpress.com).

9 „Practitioners might be asked, for example, »If you have a problem of type x, who would you go to for advice?« Or they might be asked to sort cards bearing the names of other domain practitioners into piles according to one or another skill dimension or knowledge category“ (Hoffman/Lintern 2006: 208).

1994: 731). Im Ansehen spiegelt sich auch die Prozesskompetenz eines Mitarbeiters wider (etwa seine Art der Problembewältigung, sein Argumentierenkönnen oder sein Arbeits- und Entscheidungsverhalten).

Schließlich stellt die in Personalakten dokumentierte *Arbeitsleistung* eines Mitarbeiters eine wichtige Informationsquelle dar. Diese ist geeignet „to trace the course of expert performance across time“ (Simonton 2006: 324). Durch vergangene Leistungsbeurteilungen im Rahmen von Zielvereinbarungen sind Mitarbeiterklassifizierungen in Humanressourcen-Portfolios möglich. „A-Mitarbeiter übertreffen in der Regel gesetzte Ziele, zeichnen sich durch ein außergewöhnliches Maß an Engagement aus (...) und haben häufig exzellente Ideen“ (von der Oelsnitz/Tacke 2009: 346). Doch auch das Wissen von B-Mitarbeitern, die die Organisation allgemein gut kennen, solide Arbeit leisten und über persönliche Netzwerke verfügen, ist unter Umständen wertvoll, was auf eine generelle Problematik verweist: Fachliche Exzellenz mag zwar im Leistungssport ausreichen, um erfolgreich zu sein, nicht aber in Unternehmen. Hier ist Expertise weniger autark und isoliert zu sehen. Sie ist vielmehr in interdependente Arbeitskontexte eingebettet, die zu entschlüsseln ebenso wichtig sein kann. Ein erweiterter Expertenbegriff hat damit kontextuelle Verflechtungen und auch Experten jenseits fachlicher Grenzen zu berücksichtigen; das sind insbesondere Macht-, Prozess- und Beziehungspromotoren (vgl. Rost/Hölzle/Gemünden 2007: 342 ff.). Diese »Experten« bleiben nachfolgend allerdings ausgeklammert. Eine ganzheitliche Sicht auf das in spezifischen Unternehmensgegebenheiten verankerte Fachwissen ist gleichwohl bedeutsam, denn der Transfer von Expertise sollte möglichst kontextgebunden bzw. -angereichert sein.

Um die Auffindung von Experten in praktischer Hinsicht zu erleichtern, setzt die NASA automatische Suchmaschinen ein. Diese analysieren Mitarbeiterprofile (nach Berufserfahrung und Ausbildung), Dokumente von Mitarbeitern (nach Relevanz und Abruffrequenz) und Datenbankeneinträge (vgl. Becerra-Fernandez 2000). Daneben lässt sich, wenngleich dies sehr aufwendig und datenschutzrechtlich fragwürdig ist, der E-Mail-Verkehr von Mitarbeitern themenspezifisch auswerten, denn Experten werden häufiger um Rat gefragt und sollten dementsprechend auch häufiger in fachspezifischen E-Mail-Wechseln auftauchen.

Bei der Identifikation von Experten in schlecht strukturierten Domänen gibt es keinen Königsweg. Allgemein ist nur zu sagen, dass retrospektive, einen mehrjährigen Zeitraum umfassende Leistungsanalysen gegenüber punktuellen Einzel-Assesments oder Potenzialanalysen vorzuziehen sind, und dass die Kombination verschiedener Identifikationsansätze gegenüber dem Einsatz einzelner Verfahren validere Ergebnisse erzielt.

4. Weitergabe und Bewahrung von Expertenwissen

Stehen der oder die Experten fest, deren Wissen es zu sichern gilt, so kann die Planung von Transfermaßnahmen beginnen. Es ist wichtig, sich an dieser Stelle nochmals die komplexen Entstehungsbedingungen von Expertise vor Augen zu halten, um sich darüber klar zu werden, dass der Transfer eine alles andere als einfach zu bewerkstelligende Aufgabe ist. Wir reden hier stets von hochspezialisierten Wissensgebieten, nicht von einfachen Handgriffen, die leicht erlernt und damit auch ersetzt werden können. Expertise ist das Ergebnis langwieriger und mühevoller Lernprozesse. Sie kann – allen Versprechungen sog. Superlearning-Ratgeber zum Trotz – nicht über Abkürzungswege erreicht werden.

4.1 Grundproblematik

In der höchsten Stufe zeichnet sich Expertise durch die spielerische Beherrschung einer Domäne in Form von Wahrnehmungs- und Handlungsautomatismen aus (vgl. Kap. 2.4).[10] *Das Wissen des Experten* hat auf diesem Level zu einem Großteil *implizite Züge* angenommen.[11] Genau hier liegt dann aber auch die Crux im Hinblick auf die Transferierbarkeit von Expertenwissen: „[T]he more competent domain experts become, the less able they are to describe the knowledge they use to solve problems (...) It appears that in many domains, the "experts" are largely unable to communicate (...) the specific knowledge that makes them experts" (Ford/Adams-Webber 1992: 130). Die Frage der Transferierbarkeit stellt sich ebenso bei denen mit Expertise verknüpften *Persönlichkeitseigenschaften* wie Disziplin oder Selbststeuerungskompetenz, die stark biographisch geprägt sind. Ähnliches gilt für die *persönlichen Netzwerke*: „It usually takes years of working for a company before an employee has built up a social network consisting of helpful informal linkages which enable him or her to solve even complicated, cross-departmental problems independently and efficiently. In other words: The knowledge about existing networks is personal, mainly experienced-based and therefore hard to retain and to transfer" (Haarmann et al. 2008: 2).

Diesen grundsätzlichen Problemen auf seiten des Transfergebers stehen solche auf seiten des Transfernehmers gegenüber. Zum einen ist zu klären, wer überhaupt als *Nachfolger(kreis)* des Experten geeignet ist. Lässt sich im Vorfeld tatsächlich exakt bestimmen, wer den Platz des Experten später einnehmen kann? Mit Sicherheit kann es nicht schaden, den Experten in dieser Frage selber um Rat zu fragen, da er am ehesten spürt, wer die notwendigen Potenziale mitbringt (vgl. Olsson 2011: 76). Zum anderen muss klar sein, dass die *»Absorptionsfähigkeit« des Nachfolgers* trotz fachlicher Nähe begrenzt ist. Ein Professor, der bereits 500 Vorlesungen gehalten hat, kann

---

10 „immediate intuitive situational response" (Dreyfus/Dreyfus 2005: 787), „abstraction and facile recognition of patterns of system behavior" (Schumacher/Czerwinski 1992: 73), „highly automized" (Gordon 1992: 101). Zu den damit verbundenen Schattenseiten (z. B. übertriebenes Selbstvertrauen, Übersehen von Details, Inflexibilität, »Fachidiotentum«) vgl. Chi (2006: 24 ff.).

11 Die Frage, ob implizites Wissen überhaupt transferierbar ist, wurde an anderer Stelle bereits hinreichend ausführlich behandelt (vgl. zu einem aktuellen Überblick Schewe/Nienaber 2011: 40 ff.). Zu einer ausführlichen Erörterung des Wissenstransfers vgl. Knörck (2009: 29 ff.).

seinem Mitarbeiter, der vor seiner ersten Vorlesung steht, zwar Tipps und Tricks geben, in der Vorlesung werden dem Mitarbeiter aber dennoch die Erfahrung und die damit einhergehende Selbstsicherheit fehlen. Ein anderes Beispiel ist wiederum die Kochkunst: „In der Internetära ist jedes Rezept jederzeit überall zugänglich (...) Aber dass die Rezepte allgegenwärtig sind, bedeutet ja nicht, dass die Zahl derer wächst, die sie umsetzen können" (Eckart Witzigmann, zitiert in o.V. 2011: 129).

Die Transfersituation hat also ihre natürlichen Grenzen.[12] Weder ist ein 1:1-Transfer zwischen dem, was ein Experte kann, und dem was er auszudrücken vermag, möglich, noch ist ein 1:1-Transfer des Wissens und der Erfahrungen[13] vom Experten auf seinen Nachfolger vorstellbar. „We should note that the analyst does *not* "acquire" something that is already "there" in the expert's head, ready to be recorded. Rather, a new entity is *created*: A body of knowledge is constructed cooperatively by the expert and the analyst, with each contributing his or her share" (Regoczei/Hirst 1992: 22). Dies hat manche Forscher dazu veranlasst, den Austausch zwischen zwei Personen generell in Frage zu stellen. So sah Niklas Luhmann in gelungener Kommunikation einen höchst unwahrscheinlichen Zustand (vgl. Luhmann 1984: 217 f.). Radikal zu Ende gedacht würde dies bedeuten, dass jeder Wissens- und Erfahrungstransfer von Anfang an zum Scheitern verurteilt, d.h. Geldverschwendung aus Sicht des Unternehmens ist. Wir möchten hier aber einer gemäßigteren, managementgeleiteten Sichtweise folgen: *Gelungener Transfer ist dann wahrscheinlich(er), wenn er frühzeitig einsetzt, über einen längeren Zeitraum und unter Nutzung möglichst vielfältiger Instrumente betrieben wird.* Dabei ist sowohl auf personalisierungs- als auch auf kodifizierungsorientierte Ansätze der Wissensbewahrung zurückzugreifen, d.h. das Wissen des Experten lässt sich auf Personen oder auf materielle Datenträger (z.B. Wikis, Videoaufzeichnungen) übertragen (vgl. Trojan 2006: 78 f.). Im Folgenden werden drei Transferphasen unterschieden:

1. *Vorbereitungsphase* (etwa ein bis drei Jahre vor dem Ausscheiden des Mitarbeiters): Der Mitarbeiter arbeitet hier noch in seinem Bereich, bekommt aber bspw. bereits einen Nachfolger zur Seite gestellt oder wird in altersgemischten Teams eingesetzt, um sein Wissen auf mehrere Personen zu verteilen. Insgesamt geht es hier um die Sensibilisierung aller Betroffenen.
2. *Hauptphase* (etwa ein bis sechs Monate vor dem Ausscheiden des Mitarbeiters): Hier wird das Wissen des Mitarbeiters mit Hilfe gezielter Erhebungsverfahren intensiv aufgedeckt (z.B. Story Telling, Think-Aloud-Methode, strukturierte Interviews). Der Mitarbeiter muss bzw. kann seiner Arbeit hier nicht

12 Schewe/Nienaber (2011: 46 ff.) benennen in einer umfassenden Literaturanalyse strukturelle und personelle »Explikationsbarrieren«. Die häufigsten strukturellen Barrieren sind demnach Zeitmangel, starre Aufbauorganisation und räumliche Distanz. Die häufigsten personellen Barrieren sind Mangel an kommunikativen Fähigkeiten, Mangel an Sozialkapital, Mangel an Vertrauen und Furcht vor Macht- bzw. Prestigeverlust; zu weiteren Barrieren vgl. Knörck (2009: 65 ff.).

13 Zum Verhältnis der Begriffe Wissen und Erfahrung vgl. Humpl (2004: 66 ff.).

mehr mit vollem Einsatz nachgehen. Einerseits wird er während seiner Arbeit beobachtet und befragt (was zu Arbeitsverzögerungen führt), andererseits wird sein Wissen außerhalb seiner Arbeit systematisch »abgezapft«.
3. *Nachbereitungsphase* (nach Ausscheiden des Mitarbeiters): Hier geht es um die Klärung der weiteren Verfügbarkeit des Mitarbeiters (Kenntnis seiner Kontaktdaten), seinen fallweisen Einsatz als Berater in Projekten, seine Einbindung in Ehemaligennetzwerken sowie die Möglichkeit sonstiger Begegnungen und Austauschgelegenheiten mit ihm (bspw. im Rahmen von Workshops oder Trainingsmaßnahmen).

4.2 Vorbereitungsphase

In der Vorbereitungsphase soll ein intensiver persönlicher Austausch zwischen dem Experten und seinem(n) Nachfolger(n) ermöglicht werden. Gemäß dem Polanyi'schen Diktum, dass wir stets mehr wissen als wir sagen können (vgl. Polanyi 1983: 4), bedarf es möglichst vielfältiger Anregungssituationen und genauer Beobachtungen, um das erfahrungsgebundene und kontextverankerte implizite Wissen eines Experten »hervorzulocken« (vgl. Gordon 1992: 112; Gueldenberg/Helting 2007: 118 f.). „[T]he tacit dimensions of an expert's deep smarts have to be *re-created* to take hold. That is, the novice needs to discover the expert's know-how through practice, observation, problem solving, and experimentation" (Leonard/Swap 2004: 94). Die *Beobachtung unter Anleitung* (guided observation, shadowing) gilt gemeinhin als die beste »Technik«, um dem Transfer von tiefgründigem Wissen zu fördern. Charles Handy berichtet über eine solche Anleitung in seiner Autobiographie. Er arbeitete damals bei Shell und hatte das Glück, gleich zu Beginn seiner Karriere auf einen jungen Geschäftsführer zu treffen, der ihn unter seine »Fittiche« nahm: „»Ich werde Ihnen sagen, was wir machen«, erklärte er. »Setzen Sie sich in den ersten zwei Monaten einfach zu mir in mein Büro. Verhalten Sie sich still und hören Sie einfach nur zu und beobachten Sie. Solange es nicht um etwas streng Vertrauliches geht, können Sie den ganzen Tag dort sitzen oder mich zu meinen Terminen begleiten. So können Sie sich ein Bild davon machen, wie das Unternehmen funktioniert, und wir können uns jeden Abend kurz hinsetzen, um über Ihre Beobachtungen zu sprechen. Wer weiß, vielleicht kann ich ebenso viel von Ihnen lernen wie Sie von mir.«" (Handy 2007: 64; ähnlich Leonard/Swap 2004: 95).

Die berechtigte Frage, die sich hier stellt, ist, ob Unternehmen heutzutage noch bereit sind, einen Mitarbeiter für zwei Monate mal eben nichts tun zu lassen. Häufiger dürften *Mentor-Mentee*-Beziehungen sein. Der französische Reifenhersteller Michelin etwa nutzt eine solche *Doublage* „to ensure that important knowledge is transferred directly from the predecessor to the successor" (Streb/Voelpel/Leibold 2008: 7). Die Deutsche Bank hat mit dem *Tandem-Modell* ein ähnliches Verfahren auf der Führungsebene installiert, das die intergenerative Zusammenarbeit und die Eingliederung von Nachwuchskräften in gewachsene Beziehungsstrukturen erleichtern soll. Daneben werden internationale und politische Gepflogenheiten sowie interkulturelles

Wissen weitergegeben. Die Zusammenarbeit des »High Potential« mit dem »Senior Professional« erfolgt entweder im täglichen Geschäft, im Rahmen von Projekten oder durch regelmäßige Zusammenkünfte, in denen inhaltsbezogene Fragen besprochen werden (vgl. hierzu ausführlicher Fischer 2007: 326 ff.).

Eine Möglichkeit, um das Wissen ausscheidender Mitarbeiter breiter zu »streuen«, ist ihr Einsatz in *altersgemischten Teams* (vgl. Oertel 2007: 274 ff.). Teamarbeit hat den Vorteil, dass Erfahrungen unmittelbar anhand konkreter Probleme weitergegeben werden können. Es findet sozusagen ein Lernen am Modell unter realen Arbeitsbedingungen statt. Mitarbeiter haben die Gelegenheit, durch gezielte und intelligente Fragen verborgenes Wissen zu Tage zu fördern (vgl. o.V. 2009: 43).[14] Auch durch den begleitenden Einsatz von Reflexionsinstrumenten (z.B. After Action Review, Action Learning, Lessons-Learned-Workshop) werden tieferliegende Wissensbestände des Experten offengelegt und den anderen zugänglich gemacht (vgl. Schindler 2002: 153 ff. zu einem Überblick über Instrumente des Erfahrungslernens auf Teamebene). In Beratungsunternehmen, die an hohe Fluktuationszahlen gewöhnt sind, bildet Projektarbeit seit jeher den strukturellen Rahmen, nicht nur, um die eigentliche Arbeit zu leisten, sondern auch, um das Lernen von- und miteinander zu fördern und damit gleichzeitig Wissensverluste durch Mitarbeiterwechsel »abzufedern« (vgl. von Krogh/Ichijo/Nonaka 2000: 242 ff.).

Schließlich können auch technologiegestützte, interaktive *Expertengemeinschaften* (communities of practice) zum Einsatz kommen. Traditionell sollen diese die innerbetriebliche Diskussion von Problemen und den Austausch von Best Practices fördern. Solche Gemeinschaften eignen sich jedoch auch, um die Sicherung und den globalen Transfer von Erfahrungen voranzutreiben. Unternehmen wie IBM haben dieses Potenzial bereits frühzeitig erkannt (vgl. Murrell/Forte-Trammell/Bing 2009: 53 ff.). Durch die Heranführung älterer Mitarbeiter an Web 2.0-Technologien (z.B. Internetforen, Weblogs, Chats, Podcasts) wird zudem ermöglicht, dass sie nach ihrem realen Ausscheiden zumindest virtuell präsent bleiben.

4.3 Hauptphase

Während durch die Vorbereitungsphase stärker der Transfer impliziten Wissens gefördert werden soll, steht in der Hauptphase die Externalisierung, also die Erfassung und Dokumentation des explizier- bzw. verbalisierbaren Expertenwissens im Vordergrund. Dazu werden in der Regel speziell ausgebildete Fachleute (knowledge engineers) oder Inhouse-Consulter sowie der oder die Nachfolger mit eingebunden. „Eine der einfachsten Methoden sind strukturierte Austrittsgespräche (...) In ihnen wird das für die Organisation kritische Wissen (spezielle Dokumente, Kontakte, Projektein-

14 Der hier Interviewte, Sven Voelpel, hat im Internet eine Plattform errichtet (WISE Demographie Netzwerk), die Erfahrungen im Hinblick auf den intergenerativen Austausch bündeln soll (vgl. http://www.jacobs-university.de/wdn).

bindungen) expliziert und dokumentiert“ (Probst/Raub/Romhardt 2010: 205). Bei der Volkswagen AG wird dieses Verfahren als *Wissensstafette* bezeichnet. Im Mittelpunkt stehen dabei maßgeschneiderte, durch Spezialistenteams organisierte, moderierte und dokumentierte Experteninterviews, in denen Fach-, Beziehungs- und Projektwissen aufgedeckt wird. Vorgänger und Nachfolger können im Vorfeld thematisch Einfluss auf das Gespräch nehmen (z.B. durch die Erstellung einer Mindmap, einer Aufgabenanalyse oder eines Ablaufdiagramms). Die Wissensstafette ist als iterativer Prozess angelegt – von ersten Kennenlerngesprächen über mehrere Intensiv-Befragungen und Gespräche bis hin zu einem abschließenden Transition Workshop mit allen Mitarbeitern (vgl. North 2011: 259).

In eine ähnliche Richtung gehen *(Leaving) Expert Debriefings*, die bereits von Unternehmen wie Siemens, der Schaeffler Gruppe oder dem Henkel-Konzern eingesetzt werden (vgl. Trojan 2006: 153 ff.; Hofer-Alfeis 2008: 46 ff.; Dückert/Hartmann 2009: 21 ff.). Auch hier bilden strukturierte Interviews und professionell durchgeführte Workshops den Mittelpunkt. Ergänzend kommen 360°-Gespräche hinzu, in denen die Rolle des Experten im Zusammenwirken mit anderen Bereichen verdeutlicht wird. Firmen- oder Abteilungswikis, die How-to-do-Seiten, Checklisten, Informationen zum Besprechungs-, Projekt- und Prozessmanagement, FAQ-Sammlungen, Wettbewerberwissen und spezielles technisches Wissen vereinen, werden dabei zunehmend als wichtige Dokumentationsformen genutzt (vgl. Dückert/Hartmann 2009: 22).

Im Rahmen von Expertenbeobachtungen wird häufig auf die *Think-Aloud-Methode* zurückgegriffen (vgl. zusammenfassend von der Oelsnitz/Busch 2008: 261 ff.). Experten sollen hierbei laut denken, während sie eine bestimmte Arbeit verrichten (z.B. beim Bedienen einer Maschine oder der Lösung eines technischen Problems). Je nach Vorgehen können während oder nach der Kommentierungsphase durch die Anwesenden Fragen gestellt werden. Das grundsätzliche Problem, kognitive Vorgänge sprachlich exakt zu fassen, kann damit jedoch zumeist nicht gelöst werden. Deswegen spielen *Fragetechniken* (sokratisches Vorgehen, Mäeutik) eine wichtige Rolle, um möglichst unterschiedliche Wissensareale des Experten anzuregen (vgl. Pepels 1999: 150 ff.).

Geschicktes Interviewen ist besonders wichtig, wenn es darum geht, Erinnerungen des Experten, d.h. arbeitsbezogene Erfahrungen aus der Vergangenheit wachzurufen. Diese sind die Grundlage bei der narrativen Weitergabe von Wissen in Form von Erzählungen, dem sog. *Story Telling*. Im Zentrum stehen dabei häufig *Critical Incidents*, worunter Ereignisse verstanden werden, die besonders starke Emotionen ausgelöst haben (z.B. sehr riskante Vorfälle oder besonders erfolgreiche Projekte). Die Aussagen des Experten werden entweder direkt mündlich weitergegeben oder sie werden aufgezeichnet, thematisch geordnet, extrahiert und in Erfahrungsdokumenten (learning histories) zusammengefasst (vgl. Kleiner/Roth 1997: 176). Die *Erfahrungsdokumente* bestehen in der Regel aus mehreren kommentierten, interessant aufbereiteten und zum Nachdenken anregenden Kurzgeschichten bzw. komprimierten Fallstudien, die zur Grundlage für Diskussionen zwischen Abgänger und Nachfolger werden können.

Der Soziologe Helmut Willke spricht von *MikroArtikeln*. Diese weisen folgende Grundform auf: (1) Thema – Problem – Headline; (2) Geschichte – story line – Kontext; (3) Einsichten – Lessons Learned; (4) Folgerungen; (5) Anschlussfragen. Entscheidend ist die Anschlussfähigkeit des Erzählten an eigene Erfahrungen: „Verstehbar ist für Leser eine Geschichte dann, wenn sie mit ihren eigenen Erfahrungen an den Erfahrungskontext der erzählten Geschichte anknüpfen können" (Willke 2007: 86).[15] Das Verfassen einer anregenden Geschichte ist gleichwohl alles andere als einfach, weshalb häufig professionelle Schreiber zu Rate gezogen werden. Außerdem ist zu bedenken, dass viele Erlebnisse mit der Zeit verblassen oder sich verzerren. Die bereits in der Vorbereitungsphase parallel zur Arbeit erfolgte Dokumentation von Erfahrungen in Tagebüchern oder Arbeitsberichten kann als wichtige Erinnerungsstütze dienen.

Eine im französischsprachigen Raum verbreitete Methode, um Erinnerungen wieder lebendig zu machen, ist die *Explicitation*. Dabei handelt es sich um eine Art Intensiv-Retrospektion von Ereignissen. Der Interviewer versucht, beim Interviewten einen Bewusstseinszustand hervorzurufen, der es ermöglicht „that they are "reliving" (...) the activity under investigation" (Urquhart et al. 2003: 66.). Dadurch sollen emotionsreiche Berichte hervorgebracht werden, sozusagen wahrhaftige Vergegenwärtigungen eines Geschehens: „[T]he event is being experienced anew, rather than just retold" (Urquhart et al. 2003: 67). Dazu hat der Interviewer einige Verhaltensregeln zu beachten: Er sollte Fragen stellen, die sich auf die Sinneswahrnehmung beziehen, eigene Bewertungen unterlassen und auch den Interviewten möglichst nicht zu Bewertungen verleiten. Das bedeutet etwa, bei der Klärung von Kausalitäten auf Warum-Fragen zu verzichten und an ihre Stelle Was- oder Wie-Fragen treten zu lassen (z.B. Was dachten, fühlten, empfanden Sie dabei? Wie kamen Sie auf die Vorstellung, dass ...?). Das Ziel ist, im Interviewten letztlich nur Erinnerungen wachzurufen, nicht aber Interpretationen zu veranlassen. In praktischer Hinsicht sollte der Interviewer daher dem Interviewten nicht Auge-in-Auge gegenübersitzen, um bei diesem ein Schweifen des Blicks zu ermöglichen. Fixationen können den Erinnerungsprozess beeinträchtigen oder verzerren, indem der Interviewte etwa unbewusst nonverbale Signale des Interviewers aufgreift. Die Methode der Explicitation eignet sich auch, um implizites bzw. wenig bewusstes Wissen des Interviewten offenzulegen sowie Einblicke in seine (meta-)kognitiven Denk- und Lernvorgänge zu liefern: „[S]everal interviewees commented on how they surprised themselves with recalling thoughts of

15 Morris/Oldroyd (2009): 16 f. sprechen von Smart Lessons, die die Weltbank zur Reflexion von Erfahrungen einsetzt. Wie auch immer gestaltet, müssen Geschichten drei Anforderungskriterien genügen: „true to the data", d.h. faktenorientiert; „true to the story", d.h. Aufmerksamkeit erzeugend und „true to the audience", d.h. für den Leser bzw. Zuhörer muss ein konkreter Nutzen erkennbar sein.

which they had not been fully aware of thinking at the time“ (Urquhart et al. 2003: 69).

Zusammenfassend betrachtet mangelt es keineswegs an geeigneten Verfahren zur Offenlegung, Weitergabe und Bewahrung von Wissen. Allein der mit den aufgezeigten Verfahren häufig verbundene Aufwand ist so groß, dass viele Unternehmen davor zurückschrecken, sie einzusetzen. Deswegen wird bevorzugt auf den direkten Erfahrungstransfer von Person zu Person gesetzt oder – und dies verweist auf die letzte Phase – das Bestreben geht dahingehend, den Experten auch nach seinem Ausscheiden in irgendeiner Form verfügbar zu halten.

4.4 Nachbereitungsphase

Eine Möglichkeit in dieser Hinsicht ist der *Rückzug auf Raten*, wie ihn der Schweizer ABB-Konzern durch die Gründung der ABB Consulting AG praktiziert. Erfahrene Führungskräfte können ihr Wissen im Bereich der Unternehmensberatung weiternutzen: „Diese grauen Berater agieren hauptsächlich in Tochterunternehmen der ABB und können damit ihr weltweites Beziehungsnetz und ihre Branchenerfahrung weiterhin voll einbringen“ (Probst/Raub/Romhardt 2010: 203). Eine Variante dieses schrittweisen Altersausstiegs bietet der Personaldienstleister Adecco seinen Mitarbeitern an. Sofern der Mitarbeiter dazu bereit ist, kann er fallweise *Arbeit in Projekten* in beratender oder führender Funktion leisten, um seinen Erfahrungsschatz zu nutzen und an andere weiterzugeben: „as a freelance consultant, he can still offer his unique know-how and access to his network“ (Streb/Voelpel/Leibold 2008: 4).

Neben dieser direkten Einbindung sind auch lockerere Formen der weiteren Beteiligung von Mitarbeitern denkbar: in Workshops, Schulungen, regelmäßigen Begegnungen oder Beziehungsnetzwerken. Die Volkswagen AG sucht beispielsweise durch die Volkswagen Management Association, die ca. 1200 ehemalige und 600 aktive Führungskräfte zählt, die Gelegenheit und den Anreiz zum Austausch von Erfahrungen auf der Managementebene zu schaffen. Die neuen Technologien (social media) bieten zahlreiche Möglichkeiten, den Kontakt zu ehemaligen Mitarbeitern weiter zu pflegen.

Am Willen zur weiteren Zusammenarbeit wird es auf seiten des Experten selten mangeln, denn Experten können aufgrund ihrer geschilderten Persönlichkeit nicht ohne Aufgaben auskommen. Wenn sie keine Aufgaben mehr haben, schaffen sie sich selbst neue. Peter Drucker hat Wissensarbeitern daher die Emfpehlung ausgesprochen, frühzeitig ein zweites »Standbein«, einen zweiten Beruf neben dem eigentlichen Beruf aufzubauen (z.B. Arbeit in gemeinnützigen Organisationen, Bibliothekar, Kirchenrat) (vgl. Drucker 2009: 49 f.). Dieser Drang, aktiv zu bleiben, sollte von Unternehmen nicht ungenutzt bleiben. Der Leistungsbereitschaft des ausscheidenden Mitarbeiters sollten zugkräftige Leistungsangebote des Unternehmens gegenüberstehen.

5. Fazit und Ausblick

Gary A. Klein (1992: 170) gelangte vor 20 Jahren zu folgender Einschätzung: „Because most organizations do not really understand how to value their own expertise, they tend to lose it. They fail to develop a workable corporate memory. The result is that they repeat errors because they fail to take advantage of lessons learned.“ Diese Einschätzung hat bis heute nichts an Bedeutung verloren. Ganz im Gegenteil: Die Folgen des demografischen Wandels erhöhen die Virulenz der getroffenen Aussage. Wieviel Wissen ausscheidender Professoren im universitären Bereich wird beispielsweise gesichert? Wie wird deren Erfahrung weiterhin genutzt? Vermutlich wenig bis gar nicht. Universitäten, Behörden, Non-Profit-Organisationen oder Unternehmen werden in Zukunft nicht umhin kommen, sich wesentlich gründlicher mit der Frage der Wissensbewahrung bzw. -weitergabe auseinanderzusetzen und dabei spielt insbesondere die Kenntnis der Hintergründe der Expertise von Mitarbeitern eine tragende Rolle.

Sie ist ein wesentlicher Bestandteil akkumulierter Erfahrungen, deren Entwicklung viel Zeit kostet, aus denen aber auch die entscheidenden unternehmerischen Wettbewerbsvorteile entspringen (sog. time compression diseconomies, vgl. Dierickx/Cool 1989: 1507 ff.). Es wäre töricht, diese Erfahrungen mit dem Ausscheiden der Mitarbeiter einfach verloren zu geben. Ihr Wert muss frühzeitig erkannt, ihr Transfer rechtzeitig betrieben werden. Der Logik der Organisationsentwicklung folgend sollte dies nicht bloß als punktuelle Aufgabe, sondern als Daueraufgabe begriffen und durch entsprechende Maßnahmen organisatorisch verankert werden.

Für die Einordnung der Expertiseforschung in das Strategische Kompetenzmanagement ergeben sich in dem Zusammenhang zahlreiche interessante Anknüpfungspunkte und Weiterentwicklungen. Zunächst sind aus der Expertiseforschung wichtige Ableitungen für innerbetriebliche Trainings- und Transfermaßnahmen zu treffen. Hierbei sollte etwa das Konzept der Deliberate Practice als Basis einer stärkenorientierten Weiterqualifizierung von Mitarbeitern aufgegriffen werden. Als nächstes ist zu klären, inwiefern es sinnvoll ist, Expertise fachlich zu verengen. Der zuvor nur angerissene erweiterte Expertenbegriff, der interdependente Arbeitskontexte berücksichtigt und weit über das rein Fachliche hinausgeht, erscheint dabei besonders vielversprechend und ausbaufähig. Wissens- und Erfahrungstransfer ist in dieser Lesart als eine umfassende, d.h. betriebs- und kontextangereicherte Aufgabe zu begreifen.

Zudem ist dem verkomplizierenden Aspekt Rechnung zu tragen, dass die Wissensgewinnung heutzutage häufig in Teams erfolgt. Wenn aber Arbeitsergebnisse kollektiv erzielt werden, also in der effizienten Verknüpfung individueller Kompetenzen gründen, dann muss auch die Weitergabe von Wissen auf Teambasis geschehen. Eine Übertragung von Person zu Person greift hier zu kurz. Erkenntnisse der Erforschung kollektiver Gedächtnisphänomene (organizational memory, transactive memory) könnten dabei wertvolle Einsichten liefern (vgl. Lewis/Lange/Gillis 2005).

Schließlich sind auch die Schattenseiten von Expertise zu beleuchten: Wo liegen die Grenzen von Leistungsexzellenz? Ist das Expertenmodell überhaupt „auf die Masse“

übertragbar und wo liegen die möglichen Gefahren? Erwähnt seien in diesem Zusammenhang lediglich die beiden Schlagworte Nachhaltigkeit und Burnoutprävention. Jedes Unternehmen braucht individuelle Hochleistung. Doch gerade durch ihren Hang zur Selbstausbeutung gilt es, Experten zum Teil vor sich selbst zu schützen (z.B. durch ein betriebliches Gesundheitsmanagement), um langfristig unternehmerischen Nutzen aus ihnen ziehen zu können (vgl. Wieland 2011).

Insgesamt kann der RBV genauso wie die Erforschung dynamischer Fähigkeiten von der Expertiseforschung in starkem Maße profitieren, denn die individuelle Ebene führt schlussendlich zu feinkörnigeren Erklärungen der unternehmerischen Kompetenzgenese und des Kompetenzerhalts.

Literatur

Bauer, U. (2011): Sozialisation und Ungleichheit – Eine Hinführung, VS Verlag für Sozialwissenschaften: Wiesbaden.

Becerra-Fernandez, I. (2000): Facilitating the online search of experts at NASA using expert seeker people-finder. In: http://citeseerx.ist.psu.edu, Abruf: 07.08.2011.

Bergmann, B. (2008): Durch die Auseinandersetzung mit Aufgaben zur Expertise. In: Pawlowsky, P./Mistele, P. (Hrsg.): Hochleistungsmanagement – Leistungspotenziale in Organisationen gezielt fördern, Gabler Verlag: Wiesbaden: 61-78.

Brinkbäumer, K./Pfeil, G. (2010): Im Imperium der Sieger. In: Der Spiegel 9/2010: 144-147.

Bueb, B. (2007): Lob der Disziplin – Eine Streitschrift, 14. Aufl., List Verlag: Berlin.

Busch, M.W. (2008): Kompetenzsteuerung in Arbeits- und Innovationsteams – Eine gestaltungsorientierte Analyse, Gabler Verlag: Wiesbaden.

Busch, M.W. (2009): T-Shaped Skills – Der Spezialist mit überfachlichen Antennen. In: OrganisationsEntwicklung, 28 (4): 73-80.

Busch, M.W. (2011): Was Personalentwicklung und Weiterbildung von der Expertiseforschung lernen können – Stete Übung macht den Meister. In: Personalführung, 44 (1): 20-29.

Chi, M.T.H. (2006): Two approaches to the study of experts‘ characteristics. In: Ericsson, K.A. et al. (Hrsg.): The Cambridge handbook of expertise and expert performance, Cambridge University Press: Cambridge: 21-30.

Chi, M.T.H./Glaser, R./Rees, E. (1982): Expertise in problem solving. In: Sternberg, R.J. (Hrsg.): Advances in the psychology of human intelligence, Bd. 1, Lawrence Erlbaum Associates: Hillsdale, NJ: 7-75.

Chua, A. (2011): Die Mutter des Erfolgs – Wie ich meinen Kindern das Siegen beibrachte, Nagel & Kimche: München.

Cooke, N.J. (1992): Modeling human expertise in expert systems. In: Hoffman, R.R. (Hrsg.): The psychology of expertise – cognitive research and empirical AI, Springer-Verlag: New York: 29-60.

Coutinho, S. et al. (2005): Metacognition, need for cognition and use of explanations during ongoing learning and problem solving. In: Learning and Individual Differences, 15 (4): 321-337.

Dekeyser, M. et al. (2008): Mindfulness skills and interpersonal behaviour. In: Personality and Individual Differences, 44 (5): 1235-1245.

Dierckx, I./Cool, K. (1989): Asset stock of accumulation and sustainability of competitive advantage. In: Management Science, 35 (12): 1504-1511.

Dreyfus, H.L./Dreyfus, S.E. (2005): Expertise in real world contexts. In: Organization Studies, 26 (5): 779-792.

Drucker, P.F. (2009): Die Kunst, sich selbst zu managen. In: Harvard Business Manager, 31 (11): 38-50.

Dückert, S./Hartmann, K. (2009): Wissenstransfer und organisationales Lernen mit Expert Debriefing und Wikis – Schritte zu einer kontinuierlichen Dokumentation und Kommunikation von Wissen. In: Personalführung, 42 (12): 20-29.

Duckworth, A.L./Seligman, M.E.P. (2005): Self-discipline outdoes IQ in predicting academic performance of adolescents. In: Psychological Science, 16 (12): 939-944.

Ericsson, K.A./Charness, N. (1994): Expert performance – its structure and acquisition. In: American Psychologist, 49 (8): 725-747.

Ericsson, K.A./Krampe, R.T./Tesch-Römer, C. (1993): The role of deliberate practice in the acquisition of expert performance. In: Psychological Review 100 (3): 363-406.

Ericsson, K.A. et al. (Hrsg.) (2006): The Cambridge handbook of expertise and expert performance, Cambridge University Press: Cambridge.

Ericsson, K.A./Prietula, M.J./Cokely, E.T. (2007): The making of an expert. In: Harvard Business Review 85 (7-8): 114-121.

Farrington-Darby, T./Wilson, J.R. (2006): The nature of expertise – a review. In: Applied Ergonomics, 37 (1): 17-32.

Feldhusen, J.F. (2005): Giftedness, talent, expertise, and creative achievement. In: Sternberg, R.J./Davidson, J.E. (Hrsg.): Conceptions of giftedness, 2. Aufl., Cambridge University Press: Cambridge: 64-79.

Fischer, P.M. (2007): Berufserfahrung älterer Führungskräfte als Ressource, Deutscher Universitäts-Verlag: Wiesbaden.

Ford, K.M./Adams-Webber, J.R. (1992): Knowledge acquisition and constructivist epistemology. In: Hoffman, R.R. (Hrsg.): The psychology of expertise – cognitive research and empirical AI, Springer-Verlag: New York: 121-136.

Freeman, J. (2002): Families – the essential context for gifts and talents. In: Heller, K.A. et al. (Hrsg.): International handbook of giftedness and talent, 2. Aufl., Elsevier Science Ltd.: Oxford: 573-585.

Freiling, J. (2001): Resource-based View und ökonomische Theorie – Grundlagen und Positionierung des Ressourcenansatzes, Deutscher Universitäts-Verlag: Wiesbaden.

Gigerenzer, G. (2008): Bauchentscheidungen – Die Intelligenz des Unbewussten und die Macht der Intuition, 3. Aufl., Wilhelm Goldmann Verlag: München.

Gladwell, M. (2009): Überflieger – Warum manche Menschen erfolgreich sind – und andere nicht, Campus Verlag: Frankfurt/Main.

Glaser, R./Chi, M.T.H. (1988): Overview. In: Chi, M.T.H./Glaser, R./Farr, M.J. (Hrsg.): The nature of expertise, Lawrence Erlbaum Associates: Hillsdale, NJ: XV-XXVIII.

Gobet, F. (1996): Expertise und Gedächtnis. In: Gruber, H./Ziegler, A. (Hrsg.): Expertiseforschung – Theoretische und methodische Grundlagen, Westdeutscher Verlag: Opladen: 58-79.

Goleman, D. (1997): Emotionale Intelligenz, 3. Aufl., Deutscher Taschenbuch Verlag: München.

Gordon, S.E. (1992): Implications of cognitive theory for knowledge acquisition. In: Hoffman, R.R. (Hrsg.): The psychology of expertise – cognitive research and empirical AI, Springer-Verlag: New York: 99-120.

Gruber, H./Lehmann, A.C. (2007): Entwicklung von Expertise und Hochleistung in Musik und Sport. In: Forschungsbericht Nr. 26, Universität Regensburg, Lehrstuhl für Lehr-Lern-Forschung: Regensburg: 1-32.

Gruber, H./Mandl, H. (1996): Expertise und Erfahrung. In: Gruber, H./Ziegler, A. (Hrsg.): Expertiseforschung – Theoretische und methodische Grundlagen, Westdeutscher Verlag: Opladen: 18-34.

Gruber, H./Ziegler, A. (Hrsg.) (1996): Expertiseforschung – Theoretische und methodische Grundlagen, Westdeutscher Verlag: Opladen.

Gueldenberg, S./Helting, H. (2007): Bridging 'the great divide': Nonaka's synthesis of 'western' and 'eastern' knowledge concepts reassessed. In: Organization, 14 (1): 101-122.

Güttel, W.H. (2006): Methoden der Identifikation organisationaler Kompetenzen – Mapping vs. Interpretation. In: Burmann, C./Freiling, J./Hülsmann, M. (Hrsg.): Neue Perspektiven des Strategischen Kompetenz-Managements, Gabler Verlag: Wiesbaden: 411-435.

Haarmann, J. et al. (2008): K.exchange – a systematic approach to knowledge transfer of the aging workforce. In: http://www.pumacy.de/publikationen/ 2008/kexchange_in_der_luftfahrt.html, Abruf: 08.08.2011

Handy, C. (2007): Ich und andere Nebensächlichkeiten, Ullstein Buchverlage GmbH: Berlin.

Heller, K.A. et al. (Hrsg.): International handbook of giftedness and talent, 2. Aufl., Elsevier Science Ltd.: Oxford.

Hofer-Alfeis, J. (2008): Knowledge management solutions for the leaving expert issue. In: Journal of Knowledge Management, 12 (4): 44-54.

Hoffman, R.R./Lintern, G. (2006): Eliciting and representing the knowledge of experts. In: Ericsson, K.A. et al. (Hrsg.): The Cambridge handbook of expertise and expert performance, Cambridge University Press: Cambridge: 203-222.

Horn, J./Masunaga, H. (2006): A merging theory of expertise and intelligence. In: Ericsson, K.A. et al. (Hrsg.): The Cambridge handbook of expertise and expert performance, Cambridge University Press: Cambridge: 587-611.

Huber, B. (1999): Experts in organizations: the power of expertise. In: Institute for Research in Business Administration, University of Zurich, http://www. sba.muohio.edu/abas/1999/huberbe.pdf, Abruf: 26.07.2011.

Humpl, B. (2004): Transfer von Erfahrungen – Ein Beitrag zur Leistungssteigerung in projektorientierten Organisationen, Deutscher Universitäts-Verlag: Wiesbaden.

Kahnemann, D. (2011): Schnelles Denken, Langsames Denken, 3. Aufl., Siedler Verlag: München.

Klein, G.A. (1992): Using knowledge engineering to preserve corporate memory. In: Hoffman, R.R. (Hrsg.): The psychology of expertise – cognitive research and empirical AI, Springer-Verlag: New York: 170-187.

Kleiner, A./Roth, G. (1997): How to make experience your company's best teacher. In: Harvard Business Review, 75 (5): 172-177.

Knaese, B./Probst, G. (2001): Wissensorientiertes Management der Mitarbeiterfluktuation – Eine Methode zur Reduzierung personeller Wissensrisiken. In: Zeitschrift Führung + Organisation, 70 (1): 35-41.

Knörck, C. (2009): Intraorganisationaler Wissenstransfer in global agierenden Unternehmen, Verlag Dr. Kovač: Hamburg.

Krogh, G. von/Roos, J. (1995): A perspective on knowledge, competence and strategy. In: Personnel Review 24 (3): 56-76.

Krogh, G. von/Ichijo, K./Nonaka, I. (2000): Enabling knowledge creation – how to unlock the mystery of tacit knowledge and release the power of innovation, Oxford University Press: Oxford.

Leonard, D./Swap, W. (2004): Deep smarts. In: Harvard Business Review, 82 (9): 88-97.

Lewis, K./Lange, D./Gillis, L. (2005): Transactive memory systems, learning, and learning transfer. In: Organization Science, 16 (6): 581-598.

Luhmann, N. (1984): Soziale Systeme, Suhrkamp Verlag: Frankfurt/Main.

Malik, F. (2006): Führen Leisten Leben – Wirksames Management für eine neue Zeit, Campus Verlag: Frankfurt/Main.

Martens, J.-U./Kuhl, J. (2009): Die Kunst der Selbstmotivierung – Neue Erkenntnisse der Motivationsforschung praktisch nutzen, 3. Aufl., Verlag W. Kohlhammer: Stuttgart.

Martin, A./Hansen, N.K. (2010): Dynamische Kompetenz als reflexiv-kreatives Handeln. In: Stephan, M. et al. (Hrsg.): 25 Jahre ressourcen- und kompetenzorientierte Forschung, Gabler Verlag: Wiesbaden: 57-85.

McClelland, D. (1987): Human motivation, Cambridge University Press: Cambridge.

Miller, G.A. (1956): The magical number seven, plus or minus two – some limitations on our capacity for information processing. In: Psychological Review 63 (2): 81-97.

Mischel, W./Ayduk, O. (2011): Willpower in a cognitive affective processing system – the dynamics of delay of gratification. In: Vohs, K.D./Baumeister, R.F. (Hrsg.): Handbook of self-regulation – research, theory, and applications, 2. Aufl., The Guilford Press: New York: 83-105.

Mistele, P. (2007): Faktoren des verlässlichen Handelns – Leistungspotenziale von Organisationen in Hochrisikoumwelten, Deutscher Universitäts-Verlag: Wiesbaden.

Morris, S./Oldroyd, J.B. (2009): Wie Projekte weiterleben. In: Harvard Business Manager, 31 (6): 16-17.

Murrell, A.J./Forte-Trammell, S./Bing, D.A. (2009): Intelligent mentoring – how IBM creates value through people, knowledge, and relationships, IBM Press: Upper Saddle River, NJ.

Neal, J.G. (1989): Employee turnover and the exit interview. In: Library Trends, 38 (1): 32-39.

Neuweg, G.H. (2004): Könnerschaft und implizites Wissen – Zur lehr-lerntheoretischen Bedeutung der Erkenntnis- und Wissenstheorie Michael Polanyis, 3. Aufl., Waxmann: Münster.

Nissen, V. (2007): Consulting Research – Eine Einführung. In: Nissen, V. (Hrsg.): Consulting Research, Gabler Verlag: Wiesbaden: 3-38.

North, K. (2011): Wissensorientierte Unternehmensführung – Wertschöpfung durch Wissen, 5. Aufl., Gabler Verlag: Wiesbaden.

Oelsnitz, D. von der/Busch, M.W. (2008): Die Think-Aloud-Methode. In: Die Betriebswirtschaft, 68 (2): 260-265.

Oelsnitz, D. von der/Tacke, O. (2009): Der WEA-Ansatz als Instrument des strategischen Personalcontrollings. In: Müller, D. (Hrsg.): Controlling für kleine und mittlere Unternehmen, Oldenbourg Verlag: München: 339-359.

Oertel, J. (2007): Generationenmanagement in Unternehmen, Deutscher Universitäts-Verlag: Wiesbaden.

Olsson, P. (2011): Erkenne dein Talent – Was wir von Spitzensportlern und Topmanagern lernen können, Edel Germany GmbH: Hamburg.

o. V. (2005): Anne Sopie Mutter über Leistung. In: Süddeutsche Zeitung, 15./16.10.2005, Nr. 238: VIII.

o. V. (2009): »Wer viel weitergibt, bekommt viel zurück« – Der Leiter des „demopass-Projekts", Sven Voelpel, im Gespräch. In: Personalführung, 42 (12): 42-45.

o. V. (2011): »Es juckt immer noch« – Der Jahrhundertkoch Eckart Witzigmann über die Licht- und Schattenseiten des Koch-Booms im Fernsehen, den Griff nach den Sternen und seine eigene Rückkehr an den Herd. In: Der Spiegel 1/2011: 128-130.

Pepels, W. (1999): Befragungsstrategie und -taktik. In: ders. (Hrsg.): Moderne Marktforschungspraxis – Handbuch für mittelständische Unternehmen, Luchterhand: Neuwied: 148-155.

Polanyi, M. (1983): The tacit dimension, Peter Smith Publisher: Goucester, Mass.

Posner, M.I. (1988): Introduction – What is it to be an expert? In: Chi, M.T.H./Glaser, R./Farr, M.J. (Hrsg.): The nature of expertise, Lawrence Erlbaum Associates: Hillsdale, NJ: XXIX-XXXVI.

Probst, G./Raub, S./Romhardt, K. (2010): Wissen managen – Wie Unternehmen ihre wertvollste Ressource optimal nutzen, 6. Aufl., Gabler Verlag: Wiesbaden.

Ready, D.A./Conger, J.A./Hill, L.A. (2010): Are you a high potential? In: Harvard Business Review, 88 (6): 78-84.

Regoczei, S.B./Hirst, G. (1992): Knowledge and knowledge acquisition in the computational context. In: Hoffman, R.R. (Hrsg.): The psychology of expertise – cognitive research and empirical AI, Springer-Verlag: New York: 12-25.

Reichelt, B. (2008): Mentoring und Patenschaft. In: Bröckermann, R./Müller-Vorbrüggen, M. (Hrsg.): Handbuch Personalentwicklung – Die Praxis der Personalbildung, Personalförderung und Arbeitsstrukturierung, 2. Aufl., Schäffer-Poeschel Verlag: Stuttgart: 391-407.

Rost, K./Hölzle, K./Gemünden, H.-G. (2007): Promotors or champions? Pros and cons of role specialization for economic process. In: Schmalenbach Business Review, 59 (4): 340-363.

Rothe, H.-J./Schindler, M. (1996): Expertise und Wissen. In: Gruber, H./Ziegler, A. (Hrsg.): Expertiseforschung – Theoretische und methodische Grundlagen, Westdeutscher Verlag: Opladen: 35-57.

Salas, E./Rosen, M.A. (2010): Experts at work: principles for developing expertise in organizations. In: Kozlowski, S.W.J./Salas, E. (Hrsg.): Learning, training, and development in organizations, Routledge: New York, London: 99-134.

Schewe, G./Nienaber, A.-M. (2011): Explikation von implizitem Wissen – Stand der Forschung zu Barrieren und Lösungsansätzen. In: Journal für Betriebswirtschaft, 61 (1): 37-84.

Schindler, M. (2002): Wissensmanagement in der Projektabwicklung – Grundlagen, Determinanten und Gestaltungskonzepte eines ganzheitlichen Projektwissensmanagements, 3. Aufl., Josef Eul Verlag: Lohmar.

Schmalt, H.-D./Sokolowski, K./Langens, T. (2000): Das Multi-Motiv-Gitter für Anschluss, Leistung und Macht (MMG) – Manual, Sweets & Zeitlinger B.V.: Frankfurt am Main.

Schneider, W. (2002): Giftedness, expertise, and (exceptional) performance – a developmental perspective. In: Heller, K.A. et al. (Hrsg.): International handbook of giftedness and talent, 2. Aufl., Elsevier Science Ltd.: Oxford: 165-177.

Scholz, C. (2011): Grundzüge des Personalmanagements, Verlag Franz Vahlen: München.

Schumacher, R.M./Czerwinski, M.P. (1992): Mental models and the acquisition of expert knowledge. In: Hoffman, R.R. (Hrsg.): The psychology of expertise – cognitive research and empirical AI, Springer-Verlag: New York: 61-79.

Sennett, R. (2008): Handwerk, Berlin Verlag: Berlin.

Shanteau, J. (1992): The psychology of experts – an alternative view. In: Wright, G./Bolger, F. (Hrsg.): Expertise and decision support, Plenum Press: New York: 11-23.

Shanteau, J. et al. (2002): Performance-based assessment of expertise – how to decide if someone is an expert or not. In: European Journal of Operational Research, 136 (2): 253-263.

Shoda, Y./Mischel, W./Peake, P.K. (1990): Predicting adolescent cognitive and self-regulatory competencies form preschool delay of gratification – identifying diagnostic conditions. In: Developmental Psychology, 26 (6): 978-986.

Siefer, W. (2009): Das Genie in mir, Campus Verlag: Frankfurt/Main.

Simonton, D.K. (2006): Histriometric Methods. In: Ericsson, K.A. et al. (Hrsg.): The Cambridge handbook of expertise and expert performance, Cambridge University Press: Cambridge: 319-335.

Sloterdijk, P. (2009): Du musst dein Leben ändern – Über Anthropotechnik, Suhrkamp Verlag: Frankfurt am Main.

Smith, F.J./Kerr, W.A. (1953): Turnover factors as assessed by the exit interview. In: Journal of Applied Psychology, 37 (5): 352-355.

Sternberg, R.J. (2002): Giftedness as developing expertise. In: Heller, K.A. et al. (Hrsg.): International handbook of giftedness and talent, 2. Aufl., Elsevier Science Ltd.: Oxford: 55-66.

Streb, C.K./Voelpel, S.C./Leibold, M. (2008): Managing the aging workforce – status quo and implications for the advancement of theory and practice. In: European Management Journal, 26 (1): 1-10.

Tannenbaum, A.J. (2000): A history of giftedness in school and society. In: Heller, K.A. et al. (Hrsg.): International handbook of giftedness and talent, 2. Aufl., Elsevier Science Ltd.: Oxford: 23-53.

Trojan, J. (2006): Strategien zur Bewahrung von Wissen – Zur Sicherung nachhaltiger Wettbewerbsvorteile, Deutscher Universitäts-Verlag: Wiesbaden.

Urquhart, C. et al. (2003): Critical incident technique and explicitation interviewing in studies of information behavior. In: Library & Information Science Research, 25 (1): 63-88.

Weiss, D.J./Shanteau, J. (2003): Empirical assessment of expertise. In: Human Factors, 45 (1): 103-116.

Wieland, N. (2011): Resilienz und Resilienzförderung – eine begriffliche Systematisierung. In: Zander, M. (Hrsg.): Handbuch Resilienzförderung, VS Verlag: Wiesbaden: 180-207.

Willke, H. (2007): Einführung in das systemische Wissensmanagement, 2. Aufl., Carl-Auer Verlag: Heidelberg.

Wollersheim, J. (2010): Exploration und Exploitation als zwei Seiten derselben Medaille: Eine systematische Zusammenführung bestehender Konzepte zur Förderung von Ambidextrie in Unternehmen. In: Stephan, M./Kerber, W. (Hrsg.): Jahrbuch Strategisches Kompetenz-Management, Bd. 4, Rainer Hampp Verlag: München, Mering: 3-26.

Ziegler, A. (2008): Hochbegabung, Ernst Reinhardt Verlag: München.

Zimmerman, B.J. (2005): Attaining self-regulation – a social cognitive perspective. In: Boekaerts, M./Pintrich, P.R./Zeidner, M. (Hrsg.): Handbook of self-regulation, Academic Press: San Diego: 13-39.

Herausgeber- und Autorenverzeichnis

Prof. Dr. Wolfgang Burr
Jg. 1966, Inhaber des Lehrstuhls für Lehrstuhl für ABWL, Forschungs-, Entwicklungs- und Innovationsmanagement an der Universität Stuttgart, Keplerstraße 17, D-70174 Stuttgart
Email: wolfgang.burr@bwi.uni-stuttgart.de
Arbeitsgebiete: Innovations- und Dienstleistungsmanagement, Resource- and Competence-based View of the Firm

Dr. Michael W. Busch
Jg. 1972, Akademischer Rat am Lehrstuhl für Organisation und Führung an der Technischen Universität Braunschweig, Abt-Jerusalem-Str. 4, D-38106 Braunschweig
Email: michael.busch@tu-braunschweig.de
Arbeitsgebiete: Kompetenz- und Teammanagement, Expertenforschung.

Dr. Silke Geithner
Jg. 1977; Technische Universität Dresden, wissenschaftliche Mitarbeiterin am Lehrstuhl für BWL, insbesondere Organisation der TU Dresden, 01069 Dresden
Email: silke.geithner@tu-dresden.de
Arbeitsgebiete: Transformation von Arbeit und die Konsequenzen für die Personal- und Organisationsentwicklung, die demografische Entwicklung und ihre Folgen für Organisationen, tätigkeitstheoretische Theorien individuellen und kollektiven Lernens

Prof. Dr. Martin Gersch
Jg. 1966, Professorship of Business Administration, School of Business & Economics, Department Business Information System, Freie Universität Berlin
Email: martin.gersch@fu-berlin.de
Arbeitsgebiete: Technology-driven change and transformation processes, Economic Theory, Information Management, E-Business, innovative teaching and learning concepts

Prof. Dr. Wolfgang H. Güttel
Jg. 1968, Professur für Human Resource & Change Management an der Johannes Kepler Universität Linz, Altenbergerstraße 69, A-4040 Linz
Email: wolfgang.guettel@jku.at
Arbeitsgebiete: Dynamic Capabilities, Organizational Routines, Replication, Ambidexterity

Prof. Dr. Jürgen Kaschube
Jg. 1960, Professor für Personal- & Wirtschaftspsychologie an der Privatuniversität Schloss Seeburg, Seeburgstr. 8, A-5201 Seekirchen am Wallersee/Salzburg.
Email: Juergen.Kaschube@uni-seeburg.at
Arbeitsgebiete: Personalpsychologie, Förderung von Innovationsprozessen, Eigenverantwortung und freiwilliges Arbeitsengagement

Dr. Torsten Klein
Jg. 1979, Geschäftsfeldentwickler der ThyssenKrupp Steel Europe AG und Lehrbeauftragter für Unternehmensführung an der Fachhochschule Köln und der Hochschule für Ökonomie und Management Siegen, Derschlager Str. 12, D-51674 Wiehl.
Email: torsten-klein@arcor.de
Arbeitsgebiete: Organisationsgestaltung, Organisationswandel, Ressourcenmanagement

Dr. Antje Koch
Jg. 1975, Mitarbeiterin der Stadtverwaltung Kamenz
Email: antje.koch75@googlemail.com
Arbeitsgebiete: Controlling, Beteiligungsmanagement

Prof. Dr. Jochen Koch
Jg. 1968, Chair of Management and Organization, European University Viadrina, Frankfurt / Oder
Email: koch@europa-uni.de
Arbeitsgebiete: Organizational and strategic paths, routines and social practices, competences and capabilities.

Dr. Stefan Konlechner
Jg. 1968, Wissenschaftlicher Mitarbeiter am Institut für Human Resource & Change Management an der Johannes Kepler Universität Linz, Altenbergerstraße 69, A-4040 Linz
Email: stefan.konlechner@jku.at
Arbeitsgebiete: Dynamic Capabilities, Organizational Routines, Replication, Ambidexterity

Kristian Kunow, M.A.
Jg. 1980, Fellow am Pfadkolleg Research Center, School of Business & Economics, Freie Universität Berlin
Email: kristian.kunow@fu-berlin.de
Arbeitsgebiete: Organizational paths, routines and capabilities, media management and transformation processes

Prof. Dr. Birgit Renzl
Jg. 1974, Professorin für Strategie & Organisation an der Privatuniversität Schloss Seeburg, Seeburgstr. 8, A-5201 Seekirchen am Wallersee/Salzburg.
Email: Birgit.Renzl@uni-seeburg.at.
Arbeitsgebiete: Wissens- und Innovationsmanagement, Strategisches Human Resource Management, Organisation

Dipl.-Kfm. Martin Rost
Jg. 1976, Lecturer an der Fakultät für Betriebswirtschaft der Universität der Bundeswehr München, Werner-Heisenberg-Weg 39, D-85577 Neubiberg.
Email: Martin.Rost@unibw.de.
Arbeitsgebiete: Kompetenzmanagement, Ambidexterity, Evaluation

Annett Schädlich, M.A.
Jg. 1976; Technische Universität Chemnitz; Forschungsakademie, 09126 Chemnitz
Email: annett.schaedlich@hrz.tu-chemnitz.de
Arbeitsgebiete: Personal- und Organisationsentwicklung, insb. Gestaltung partizipativer Veränderungsprozesse in KMU, Organisationales Lernen

Dipl.-Kffr. Tanja Schulze
Jg. 1985; AZ Vermögensverwaltung GmbH&Co.KG, 09526 Olbernhau; ehemals Technische Universität Chemnitz, Lehrstuhl für Organisation und Arbeitswissenschaft
Email: schulzetanja@hotmail.de
Arbeitsgebiete: Personal- und Organisationsentwicklung, Gestaltung organisationalen Wandels in KMU, Aufbau und Implementierung von Controlling- und Managementinstrumenten

Prof. Dr. Dietrich von der Oelsnitz
Jg. 1964, Direktor des Instituts für Unternehmensführung und Inhaber des Lehrstuhls für Organisation und Führung an der Technischen Universität Braunschweig, Abt-Jerusalem-Str. 4, D-38106 Braunschweig
Email: d.oelsnitz@tu-braunschweig.de
Arbeitsgebiete: Strategische Unternehmensführung, Experten- und Leadershipforschung.

Jahrbuch Strategisches Kompetenz-Management

Band 1

Jörg Freiling, Hans Georg Gemünden (Hrsg.):

Dynamische Theorien der Kompetenzentstehung und Kompetenzverwertung im strategischen Kontext

ISBN 978-3-86618-141-0, Rainer Hampp Verlag, München und Mering 2007, 335 S., € 32.80

Band 2

Jörg Freiling, Christoph Rasche, Uta Wilkens (Hrsg.):

Wirkungsbeziehungen zwischen individuellen Fähigkeiten und kollektiver Kompetenz

ISBN 978-3-86618-287-5, Rainer Hampp Verlag, München und Mering 2008, 172 S., € 22.80

Band 3

Heike Proff, Christoph Burmann, Jörg Freiling (Hrsg.):

Der kompetenzbasierte Ansatz auf dem Weg zu einer „Theorie der Unternehmung"

ISBN 978-3-86618-357-5, Rainer Hampp Verlag, München und Mering 2009, 192 S., € 24.80

Band 4

Michael Stephan, Wolfgang Kerber (Hrsg.):

„Ambidextrie": Der unternehmerische Drahtseilakt zwischen Ressourcenexploration und -exploitation

ISBN 978-3-86618-494-7 Rainer Hampp Verlag, München und Mering 2010, 284 S., € 27.80

Band 5

Dietrich von der Oelsnitz, Wolfgang Güttel (Hrsg.):

Kooperationsorientierte Kompetenzen

ISBN 978-3-86618-648-4, Rainer Hampp Verlag, München und Mering 2011, 140 S., € 22.80

Strategische Allianzen, Joint Ventures, international aufgestellte Franchise-Systeme und netzwerkartige Wertschöpfungspartnerschaften gehören mittlerweile zum Standardrepertoire des Strategischen Managements. Parallel dazu sind kooperative Systeme auch in der Forschung zu einem Hauptthema geworden. In diesem Sammelband wird die Kooperationsthematik unter einer ressourcen- und kompetenzorientierten Perspektive betrachtet. Im Mittelpunkt stehen die *skills* und *capabilities*, die heutzutage zum erfolgreichen Management überbetrieblicher Kooperationen erforderlich sind. Deren Analyse wird durch einen ausgewählten Branchenfokus (Filmindustrie, Glasfasernetzindustrie) vertieft.

Strategic alliances, joint ventures, international franchise systems and network-organized value added partnerships have become the standard repertoire of strategic management. Cooperative systems have also developed as a main topic in the research area. This reader views the theme of cooperation from a resource based and competence oriented perspective. Skills and capabilities are in the focus of successful management of inter-organizational co-operations. Their analysis will be enlarged by focusing selected industry sectors (film industry, fiberglass net industry).

Zeitfracht Medien GmbH
Ferdinand-Jühlke-Straße 7
99095 Erfurt, Deutschland
produktsicherheit@kolibri360.de